SELLING SNAKE OIL

INVESTMENT LESSONS FROM THE WORLD'S GREATEST FRAUDS

Mo Lidsky

gatekeeper press

Columbus, Ohio

Selling Snake Oil: Investment Lessons from the World's Greatest Frauds

Published by Gatekeeper Press
2167 Stringtown Rd, Suite 109
Columbus, OH 43123-2989
www.GatekeeperPress.com

ISBN (hardcover): 9781642373653
ISBN (paperback): 9781642373646
eISBN: 9781642373639

Printed in the United States of America

Demand for snake oil's plummeted,
The salesman's lost his job.
He checks the worldwide network
For suckers he can rob.

His eyes light on the British Isles
Where greed and sloth is rife.
He utilises all his wiles
To build a brand new life.

With worthless shares and dodgy loans
He earns a massive bonus.
Never mind inflated homes,
The jobless and the homeless!

Fools go on admiring him,
Until the great big crash.
Then they yell at government
"Oi! You lot! Where's our cash?"

The ministers and experts,
Like headless chickens running,
Scurry round in circles–
They didn't see it coming!

The con man's made his packet,
Cashed it in and fled,
Laughing while the rest of us
Are calling for his head.

Martin Brown

In loving memory of JL and EL,
two of the sweetest and
most beautiful souls I've ever encountered

CONTENTS

ACKNOWLEDGEMENTS..7

PREFACE...9

INTRODUCTION..13

THIRD-PARTY VERIFICATION..19
  How Ivar Kreuger's Matches Set the SEC on Fire............................20
  Stanley Goldblum: If They're in on the Scam, Keep
    Them on Payroll..26
  The Count Who Sold the Eiffel Tower..34
  Bre-X Minerals and the Canadian Gold Rush....................................40
  Marc Dreier: The Man Most Likely to Succeed . . . in Jail.................47
  Sucker Day: In Commemoration of F. Bam Morrison......................55
  Choosing De Niro Over Dinero and the Valuation Practices
    of Edward Strafaci..62
  Horses, Libraries and Hockey: The Story of WG Trading.................68

CHECKS AND BALANCES..73
  Antigua's CD Player: The Story of Sir Allen Stanford........................74
  The Talented Xanthoudakis Who Could Make Money Disappear........81
  Calisto Tanzi's Spoiled Milk: The Rise and Fall of Europe's Enron.....88
  America's Most Notorious Moral Warrior: Charles
    Keating and the Savings & Loan Scandal....................................94
  Want to Make it Big? Start a Charity!..103
  "Give, and I Shall Taketh From You": The Lies of Gerald
    "Double Your Money" Payne...108

COMPLIANCE & REGULATION...113
  Rudy Kurniawan vs. Bill Koch: Guess Who is Still Standing?...........114
  Sovereign Promises: Sir Gregor MacGregor & the
    Dominion of Melchizedek...121
  Martin Frankel: The Anxious Nerd who Forced a Global Manhunt....129
  Look Out for the Repeat Antics of Roc Hatfield............................137
  The Rise and Fall of Panama's Escape Artist: Marc Harris...............141
  YBM Magnex: The Story of the Brainy Don who Loved Canada.......147

QUALITY OF PEOPLE... 153
   Richard Whitney: The Dark Knight of Wall Street........................ 154
   Martha's Rush to the Door: A Case Study in Insider Selling 161
   John Mabray and Ben Marks's Two-Faced House in Two Countie.............. 167
   The Man Who Couldn't Face the Music.. 173
   Ferdinand Ward: How to Fool a President and Become the
      Best-Hated Man in America 179
   Whitaker Wright: A Ballroom Under a Lake is of Little Consolation.................. 186
   Rape, Plunder and Loot: The Story of the Fugitive Financier 194

VALIDITY OF OPPORTUNITY... 203
   Charles Ponzi: The Man who Promoted Peter and Paul................ 204
   Oprah's Carpet Cleaning Mogul Stealing Grandma's Jewelry:
   The Crazy Life of Barry Minkow.. 211
   Even the Jargon Couldn't Save Him: How Kirk Wright Got Sacked.................... 217
   The Crocodile Tears of Lawrence Salander 224
   The Salad Oil King Who Toppled AMEX and Elevated Buffet.................... 231
   Boiler Rooms and Superloaders: How Walter Tellier Ruled the '50s 238
   Nami's Yen: Came Down from Heaven and Went Up in Smoke.................. 245
   An Eccentric Vigilante's War on the World's Biggest Pigeon Fraud 251
   William Miller: The 520% Man.. 259
   From Cowsheds to Laundromats: The Rastogi's Imaginary Empire 265
   Rudy Giuliani's Big, Greedy Fish: The Story of Ivan Boesky 270
   The Taped Insider: A Glimpse into the Rise and Fall of Raj Rajaratnam....... 278

CONSISTENCY & ALIGNMENT 283
   The Defrauded Fraudster: The Unbelievable Bayou Story.................. 284
   Wood River's Sunset in Sun Valley.. 294
   Subprime-Rich and Cash-Poor: The Story of Ralph Cioffi
      and the Downfall of Bear Stearns 301
   The Unsafe Harbor of Portus Asset Management 307
   The Only Hitter with a .966 Batting Average: Bernard L. Madoff 314
   Being Too Early Doesn't Count: Michael Berger's Doomsday Bet.................. 321
   Computer Associates: Creating the 35-Day Month 328
   Turning the Tables on the Legend of Sir Francis Drake.................... 335
   How to Manipulate $360 Trillion: The Curious Case of
      LIBOR and Thomas Hayes... 342

THE FUTURE OF FRAUD 349

CLOSING THOUGHTS 367

APPENIDIX I: RED FLAGS BASED ON KEY TAKEAWAYS.................... 371

APPENDIX II: REFERENCES BY CASE.. 375

APPENDIX III: SUGGESTED READINGS THAT INSPIRED THIS BOOK....396

ACKNOWLEDGEMENTS

THERE IS NEVER a shortage of people to thank for every piece of advice or recommendation, and for the latitude my partners, family and friends have given me to focus on my writing. I am deeply grateful to all those that took the time to read and offer meaningful feedback on early drafts of this book. They include Chuck English, Howard English, Shimmy Brandes, Wayne Nates, Stuart Schipper, Fenyrose Romano, Eddie Tobis, Noah Soberano, Ashley Faintuch, Vincent Duggan, Davee Gunn, and Jeremy Rosmarin. I am especially grateful to Jim Chanos, whose thought leadership on this topic is globally renowned. It was over lunch in Newport some years ago where Jim offered to send me his curriculum on the corporate fraud class he teaches at Yale. This gesture simultaneously flooded my home library with books and served as the impetus to move this project forward.

There are, however, three individuals to whom I am most indebted for helping make this book a reality. This book could not have been completed without the tireless efforts of my right-hand researcher and support writer, Aaron Weber. He has ensured that all the key cases are properly prepared and that the stories are engaging enough to be truly memorable to the reader. His tireless efforts on this project the past two years cannot be overstated.

This book was nothing more than an idea that sprung up over drinks with my dear friend and mentor, Michael Lax. Shortly after my meeting with Jim Chanos, I mentioned to Michael my desire to write something specifically for private investors on the topic. To which Michael smiled wryly and responded, "Finally, a book of yours people might actually read!" It was with that affectionate tease and encouragement that I got started, and Michael has continued to serve as a critically helpful advisor throughout the process.

Finally, none of my professional, communal or vocational projects would have been possible without the unendingly generous support of my extraordinary wife, Naomi. She has endured late nights and pre-dawn alarm clocks, put up with my relentless travel and my neglect of domestic responsibilities to write, research, and edit. She has masterfully managed a busy household of five amazing (and adorably precocious) children and miraculously kept all of us physically and spiritually nourished throughout.

My profound and eternal thanks to each of you.

PREFACE

HE ARRIVED TO pitch us that morning, and it began as any other investment manager meeting. After a few pleasantries and a bit of social geography, connecting some overlapping contacts, we dove into the strategy. The middle-aged man, who appeared seasoned and well heeled in financial services, presented an opportunity with structured notes. It was a seemingly brilliant strategy that allowed us to capture virtually all the upside in the market, but no downside unless the market lost over 40%. Not only that, if the market returned less than 6% during the period, the return was doubled.

As I and two of my analysts were contemplating how the strategy worked . . . BAM! A sudden thud on the desk interrupted our train of thought. It was my then partner, Ian Rosmarin, who slammed the table with his open palm. Ian, who would generally be described as a soft-spoken, sagacious and gentlemanly South African, appeared irked and irate. As blood seemed to gather at his increasingly red forehead, he told our presenter that morning, "Stop. We've heard enough. This is not real; you know it, and I know it, so there's no sense in continuing the conversation. Please leave."

The man corked back as if he had just been slapped in the face. Within a moment, he fired back at Ian for insulting his intelligence, his experience, and clearly not understanding the opportunity. Tempers flared as the presenter fought back with the fervor of a wounded dog, but after a brief battle he stomped out of our office in a huff. I was mortified. Along with our analysts I was embarrassed by Ian's brashness and confused by his confidence that this wasn't "real." We all sat in the same room, heard the same facts, and nothing about it screamed "SCAM!" Of course, we've seen many structured note opportunities that offered Pleasantville until you read the sobering fine print. And there were few we ever liked, but to accuse someone of being a charlatan was something else altogether.

After the shamed presenter left, we asked Ian what in the world prompted him to react as he did. He vaguely referred to some similarily sketchy deal with Lloyd's of London some twenty-five years prior. Without really understanding him, we thought Ian had lost his marbles. There was nothing about the presentation that suggested fraud. But the hectic tempo of that day quickly diverted our attention, and this incident was virtually forgotten.

Two and a half years later, in the summer of 2014, I was attending a charity golf tournament. Before the afternoon tee-off, my golfing buddies and I were enjoying lunch in the clubhouse. One of them received a call. After picking up the phone, he said to me, "Mo, you'll have to go on without me. This conference call may take a while." I asked him why he scheduled a call at tee time, to which he responded, "I normally wouldn't, but losing $5 million makes you do a lot of things you wish you didn't."

My friend worked as the chief investment officer in one of Canada's largest family offices. As he was waiting for the others to join the conference call, I asked him what happened, and he relayed to me the story of a middle-aged man, seasoned in financial services, who sold him $5 million of fraudulent structured notes. As this story sounded familiar, I asked him to name and describe the culprit. Sure enough, it was the same schmuck Ian kicked out of our office some two and a half years prior.

Once again, I was mortified. This time, however, it was not with the shame of inhospitality, but with the shame of ignorance. How did I sit in the same room and hear the same facts while remaining clueless to what was going on? What did he see that I didn't? How did some money-losing lesson twenty-five years earlier provide him with the sensitivity to recognize the fraud? And, most dramatically, how could I have been so blind to it? As the CEO of an investment research and consulting firm, I should be among the first to the scene. I should be able to spot frauds as a doctor spots common colds. Yet, I wasn't there. Besides being humbled by my ignorance, that experience also exposed my vulnerability. On that summer day, my fixation on fraud began.

In the weeks after this event, I went to local libraries and bookstores in search of books on investment fraud. I wanted to get up to speed on every innovative investment scam ever executed. However, virtually every book I came across was focused on blue-chip corporate frauds, the likes of Enron, WorldCom, Sunbeam and Nortel, rather than the more transaction-oriented frauds private investors would likely be exposed to: funds, limited partnerships, structured notes and other direct deals.

Furthermore, each book was focused on accounting or forensic analysis, rather than red flags that any ordinary investor can identify, irrespective of their background and experience.

I am not an auditor, nor will I ever be one. But if the trained auditors from the world's largest accounting firms missed (or were accomplices in) manipulated numbers on the audited financial statements, it is highly unlikely that a common investor would catch those misrepresentations. Instead, I wondered how I and other investors could cultivate the sixth sense to detect instances of investment fraud.

Over the next several years, I immersed myself in the history of financial fraud, digging up both classic and esoteric cases of deception, chronicling and categorizing those cases, and ultimately applying their lessons by helping others make better investment decisions. Through this process I found my own sensitivity and vigilance elevated, which resulted in identifying dozens of fraud cases before they could impact me or my clients.

The purpose of this book is to help you do the same, to save you thousands of hours of reading and researching, while developing a heightened awareness of financial shenanigans. As Arthur Conan Doyle wrote in *A Study in Scarlet*, "There is a strong family resemblance about misdeeds, and if you have all the details of a thousand at your finger ends, it is odd if you cannot unravel the thousand and first."

The cases in this book include the most creative financial misdeeds ever committed. By delving into them, you will be empowered to make better investment decisions and equipped to confront the frauds that lie (no pun intended!) ahead.

INTRODUCTION

EVERY SINGLE FRAUD has at least three basic ingredients: the perpetrator, the opportunity to perpetrate fraud and the victim. We cannot do anything about the first two. The fraudster, in particular, often has no conscience. In many cases, they are psychopathic, lacking empathy and basic neural wiring that would prevent most people from stealing from charities, retirees, and friends who entrust them with everything they have. We cannot even relate to their sickness. Furthermore, the opportunities to perpetrate fraud will always exist, as loopholes and vulnerabilities will endure. However, we can do a lot about the third ingredient—we can avoid being the target.

Frauds range from simply ordering something that you'll never actually receive, to various lottery scams, to more sophisticated debt consolidation scams. Not only are frauds varied, they are often situation dependent. Large organizations may experience forms of sophisticated corruption, whereas small organizations may be subject to more pedestrian frauds like skimming and cash larceny.

The focus of this book will be on investment fraud and how affluent investors can detect and avoid investment fraud. I specify affluent investors because many of the offerings discussed in this book are not offered by prospectus and therefore only available to high net worth investors whom the regulators deem as being sophisticated or "accredited."

In the pages ahead, I will attempt to deconstruct some of the most innovative frauds ever commited into the six factors that investors need to contemplate when considering opportunities. They include:

- Third Party Verification
- Checks & Balances
- Compliance & Regulation
- Quality of People
- Validity of Opportunity
- Consistency & Alignment

To maintain your interest and help anchor these six factorrs of fraud in your conciousness, this book will be heavily case-oriented, focusing on the most salient and salacious stories that embody their messages.

Our Challenge

In the aim of shielding ourselves against the effects of fraud, we, as investors, face both an external and an internal challenge. Externally, we have four methods of protection against invest-ment fraud. They include:

- law enforcement protection (e.g. police, FBI)
- legal protection (e.g. suing the perpetrators)
- regulatory protection (e.g. Securities and Exchange Commission)
- due diligence protection (e.g. your cautious research).

The problem with legal and official enforcement is that they arrive only after all the pain of loss has been experienced, and only if it was actually reported (and if there were any assets left to pursue). Regulatory protection has also proven to be woefully helpless. Having spent the last several years studying hundreds of fraud cases, I was shocked to discover how many of these cases were known to the regulators long before they unraveled.

That leaves us with the only protection we can count on: our vigilance in employing proper due diligence and taking every necessary precaution. That starts with education; education that is achieved by learning from the mistakes of others, rather than our own.

That leads to our internal challenge, the human frailties all of us share. We all think we are smarter, less likely to be deceived, not as greedy as "the other guy." Yet most of us look for shortcuts; we're often too lazy to do the homework, too uncomfortable to ask the difficult questions, too influenced by first impressions, have too much regard for authority, too reliant on our emotions and too trusting with our existing relationships. All of these cause us to ignore that little voice inside our heads that says this is simply too good to be true. After the fact, the voice comes through with crystalline clarity, saying, "I should have seen it . . . ," or "The warning signs were obvious . . . ," and "How could I have missed that?"

Frauds affect everyone from pigeon farmers in Canada to US presidents and European royalty. They span from the seedy inner sanctums of the Russian mafia to the highest echelons of Wall Street. In this book, you will encounter individuals and stories that will both shock you and make you question humanity. However, these are stories that must be told, for when it comes to fraud, ignorance is far from bliss. Benjamin Franklin once said, "An investment in knowledge always pays the best interest." And there is one thing I can promise you. When you turn the final page of this book, you will be equipped to collect on that interest by making far better investment decisions in the future.

So let's dive right in.

* * *

THIRD-PARTY VERIFICATION

HOW IVAR KREUGER'S MATCHES SET THE SEC ON FIRE

I N THE **1920s**, Ivar Kreuger was known as the Match King. He controlled ninety percent of the world's match production and the stocks of his company, Kreuger and Toll, were the most-owned securities in America. He was also known as the savior of governments and a national status symbol in his homeland of Sweden, to whom Kreuger lent money in the post-World War I years. That is, until the Match King was exposed as a massive fraud and prompted some of the greatest changes in the field of accounting that we have today.

Ivar was born as the oldest of six children to Jenny and Ernst August Kreuger, a match entrepreneur living in Kalmar, Sweden. After taking private lessons for school and graduating two years early, the ambitious Ivar arrived in New York at the age of twenty and began his career as a construction engineer. He returned to Sweden in 1913, taking over his father's match company while also founding a construction engineering firm, Kreuger and Toll, with Paul Toll. He moved his match company into Kreuger and Toll and went on a buying spree purchasing other Swedish match companies. As Kreuger and Toll grew, they developed the ability to produce better matches at cheaper prices, putting their competition at an extreme disadvantage and forcing them to sell themselves to Kreuger. Before long, he had expanded through the rest of Europe. But Kreuger wasn't satisfied with that. He wanted absolute monopolies, and World War I was his inspiration.

In the aftermath of the war, most European companies were in extreme debt, so Kreuger began lending massive amounts to governments, doling out a total of $253 million (the equivalent of over $3.2 billion in 2018). According to *The Economist*, he lent $125 million (over $1.5 billion in 2018 dollars) to Germany alone. In exchange, he received monopolies in fourteen countries and trading concessions in many others. However, Kreuger needed to finance these loans and even his match business couldn't provide him with enough cash. Setting up the International Match Company (IMCO) in New York, he began selling shares of Kreuger and Toll on American stock markets and made his shares attractive by attaching twenty-percent dividends to them. But even as he made more loans for more monopolies, Kreuger needed to pay dividends to his growing number of shareholders and his match profits could not cover them.

That didn't bother Kreuger though. He simply paid his shareholders from capital, oftentimes from the payments of subsequent investors, a typical pyramid scheme. People would press to see his financial statements and Kreuger would refuse, knowing that the enticement of twenty-percent dividends would make them buy the stock regardless. Audits were not mandatory for corporations at that time and many other companies employed similar levels of secrecy. Kreuger even brashly told an interviewer that his success was based on "silence, silence, and more silence." In total, Kreuger raised about $150 million from American investors over a ten-year span, and IMCO's share prices rose 1100% from 1923 to 1930.

Behind the scenes, Kreuger inflated the value of his assets, claiming $400 million in "other investments," which, for the most part, didn't exist. He also created Class A and Class B shares, where the voting rights were far more limited, allowing him to keep on selling stock while maintaining his control over IMCO. And in retaliation for Mussolini declining him a match monopoly, he forged $142 million in Italian government bonds that were barely worth the paper they were written on. Even when the market crashed in 1929, Kreuger's stocks were still among the most widely held securities in the world.

As his operation grew, so did his persona. Hailed around the world for his government loans, Kreuger was given the French version of knighthood after giving a $75 million loan to France. He was on the cover of *Time*, visited the White House regularly, and served as an adviser and confidant to both President Hoover and King Gustav of Sweden. He received an honorary degree from Syracuse University and was so active at the League of Nations that he was suggested for a Nobel Peace Prize.

But even IMCO was beginning to feel the effects of the crash. Investors weren't throwing in as much money as they used to, and Kreuger needed those investors to pay his dividends. Banks also began to wake up and told Kreuger that they were not "as completely informed about the company as they should be," questioning his listings of "real-estate investments outside Sweden," "other industrial shares," and "loans secured by real-estate mortgages." Kreuger kept a confident face, but inwardly, he was nervous. He tried merging one of his companies with International Telephone and Telegraph (ITT) to raise money but ITT requested an external audit. Reluctantly, Kreuger complied, but the audit found gaps in his accounts. While some thought he'd survive due to his Italian bonds, Kreuger knew that he had forged them.

On March 12, 1932, Ivar Kreuger was found dead in what was largely believed to be a suicide (though some contend that he was murdered), and the still-ignorant public mourned the loss of a perceived hero. It took five years for Price Waterhouse to fully pour through his 400 companies, and uncover the truth. They reported that Kreuger made a "gross misrepresentation" of his assets, and it was estimated that $750 million of his investor's money was missing. Auditors knew that Kreuger had taken at least $100 million for himself, but as for the rest, they had no explanation. The fact that this transpired during the Great Depression only exacerbated its magnitude. In 1932 and 1933, five English books were published and over 300 *New York Times* articles had featured Kreuger.

But amid all of the chaos and loss, there was one silver lining. As a result of Kreuger's actions, America passed the Securities Acts of 1933 and 1934, which finally mandated corporations selling publicly traded securities to have an auditor.

Key Takeaways

The most difficult lesson that the Kreuger case imparts is that even those who were already successful from legitimate businesses, as Kreuger was, could evolve into swindlers out of pressure or desperation. Kreuger built a legitimate fortune for himself, and was certainly an innovative trailblazer, even introducing various financial structures still employed today.[1]

His mistake was making promises that were nearly impossible to keep, and investors should have taken note. Most people would be hard-pressed to name who is today's Match King, Cellophane

---

[1] Among other innovations, Krueger was given credit for creating the class B nonvoting shares, convertible debenture derivatives and participating preferred shares.

Sultan, or Tissue Titan. Whoever they are, it's unlikely that they are in the position to single-handedly bail out sovereign nations in exchange for their monopolies over tissues, cellophane or anything of the sort. Promises that are unlikely or nearly impossible to be kept foreshadow acts of desperation, and desperation foreshadows fraud.

The second, and more obvious, takeaway here is that there is hardly an investment scenario where financial opacity, or the absence of full transparency, is warranted. According to Kreuger's biographer, Robert Shaplen, Kreuger was "the last of a free-wheeling breed" that existed before the Securities Acts of 1933/4 and "the things he was able to do in carrying out his swindle would never again be possible."

The Match King author Frank Partnoy points out that in one of Kreuger's financial statements, "half the company's profits were listed simply as 'earnings from various transactions'." It is for this reason that professors Flesher and Flesher note that while Kreuger was undoubtedly the largest swindler of his era, his fraud contributed greatly for the accounting we have today and the requirement for public companies to employ an independent auditor to ensure that claimed assets actually exist and are being valued appropriately.

Yet, as *The Economist* wisely noted in 1960, the way regulators adapt to fraudsters, fraudsters adapt even faster to regulations. In fact, it was a somewhat forgotten fraud case in the 1960s that reminded Americans just what shenanigans could fool even the best of auditors. This was the case of Stanley Goldblum.

* * *

WHY AREN'T MORE PEOPLE REPORTING FRAUD?

Most victims are shockingly oblivious to the fact that they have been defrauded. For example, in the summer of 2014, authorities in London discovered the "Suckers List"–a 160,000-person database of people that were repeatedly scammed. This list was auctioned, sold and circulated among the underground world of European swindlers. When investigators began reaching out to the individuals on the list, many were surprised and incredulous, claiming that they have never been fooled or defrauded.

STANLEY GOLDBLUM: IF THEY'RE IN ON THE SCAM, KEEP THEM ON PAYROLL

Born in 1927 in the Pittsburgh area, Stanley Goldblum and his family moved to Los Angeles while he was in high school. He did well at school, was a recreational bodybuilder, and had a brief army stint in South Korea. Leaving right before the Korean War began, he returned to California, married his first wife, and attended UCLA for two years before dropping out with plans to make it big.

But that allure died quickly as Goldblum unsuccessfully bounced around various industries, at one point working as a porter dragging meat for Los Angeles' Cherry Meat Packing Company. Even when he settled into the insurance industry, he struggled. But the tall and fit Goldblum made sure to be around the right people and charmed whomever he could. Eventually, that strategy paid off with Gordon McCormick.

McCormick was a successful insurance salesman who was looking to start his own company. In 1958, he contacted Goldblum about joining his company and two years later founded Tongor Corporation with a simple idea. In the 1960s, mutual funds were "in," with expectations of big gains that exceeded the returns of a 3% guaranteed insurance policy. At the same time, people still liked the security of insurance plans with guaranteed returns, something that mutual funds didn't offer. So, reasoned McCormick, why not try packaging a mutual fund *with* an insurance policy and sell the combination to investors?

The pitch to investors went as follows: If you want to buy an insurance policy, why pay cash out of pocket for the policy when you can purchase mutual funds and use the shares as collateral for your insurance payments? In this strategy, you keep the fund shares for ten years until you amass a sizable profit and then cash in the shares to pay off your insurance policy loan plus its interest, keeping the extra profits for yourself. When all is said and done, you receive a paid-off insurance policy *and* profits from a mutual fund.

But McCormick's pitch decidedly ignored various scenarios, like what if the mutual fund makes profits, but not enough to cover the added interest expenses from the policy loan? Or, if one is less optimistic, what if the fund loses money and leaves you with losses plus an interest-bearing loan to pay off? Such questions were swept under the rug by Goldblum and a team of youthful, energetic salesmen who earned large commissions for every sale. The company saw great success, and Goldblum was quickly appointed as sales manager and administrator of the now-renamed Equity Funding Corporation. McCormick promised stakes of ownership to Goldblum and Ray Platt, a fellow manager whose love for drinking and gambling didn't stop him from being an integral part of the company's expansion.

McCormick set up New York offices and Goldblum and Pratt arranged contracts with almost sixty New York brokerages to trade for their mutual fund program. They amassed 1500 agents to sell their package and Equity Funding was quickly called a "darling of Wall Street" according to the *Village Voice*. But on the inside, internal strife was brewing. McCormick was so focused on expansion that he led the company into a series of debts and didn't follow up on his promised ownership stake to Goldblum and Platt. The two disgruntled employees teamed up with two other disgruntled higher-ups: Eugene Cuthbertson, a senior manager, and Mike Riordan, a powerhouse salesman. The team of four blackmailed McCormick, saying that unless he sold the company to them, they'd spill the beans about Equity's true nature.

The blackmail worked and for a $56,000 payment to McCormick, the four of them became the new owners, but Platt became a problem. He had started using company stock to pay his gambling debts and his unscrupulous nature ruined a few potential contracts. Goldblum, Cuthbertson and Riordan combined to give Platt the door but then faced an even more daunting problem: The high commissions to salesmen were ruining their profits, and they didn't have enough cash to pay for all the insurance premiums. Even taking the company public for $600,000 didn't generate enough cash. The SEC compounded things by ruling that their mutual fund/insurance package was a "security" and due to their going public they now needed to comply with the Security Act of 1933 requiring more disclosure than they were comfortable with.

Cuthbertson had no working solution, but the team of Riordan and Goldblum began to cook the books by claiming profits on sales that had yet to take place. Instantly, they added almost $6.7 million to their assets in the form of fake loans. Their auditor, a little-known firm whose only major client was Equity Funding, approved the books without a fight. Goldblum and Riordan then submitted their false documents to the SEC. The news that Equity Funding had more assets than originally expected caused even more shareholders to jump on the Equity bandwagon. Their stock rose from its initial offering of $6 to $10 in 1964 and by the next year, Gene Cuthbertson was the next executive pushed out of the company.

With just Goldblum and Riordan in charge, Equity soared. The stock rose to over $80 in the next five years while the duo unabashedly cooked the books and openly lied in their prospectus. In one particular example, their 1966 prospectus claimed that they sold $226.3 million of Pennsylvania Life's life insurance plans while Pennsylvania Life's own prospectus said they only sold $58.6 million.

While Pennsylvania did bar Equity Funding from selling their packages in their state, everyone else continued to buy their packages and Goldblum became fabulously wealthy. He divorced his longtime wife and mother of their two children, and then proceeded to marry his much younger sister-in-law. Together, they moved into a lavish Beverly Hills house and were neighbors with actor Paul Newman. (In a strange coincidence, Newman happened to have sold a horse farm to another famous fraudster, Paul Greenwood, who we will meet later in this book.)

Under Goldblum and Riordan's direction, Equity began a massive expansion, acquiring numerous companies both in America and abroad. Some insurance-related acquisitions made sense. Others, like a spaghetti factory in Rome or a copper mine in Zambia, couldn't be more random. However, all were pawns in the fraud. For example, in one of their acquisitions, Investor Planning Corporation (IPC), they recognized all of their projected income from sales in their financial statements and then proceeded to sell off the collection rights to another company for more than $13 million before there was anything to collect.

In early 1969, Mike Riordan was killed in a Los Angeles mudslide. Goldblum, now in sole charge of the company, would not let Mike's death slow them down. A year later, Equity was listed on the NYSE.

Goldblum set the tone for Equity's culture. While it was known as a good place to work, it was also an environment promoting financial dishonesty. In one particularly egregious example, quoted in *The Forewarned Investor,* one Equity employee who worked on selling Equity policies to reinsurance companies,[2] came up with the idea of selling them fake policies to inflate profits, another came up with the idea of printing fake share certificates of blue chip companies to strengthen the balance sheet, and the rest of Equity followed suit. This idea took off, with Equity eventually selling as much 56,000 fake insurance policies to top reinsurance companies.

In the ensuing years, Equity propped up their profits even more with fraudulent financial statements. They began using IBM computers to save time which allowed them to forge even more documents. Rumors started to circulate around Wall Street that maybe Equity wasn't as sound as it appeared, but it wasn't enough to curb the tide of investor enthusiasm. That required just one disgruntled employee.

Ronald Secrist was heavily involved in the reinsurance scam until he was fired as part of a cost-cutting downsizing. He told a respected analyst named Ray Dirks about the reinsurance scam and Dirks didn't waste time. He gathered other former Equity

---

[2] Reinsurance companies are organizations that buy other insurance companies' policies, assuming the ability to collect payments and the risks of paying out the policies.

employees and soon the fraud picture was clear. He told his own clients to drop their Equity shares, and as they began selling off their shares, the rumors on Wall Street grew. Soon, regulators in Illinois and California hired private investigators to look at Equity. With Equity's stock price falling quickly from $27 to $14, even Goldblum knew that his time was running out.

In what *The Forewarned Investor* called a precursor to Watergate, Goldblum and his new main accomplice Fred Levin installed listening devices in the offices of investigators. At the same time, the Los Angeles SEC office interviewed Dirks along with other former Equity employees and stopped the trading of Equity shares. Even as regulators descended upon Equity like crows and demanded Goldblum's resignation, Goldblum insisted all was well. He even asked the board for a rich compensation package in exchange for his resignation. His board members weren't total fools, and soon Goldblum along with twenty-one others were arrested on fraud charges. Goldblum remained steadfast, denying the $10 billion in claims against him, until his day in court when he shocked the world by pleading guilty in exchange for a four-year sentence.

Key Takeaways

There were numerous problems with Equity Funding. The fact that Equity seemed to be under investigation, even in the 1960s, was one massive red flag. Over the years, they accumulated two IRS and three SEC investigations, were barred from selling in Pennsylvania due to vast exaggerations in their prospectus, and their entire mutual fund/insurance offering was premised on the unreliable claim that mutual funds would consistently out-perform interest rates.

The main takeaway from Equity Funding is that third-party verfications from auditors are not enough if those auditors are compromised in any way. Equity's original auditor was a small outfit and Equity was by far their largest client. They would hardly be interested in killing their golden goose. Such a conflict of interest would invariably cloud both judgment and independence. How else can you explain the inability to spot 64,000 phony insurance policies, $25 million in counterfeit bonds and $100 million of missing assets?

Goldblum was aware of this; even when his auditor was bought by a larger accounting company, he insisted that his original auditors remain on board. Some of the auditors even became board members at Equity, furthering the conflict of interest.

Bottom line: while a small accounting firm may be perfect for your personal filings, it certainly isn't for your favorite publicly traded company.

* * *

HOW PREVALENT IS FRAUD?

The short answer: far more than you think. According to the Association of Certified Fraud Examiners, all forms of fraud around the world cost over $3.7 trillion USD per year, or almost 5% of global output. By some estimates, in any given year as much as 7.7% of the population in developed economies find themselves victims of some form of fraud.

A survey conducted by the British Columbia Securities Commission discovered that 29% of those who claim to be active investors over the age of fifty have already been victims of investment fraud. The effect of that, according to a 2016 study conducted by the Association of Certified Fraud Examiners on the prevalence and impact of fraud, totaled an average loss of $2.7 million per case and a median loss of approximately $150,000 per case.

THE COUNT WHO SOLD
THE EIFFEL TOWER

Few edifices are more famous than the Eiffel Tower. Now considered a national symbol of France and an attraction for almost seven million visitors each year, it may be hard to believe that this landmark was once "sold" to gullible businessmen by a smooth con man for the modern-day equivalent of $1 million. But that con man was no ordinary person, he was the exceptionally charismatic "Count" Victor Lustig.

Born in 1890 into what he later claimed to be the "poorest peasant family," Lustig began stealing at a young age just to survive. He spent his teenage years pickpocketing and street hustling before moving on to greener pastures, the trans-Atlantic Ocean liners. Fluent in five languages and charming, Lustig began targeting the "newly rich" first-class passengers in a variety of schemes. His favorite was a "money box" which had the ability to print fake money. He would show customers how it could print, while at the same time complaining that it took too long to do so. The gullible and greedy all hurried to buy it, some paying as much as $30,000 only to discover that it had the ability to print two bills and no more.

Lustig continued his scheming ways when he arrived in America at the end of World War I and quickly became a millionaire. In November of 1919, he secretly married a Kansas woman named Roberta Noret and funneled much of his gains to her and his eventual family. At the same time, he spent the remains on gambling and other lovers. He conned so many that detectives in over forty cities knew him as the "Scarred One" due to a large scar on his left cheek. Lustig boasted incessantly about his feats, even penning his own "Ten Commandments" for how to be a swindler. But his most famous con was his sale of the Eiffel Tower, done in classic Lustigian style.

He arrived in Paris in May of 1925 and procured documents that showed him to be the Deputy Director of the Ministry of Postal Services and Communications. After making his way to the Hôtel de Crillon, a historic luxury hotel located in a building constructed in 1758 upon the orders of then-King Louis XV, he sent for Paris' leading scrap metal dealers and invited them to dinner. Treating them to a deluxe Hôtel de Crillon meal, he announced that he would share with them a great secret, one that could not be revealed to the public. The City of Paris planned to dismantle the Eiffel Tower and sell its pieces as scrap metal. The idea wasn't as unexpected as it may seem, as newspapers had recently reported that the tower was a financial strain on the city. In fact, it had been built for the 1889 Paris Exposition and was originally meant to be taken down in 1909. When you add the fact that it was in poor condition and factor in Lustig's charisma, it is not surprising that the metal dealers were convinced. Eventually a bidding war to secure the contract ensued, and the "contract" was ultimately "won" by Andre Poisson.

The fact that Poisson won was already a victory for Lustig. Poisson had recently arrived in Paris and Lustig suspected that he was anxious to make a big splash, making him a ripe target for a fraudster. That thought was only confirmed when Lustig had given all of the metal dealers limo rides to the tower and noticed that among them, Poisson was the most interested in it. Even before the bidding war began, Lustig knew that Poisson was his mark, and within a short matter of time, they were ready to strike a deal.

Then Poisson's wife got involved. She was suspicious about Lustig's request for secrecy and the speed in which the transaction was taking place. But being so acutely aware of human nature, Lustig turned this entirely to his advantage. He arranged a meeting at the Poisson home where the suddenly "transparent" Lustig said he had a grave confession to make. He was not the fancy limo-riding official he claimed to be. He was not a gloriously rich or powerful French aristocrat. He was an ordinary government worker who did his best to impress, all while making a low-level salary that really wasn't sufficient to support him, and thus wanted to keep at a very low profile while arranging deals. This form of talk was familiar to the Poissons. Lustig was an ordinary man just looking for a bribe. Mrs. Poisson let go of her suspicions.

The bribe not only allowed the deal to go through, it also gave nearly quadruple the money to Lustig, as he ended up taking a $50,000 bribe from Poisson to ensure that he would win the contract added to the already $20,000 "contract" that Lustig forged. The total of $70,000 is equal to more than $1 million in today's currency. Less than an hour after receiving the money, Lustig vanished from Paris, leaving Poisson with nothing but a worthless piece of paper. Despite all of Poisson's losses, he didn't report anything to the police for fear of having the entire Parisian business sector laugh at him.

In a remarkable display of arrogance, about six months later, Lustig returned and tried performing the same scam on five other scrap metal dealers. This time, however, one of them got suspicious, contacted the police and Lustig was forced to flee.

Lustig returned to America, swindling people along the way and even allegedly pocketing $5,000 from legendary Chicago mobster Al Capone. Eventually, his schemes got far too audacious. After scamming a Texas sheriff with his favorite money printer scheme, Secret Service agents decided they had enough and made catching Lustig a priority. He was arrested in 1935. Though he did escape prison temporarily, he was recaptured and sent to Alcatraz, where he spent the remainder of his life until he died from pneumonia at the age of fifty-seven. While it is far from an honorable legacy, Count Victor Lustig will be forever remembered as "the man who sold the Eiffel Tower."

Key Takeaways

Lustig was certainly not the only one to sell famous landmarks to gullible people. George Parker, a well-known American con man who preceded Lustig, built a swindling career by selling landmarks, such as the Brooklyn Bridge to uninformed tourists. Like Lustig, he produced false documents. Yet Parker's documents were bold enough to claim that he was the owner of the Brooklyn Bridge and not simply a government agent. Parker was so convincing that he often sold the unsellable bridge multiple times a week. Police had to constantly pull people off the bridge when they began erecting tollbooths to collect the gains from their sham purchase. Like Lustig, Parker tailored his scam toward the wealth of his intended targets, selling the bridge for up to $50,000 when he could tell they were wealthy and only $50 when he saw they didn't have the money to spare.

As seen in these stories, documents that accompany a smooth-talking salesman are hardly enough. When someone is selling you something claiming to be the owner or an agent of the seller, independent verification is an absolute must. Relying on the references of the vendor or agent is equally insufficient, as you can easily be speaking with a friend or a co-conspirator.

Another salient takeaway is the need to verify that the acquired object has actually been sold before. In the art world, the provenance traces back the transaction history of the artwork to its original maker. In real estate, there are titles and deeds.[3] With operating businesses, there are corporate records and sale of business agreements. In every asset sale, there is a paper trail that is either publicly available or independently verifiable. When a sale is proposed that has no reference to prior transactions, as with the Eiffel Tower or the Brooklyn Bridge, extreme skepticism is necessary. Failing to do so will leave you in the company of Andre Poisson and countless New York tourists, with nobody to blame but yourself.

* * *

---

[3] Having title to an asset allows one to legally transfer that asset to others, and a deed is the legal document that transfers title from one entity to another.

HOW OFTEN DO PEOPLE REPORT FRAUD?

Whistleblowing on financial frauds is surprisingly rare. In fact, according to the Financial Industry Regulatory Authority (FINRA) only 12% of investment fraud victims report it, allowing the fraudster to try performing the same trick again.

BRE-X MINERALS AND THE CANADIAN GOLD RUSH

Never underestimate the power of investor FOMO (fear of missing out). Many investors missed out on the opportunity of a lifetime when, in 1994, a little-known Canadian mining company claimed to find a huge nickel deposit in Newfoundland. The company, Diamond Field Resources, ended up owning the world's largest nickel deposit and the only mainstream investor to benefit from it was an American mutual fund. The Robertson Stephens Contrarian fund, which only allocated a tiny percentage of their investments in Diamond Field, still witnessed their portfolio multiply in value forty times over. Investors kept their eyes open for the next Diamond Field and by the late 1990s it appeared that they had found it in Bre-X Minerals.

Bre-X was founded in 1989 by David Walsh as a thirty-cent penny stock on the Alberta Stock Exchange. It had all the properties of a venture capital start-up. There was no prospectus and investors who gave their money were essentially leaving it to Walsh's discretion on how to use it. The company went nowhere for four years. Walsh had first gone to a mine near Echo Bay in the Northwest Territories hunting for gold and found nothing. He then searched in a previously gold-laden area in Quebec in 1992 and then reverted back to the Northwest to search for diamonds, which also yielded nothing. Having made no profits by 1993, Walsh knew that he needed money and flew to Indonesia to meet John Felderhof, a mining consultant based in Jakarta.

Felderhof, who had previously found a gold-copper mine in New Guinea but also failed in numerous Indonesian ventures, recommended looking into an area near the Busang River. The area had previously been scoured for gold with unglamorous results, but Walsh still purchased the land. He appointed Felderhof as Bre-X's chief geologist and general manager and Felderhof recruited Filipino geologist Michael de Guzman to serve as project manager. That August, they began digging and, unlike the previous Busang explorers, Bre-X claimed promising results. By late September, their estimates showed about three to six million ounces of gold which then grew to a whopping seventeen million, translatable into roughly $10 million of annual profits after taxes.

Bre-X put out a series of online posts, press releases, and other forms of self-promotional content that would have been illegal to include in any Bre-X-produced marketing material. Naturally, it was posted unofficially on the internet. Astoundingly, as time passed, Bre-X somehow managed to find more and more gold. It seemed as though the gold chunks were mating. In 1995, they had a new estimate of thirty million ounces, followed by estimates of thirty-nine, then forty-seven and seventy-one million by 1997. All in all, Bre-X issued over 150 press releases promoting their findings.

Unfortunately, the public bought in. Share prices rose from fifty cents in 1993 to $28 in 1996. Even when *Financial Post* reporter Peter Kennedy questioned Bre-X's testing methods and caused a slight tremor of doubt, Walsh and Felderhof responded with a barrage of press releases to drown out Kennedy's lone voice. Bre-X soon issued a 10-for-1 stock split and entered the

NASDAQ, lending it further credibility. By 1997, the share prices reached a maximum of almost $300. Even the biggest American mutual companies bought in, with American Express Financial Advisors, Fidelity Investments, Invesco, and US Global Investors all holding shares.

With a market capitalization of $6 billion,[4] the Indonesian government also wanted a piece of the action. And to apply pressure on Bre-X, it revoked the company's exploration permits. In 1997, a deal was announced that gave the Indonesian government and other related parties 40% of the business, and another 15% was owned by American firm Freeport McMoran, leaving the remaining shareholders with 45%. Everything looked rosy for Walsh, Felderhof, de Guzman, and company, but then things began unraveling fast.

On March 19, after penning ten pages of suicide notes, de Guzman fell out of a helicopter over an Indonesian jungle. Just two days later, Freeport McMoran announced the results of their due diligence conducted before finalizing the Bre-X deal. They found that the gold deposits were completely insignificant and the samples had been salted with gold. Freeport McMoran backed out from the deal and Bre-X hired Strathcona Minerals to perform an independent analysis. Their due diligence produced even sharper claims that Bre-X's claims of gold were definitely false.

Bre-X's share prices had already been falling but the day after Strathcona made their findings public, 69.3 million shares of Bre-X were traded, and its price fell to a measly nine cents.

---

[4] Values in Canadian dollars

Bre-X went bankrupt and shareholders lost $3 billion, with the main losers being an array of Canadian public institutions that included the Ontario Teachers' Pension Plan. The public turned to Walsh, only to be more unpleasantly surprised.

Apparently, Walsh had sold $34 million worth of his shares in 1996 and issued statements blaming Felderhof along with de Guzman. Walsh fled to the Bahamas, where he died in 1998. It was also discovered that Felderhof, who had been publicly announcing that their deposit could net as much as 200 million ounces of gold, also sold off an astounding $87 million of his shares. A forensic investigation hired by Bre-X after Freeport's due diligence concluded that it was, in fact, de Guzman and fellow Filipino Cesar Puspos who salted the samples. Nonetheless, the government still attempted to seize Felderhof for insider trading. Though after a long trial that ended in 2007, he was eventually acquitted, as it seemed that he was actually duped by de Guzman and was merely selling high. He currently lives in the Cayman Islands, which has no provisions for white-collar extraditions back to Canada.

To this day, many believe that de Guzman faked his own death, as his body was recovered four days after he supposedly jumped from the helicopter. Upon discovery, his body was swiftly cremated without confirmation of dental records, DNA tests or any confirmed fingerprints. Even more suspiciously, eight years after his passing, one of his widows (he was a known womanizer with at least four wives), claimed to receive a check of $25,000 from her late husband.

While Michael de Guzman's life status remains a mystery and no one involved with this multi-billion dollar fraud has been brought to justice, the story offers investors some brutally expensive lessons. The greatest shame would be not heeding them in the future.

Key Takeaways

The main takeaway from the Bre-X fiasco is shockingly simple: when someone claims to have an asset, make sure they actually do. This may sound obvious, but experience with countless other frauds, especially extreme examples such as the sale of the Eiffel Tower, suggest that third-party verification on asset ownership is as critical as it is rare. Everyone was so obsessed with finding the next Diamond Field Resources that they welcomed the concoction. This was such an obvious governance gap that in the aftermath of the Bre-X fiasco, Canada passed the National Instrument 43-101, requiring mining companies to have a "qualified person" sign off on a mineral deposit to ensure that it exists.

Besides verification of asset ownership, it would be prudent (and even more rare) to secure third-party verification of the operators' or principals' alignment of interest. Knowing that the insiders were selling stocks would have offered meaningful insight into the future prospects of the company, and perceptive investors would have gotten the message much earlier than they did.

Another critical contributor to establishing the Bre-X story was the flood of press releases, by which a flimsy fantasy became reality, affirming fiction spun by the company themselves. In an online world, where fiction can be mass-produced, trusting unknown sources—regardless of their variety and pervasiveness—can easily lead investors into oblivion.

Particularly in industries that are more speculative—e.g. mining, energy or commodity exploration, etc.—proper, independent due diligence takes on added significance. Speculative and binary arenas are, by definition, offering a promise of extraordinary rewards in exchange for the prospect for permanent capital loss. In these instances, so much is riding on the exuberant belief of investors that charismatic and persuasive entrepreneurs may be highly incentivized to bend the borders of truth to further that belief.

* * *

Only when the tide goes out do you discover who's been swimming naked

—Warren Buffett

MARC DREIER: THE MAN MOST LIKELY TO SUCCEED ... IN JAIL

Most people would jump at the opportunity of having their life story as the subject of a film. But as the film crew for the 2011 documentary *Unraveled* interviewed the Yale and Harvard-educated lawyer Marc Dreier, his blue eyes were downcast. He was visibly unhappy. He had recently been caught orchestrating a massive fraud that would probably have been plastered on the front page of every newspaper if some guy named Bernie Madoff wasn't caught five days thereafter.

By every indication, Dreier started off honest. After attending Long Island's Lawrence High School and being voted "most likely to succeed," Dreier attended Yale for his bachelor's before moving on to Harvard Law School, graduating in 1975. He worked as a defense litigator at the New York firm Rosenman and Colin for many years. Former colleagues reminisce at how unusually ambitious and selfish he was, but also acknowledge that he was highly "personable" and "a shining star." He worked at two more firms before teaming up with Florida lawyer Neil Baritz to start his own firm, Dreier and Baritz, in 1996.

Their first client was a big hit, the reclusive but fabulously wealthy Sheldon Solow, one of New York's most prominent real estate developers. When he hired team Dreier, it appeared like the "most likely to succeed" prediction was coming true. But even as Dreier tried expanding and amassing a dozen lawyers under him, he was not nearly as successful as he would like to be. When Neil Baritz left the firm in 2002 due to personal reasons, *New York* magazine writer Robert Kolker theorized that Dreier had seen enough of his quasi-mediocrity. Despite being strapped for cash and in the middle of a lengthy divorce, he renamed his firm Dreier LLP and embarked on a massive expansion to make his mark.

Wanting to attract the top talent, he decided to form a new-school style of law firm. Instead of other lawyers being partners in the firm with him, where they would have to demonstrate skill in order to make profits, Dreier was the only partner and paid his lawyers a guaranteed salary. To attract the talent he desired, the salaries needed to be high, much too high for a cash-strapped lawyer to afford. To finance his new idea, Dreier began factoring receivables for cash, but even that wasn't enough. Trivial things like paying bills could hardly dissuade Dreier from achieving the success he longed for. So he found a new way of doing it. It just happened to be fraud.

In his attempt to live the high life, Dreier attended many a party and found all of them flooded with young, fantastically wealthy hedge fund managers trying to find the next big investment hit. All he needed to do was create an investment to get them excited about. He couldn't afford to give them any real assets, so he decided to sell them debt, something like an IOU note attached with an eight or nine percent interest. But why would billionaire hedge fund managers want to take on debt from Dreier LLP, still a relatively unknown firm?

The answer came like a lightning bolt: *Sheldon Solow.* His first and favorite client was mega-wealthy, well respected and Dreier knew everything about him. Better yet, Solow was reclusive enough that people wouldn't ask too many questions. With nothing but a Microsoft Excel spreadsheet, he composed a Solow Realty financial statement as well as a one-year IOU note. Still nervous, he decided to aim high enough to finance his expansion but not too high. He made the note $20 million. Recruiting a friend, he approached the highly successful Connecticut hedge fund Amaranth (which would later collapse in Herculean fashion in 2006) and offered the note, claiming that Solow Realty needed the $20 million to finance the expansion. Amazingly, no questions were asked, and Dreier LLP now had $20 million in cold cash.

Dreier expanded the office space and set out hiring more lawyers. By the end of 2004, he had almost fifty of the brightest legal minds working for him and with their high guaranteed salaries; they couldn't care less about asking how Dreier could have afforded it. Of course, Dreier did spend some of the money on himself, buying a beachfront house in the Hamptons among other luxuries. But the ever-ambitious Dreier wanted even more, and he soon issued more notes of $40 and $60 million to other hedge funds while also renewing the ones that were already sold on an annual basis.

In 2006, he opened up a Los Angeles office for entertainment lawyers and soon got the representatives of the Olsen twins, Jay Leno, football player Michael Strahan and Yankees pitcher Andy Pettite, among others. Always wanting to make a splash, he paid $300,000 monthly for an office for them in the LA skyscraper used in the 1988 hit action movie *Die Hard*. He lined the office walls, both in LA and New York, with an array of expensive paintings and by the end of 2007, he had 175 lawyers working for him and his firm occupied eleven floors of his Park Avenue building. Dreier himself bought a $10 million apartment in Midtown Manhattan and an $18 million yacht that came with a ten-man crew.

But as is the case with many frauds, the market cycle primes their undoing. In Drier's case, it was the subprime mortgage crisis. When Ralph Cioffi and Matthew Tannin's hedge funds at Bear Stearns collapsed (the subject of a later chapter), hedge fund managers began thinking twice about the performance of their investments. Some of Dreier's buyers asked to cancel their annual note renewal, and Dreier had to appease them by raising interest rates to as high as 12%. But by 2008, when the rest of Bear Stearns blew up and the "recession" was renamed "The Great Recession," Dreier's clients had enough and requested back a staggering sum of $225 million.

Dreier was able to raise some money by getting new note buyers, but this time he had to be a lot more flamboyant. With the Wall Street crisis escalating, hedge fund managers wanted to meet with Solow executives before buying their notes. While one would think that would surely stick a dagger into Dreier's plan, the smart lawyer adapted well. He paid former client Kosta Kovachev to pose as a top Solow executive in Solow's actual offices and Dreier even did some impersonations himself.

But even after he got more buyers, Dreier was still well short of his cash requirements. Desperate, he withdrew $45 million dollars from his clients' escrow accounts but was quickly caught when one of his partners needed $38 million of those monies for a transaction. After a brief trip to the United Arab Emirates to try to attract Arabian investors, Drier returned to the US and tried selling a $44 million note to a New York hedge fund, this time issuing it from a different and highly reputable former client, the Ontario Teachers' Pension Plan (OTPP). Like some of his other investors, this hedge fund manager wanted to meet the OTPP representative himself and have him sign the papers. The hedge fund manager would travel himself to Toronto for the meeting.

What Dreier did next is legendary. He flew to Toronto and met an OTPP lawyer, asking for his business card at the meeting's end. Remaining in the OTPP building, he requested a conference room for a short period while waiting until his private jet was ready to depart. The OTPP agreed. Dreier then brought the manager, who had yet to meet him in person, into the conference room and calmly offered up the business card he just received. Hoping that nobody would come in and discover the impersonation, Dreier quickly signed the papers, but the manager was suspicious. On his way out, he asked a receptionist if the man he had just met was an OTPP lawyer. She said no.

In the meantime, Dreier returned to his private plane and received a call that someone had been impersonating an OTPP employee. Amazingly, nobody had connected the dots to ascertain that it was Dreier himself who had been the impersonator. Instead of safely flying back to New York to deny the incident, Dreier instead returned to the OTPP building, where he was promptly arrested by Toronto police. When he was sent back to the US a few days later after being released on bail, the FBI arrested him with a clearer picture. Turns out, one of his note buyers had contacted Solow Realty about an overdue note, only to have Solow deny that they ever issued it.

At the end, thirteen hedge fund managers had given Dreier over $400 million and he had amassed nearly $300 million more from other investors. Prosecutors recommended sentencing Dreier to 145 years in prison, just five years short of Madoff's sentence, but the judge rejected such as harsh sentence based on the fact that Dreier stole from fewer people.

In the end, he was sentenced to twenty years in a Minnesota federal prison, with his scheduled release coming at the age of 86. Marc Simon, an entertainment lawyer also involved in film-making, directed and produced the aforementioned documentary on Dreier entitled *Unraveled*. The film was nominated for the best documentary feature at the Los Angeles Film Festival but regrettably, this success was no consolation to the investors whose millions were lost.

Key Takeaways

The lesson from the Dreier case is that any time you entrust capital to someone presenting or claiming to be involved in a certain transaction, whether it is debt issuance or the sale of an asset, verify the involvement of the beneficiary or counterparty. It is critical to verify that the one making the pitch is actually affiliated with the counterparty in the manner they claim to be affiliated. In this case, Solow was Dreier's client, but in no way did Solow ever ask Drier to issue debt on his behalf.

Usually, doing this will require you to do some independent due diligence and gather information not readily given by the person making the pitch. In Dreier's case, that would have meant his investors calling up Solow Realty to make sure they were in fact issuing the supposed promissory note. It might have been bothersome, but it would have saved many people an awful lot of money.

* * *

WHO COMMITS INVESTMENT FRAUD AND WHO ARE ITS VICTIMS?

Investment fraud accounts for only 6% of all incidences of fraud, but it's the most visible, the most dramatic, and has arguably the most resounding impact on society.

Investment fraud is also the most easily profiled. Those that commit investment fraud are typically male (87%), between 36-55 years old (76%), work in finance or in a finance-related role, hold a senior management position, and have more than ten years of experience.

At the same time, those who are victims of fraud tend to be male, earn more than $75,000 per year, (quite surprisingly) have higher educational attainment than non-victims, and are over the age of fifty.

Those who are most likely to be affected by fraud are, contrary to most people's beliefs, not the young nor the elderly. They are the middle-aged boomers and those who are too busy with generations above and below them to take notice.

SUCKER DAY: IN COMMEMORATION OF F. BAM MORRISON

I f you travel to the Oklahoma town of Wetumka on September 24, you might be in for a humorous surprise. You will find the town's residents lining the streets, celebrating their local festival: Sucker Day. A curious but well-earned name for a holiday, as the town was indeed suckered by the infamous fraudster, F. Bam Morrison.[1]

A tall and likable fellow with a perpetual smile, Morrison showed up in Wetumka shortly after the July 4th celebrations in 1950. With a population of 2,500 that has since decreased, Wetumka was a small happy-go-lucky town, an hour and a half drive from the hustle-and-bustle of Oklahoma City. As Morrison smiled and waved at the pleasant local folks, he couldn't be more pleased with his surroundings. As criminologist Robert Jay Nash writes, Wetumka was "an untouched suckerland and a con man's paradise."

Very quickly, the newcomer began announcing his news. He was a representative of Bohn's United Circus, a traveling circus that made stops all over America. The smiling Morrison was pleased to announce that Bohn's would be making a stop in Wetumka on July 24, just a few weeks away. The circus would bring tourists to the town. It would allow local stores to advertise. It would purchase supplies, like hay for the animals, from

---

[1] To some accounts, J. Bam Morrison

the local community. He claimed that Bohn had a precondition of only buying from local advertisers, and besides the fun associated with a circus coming to town, it would also be the largest financial boon the local community ever experienced.

The town exploded at the good news. Wetumka would be put on the map. They would rake in the dough.

Local storeowners began buying advertising space as they ordered the supplies for the upcoming day. The chief farmer, Argie Taylor, ordered truckloads of hay and the local grocer ordered 100 pounds of hot dogs. Boy Scouts were enlisted to sell tickets and those who would buy from the cheerful Morrison were likely to get an advance-payment discount, and some distinguished members of the community, like the local doctor, even received free tickets. Morrison struck one deal with the local restaurant to feed the entire circus and another with a local hotel to house them. Of course, all of the payments were made in hard cash, which the smiling and nodding Morrison would pocket on behalf of Bohn's.

Mr. Morrison enthusiastically helped along with the preparations, but a few days before the circus he announced that he, unfortunately, had to temporarily leave them to prepare the next town for the next stop on Bohn's circus tour. But no worries! The circus would be coming in just a few days! He told them, "Just keep on preparing, and I'll see you on opening day," as he left with his pockets full of cash.

By the time July 23rd rolled around, the town was bursting with excitement. By that night, a few skeptics began wondering why nobody from the circus had showed up. The skeptics were in the minority, though, and by the next morning, the streets were filled with local residents waiting for the incoming circus. Needless to say, they remained waiting for quite some time until Argie Taylor received the news that Morrison had sent him something in the post office. In a scene worthy of Hollywood, Taylor arrived at the post office and paid the fee to open his package. It was a pile of hay accompanied by a hand-written note, saying "Regards, J. Bam Morrison."

The news made its way around town. There would be no circus. There probably was no real Mr. F. Bam Morrison and perhaps no Bohn's Circus. But the ever happy-go-lucky town of Wetumka would rise above the challenge. Upon the advice of the local newspaper publisher, who had himself published full-page ads for the circus, the mayor declared the day to be the first annual Sucker Day. The crowds celebrated their own foolishness and merchants gave out their loads of supplies. The celebration repeated itself year after year and soon gained national attention, with an article about the scam and the subsequent holiday being featured in *Time* magazine. In an ironic twist of fate, the festival actually began attracting people to the city and did eventually become a big moneymaker for the town.

As Wetumka kept on celebrating, Morrison kept on scamming. He tried performing the same scam in other cities, but was eventually caught by a sheriff in Warrensburg, Missouri. The sheriff called up the town of Wetumka, asking them if they wanted to add their own charges to the case. Having already seen the success of the Sucker Day parade, the Wetumkans laughingly forgave Morrison and didn't press their own charges. One merchant even invited him to serve as the Marshall for the Sucker Day parade when he'd eventually be released. Sure enough, when Morrison was released from his Missouri jail, he called up the merchant to take him up on the offer, if the merchant would be willing to send him the money to travel.

The merchant laughed. "That much of a sucker, I'm not," he said, before hanging up.

Sucker Day has been celebrated every year since on varying dates with the exception of 2003, when town officials supposedly could not raise enough money from sponsors. According to a Facebook post, 2016's celebration took place on September 26th and in some years, people went around selling $10 bills for $9 as part of the festivities.

As for F. Bam Morrison, seeing that he could no longer make money on the circus scam, he tried for a new, more perverted version. He traveled to Lexington, Virginia, claiming to be a casting director for Universal Studios by the name of Mel Greenberg. Driving a shiny new car into town in 1974, again in the summer, he claimed that the town was chosen to be the filming location of an upcoming Civil War epic featuring the star-studded duo of Burt Reynolds and Audrey Hepburn. Claiming that they were looking for locals to fill the supporting cast, Morrison enlisted the most macho-looking men to play the role of warriors, with promises of $22- to $34-per-hour pay. Then he introduced a bit of perversion. He told the ladies that they were looking for one pretty girl for a larger supporting role that would come with a $12,000 payment, but one that would entail a nude bathing scene. So, Morrison sat in his motel room while watching female hopefuls bathe nude before him. There was always a female accompanier, as, of course, Morrison had no ill intentions. Of course, of course.

But the people of Lexington were less trusting than those out in Wetumka. They called up Universal Studios and found out that there was no Mel Greenberg working for them. Disappointed, town prosecutor Eric Sisler called Morrison into his office, but somehow, the smooth-talking Morrison managed to convince Sisler that he was not lying. For all of his naïveté, though, Sisler did order Morrison to put a halt to the nude tryouts.

The normally cheerful Morrison returned to his motel in a bitter mood, claiming that he was fed up with Lexington. He packed his bags, cashed some checks and left Lexington, never to be seen again.

Key Takeaways

Morrison's expertise seemed to be "brand bastardization." He gave himself credibility not only with his winning personality, but also with his claims of being affiliated with larger brands. In the case of his Lexington fraud, his chosen brand was a very well known and real one, Universal Studios, but in Wetumka, his brand most likely didn't even exist. If you google "Bohn's United Circus," the only results will be those related to Morrison. Nonetheless, a fraudster will still use a concocted brand name to sound more prestigious. If Morrison would have claimed that his own private circus was coming to town, people would have been far less enthused. There is something to be said about a brand name.

The former is much easier to avoid. All it takes is a quick call to the brand to ascertain whether the advance salesman actually works for them. In the case of Lexington, the locals did precisely that. In the Wetumka case, there is no brand to call up and no way to verify whether the salesman is telling the truth.

In scientific circles, a hypothesis must be falsifiable. In other words, the only way that something could be proven to be true is if we know how something can also be proven untrue. This is equally critical in assessing any investment opportunity. For Morrison's most successful fraud, he chose to make up the name of a circus so there was no way to prove him wrong. He was banking on the naïveté and limited resources of the small-town folk to ably disprove the existence of Bohn's United Circus, and he was right.

The lesson for investors is to make sure that every claim has a way of being both confirmed and discredited. Without a method of disproving someone's claims, there is simply no meaningful and reliable way to conduct due diligence on any new opportunity. For all of the fun that Wetumka residents enjoy each year, you probably wouldn't want a Sucker Day of your own.

* * *

WHAT ARE THE COSTS OF FRAUD?

Aside from the financial loss and its impact on the victims, what is often forgotten is the second-order consequences of fraud weighed against those who are close to the action.

These are the broken marriages, the resentful children, the shamed (and often innocent) spouses, and the hopeless retirees with no promising path forward.

Most people never see the bewildered partners or the clueless former employees whose integrity (and employability) are forever in doubt by mere association.

According to a FINRA 2015 study, the indirect costs to those who were close to a fraud include: severe stress (50 percent), anxiety (44 percent), difficulty sleeping (38 percent) and depression (35 percent), declared bankruptcy (9 percent) and of course the indirect financial costs associated with the fraud, such as late fees, legal fees and bounced checks.

CHOOSING DE NIRO OVER DINERO AND THE VALUATION PRACTICES OF EDWARD STRAFACI

Ken Lipper was well known in New York circles. Born in the Bronx, Lipper attended Colombia and then Harvard Law through scholarships, topping that off with a Master's from NYU's law school. Marrying Evelyn, the daughter of oil tycoon Joseph Gruss, Lipper's connections now matched his education. Branching into investing, he became a partner in Lehman Brothers at the ripe age of thirty-two. By the late 1980s, he was active in the New York political scene and founded his own firm, Lipper and Co., which went on to become one of the largest firms specializing in mergers and acquisitions.

If that wasn't enough, he also served as deputy mayor of New York under Ed Koch and even dabbled in Hollywood. He was heavily involved in the production of Oliver Stone's *Wall Street*, later penning the book version, and co-produced an Oscar-winning documentary with Steven Spielberg entitled *The Last Days*. While he wouldn't advertise it, he also co-wrote and co-produced a movie named *City Hall,* starring his childhood friend and dream collaborator, Al Pacino, that unfortunately flopped at the box office.

At first, his involvement in Hollywood helped out his investing. Lipper and Co.'s $4 billion of assets under management included money from Julia Roberts, Liam Neeson and former Disney CEO Michael Eisner. He bought an office in Los Angeles and the former deputy mayor soon became a man of Two Cities. But his wife Evelyn had no interest in the Hollywood glitz and soon requested a divorce. Friends recalled how Lipper was now hanging around the "Robert De Niro crowd" in a full-blown "mid-life crisis." What nobody realized was that a much more ominous crisis was happening within Lipper's own firm, a crisis orchestrated by a single employee.

Edward Strafaci, who had been working for Lipper and Co. for thirteen years, was now the firm's top portfolio manager and its Chief Compliance Officer. Apparently dissatisfied with his salary of $150,000 plus added bonuses, Strafaci had developed an interesting habit of inflating assets. Since Strafaci's bonuses were tied to the performance of the fund, his desire to increase his salary prompted him to overvalue the fund's assets. It was an easy task, as there was no independent administrator valuing Lipper's assets. Strafaci, using pricing methods that were laid out in the fund's memorandum, was valuing them in-house.

Strafaci began ignoring the memorandum and pricing Lipper's convertible securities over 10% above their actual worth. This created a domino effect that caused the fund itself to be overvalued by more than 40%. Of course, Strafaci didn't care. To the contrary, his bonuses were soaring. In 1998 and 2001, his added bonuses were $850,000 and over a million dollars in both 1999 and 2000. The overvalued figures of the fund were sent to the SEC, investors and prospective investors. Even in 2000 and 2001, when Lipper Holdings suffered bad losses, Strafaci's numbers depicted passable gains.

It all came to an end on January 14, 2002, just a few days after Strafaci cashed his hefty bonus check and the fund's auditor, PricewaterhouseCoopers, began their audit. While Lipper was busy in Los Angeles working on a Hollywood project and meeting with clients, Strafaci and a fellow worker in the pricing department abruptly resigned. An internal review followed, finding the assets to be severely overvalued and that the firm had suffered a loss of 40% since 2000. Lipper sent a letter conveying the news to his investors, sending an even more damning letter just a few months later. Apparently, the losses in the past year and a half now amounted to over 47%.

A crowd swarmed around Lipper and two of his institutional investors immediately formed lawsuits. Lipper wrote to investors that he had no idea that the funds were being overvalued and hinted that Strafaci was the one to blame. Strafaci was sure to deflect it. According to a *Business Week* cover story, when Strafaci was asked about blame, he calmly replied: "We don't bear any responsibility at all. Clients have to go to Ken Lipper if they're mad. He's the CEO."

The SEC begged to differ and Strafaci was soon arrested. Knowing that he couldn't pin this on Lipper, Strafaci ended up pleading guilty to overstating the value of the funds and was sentenced to six years in prison. Lipper, who himself had funds for his four children tied into the firm, was acquitted of all wrongdoing but his reputation was severely hit. Even as a horde of his former employers, including Ed Koch, rushed to defend him, many were skeptical and thought it was simply an act of one rich mogul covering up for the other one.

A long legal battle ensued as Lipper fought to clear his name. Investors claimed he was negligent while running his hedge fund, paying too much attention to Hollywood while ignoring the business of his own hedge fund. They further charged that he gave preferential withdrawals to his buddies while leaving the rest of the firm to run dry. Lipper adamantly denied both claims. After a nine-year legal mess, Lipper won and recovered the $14 million spent in legal fees defending himself. He also recouped $6 million from the auditor, PwC, due to his own investments in the firm while relying on their audits.

With his reputation cleared, Lipper returned to investing after a ten-year hiatus and began writing a book about his experiences. In 2013, New York Governor Andrew Cuomo appointed Lipper to the Board of Commissioners of the Port Authority of New York and New Jersey, an area where Lipper was heavily involved when serving in the Koch administration.

Key Takeaways

The size of the fraud as well as Lipper's reputation made this case the story of New York for quite some time.

Notwithstanding Lipper clearing his name, the fact remains that his various extracurricular activities undoubtedly distracted him from the portfolio. How else can one explain a portfolio manager overstating countless trades over a four-year period without an engaged chairman having a clue? As such, prudent investors should ensure those they rely on to manage their capital are doing so with unmitigated focus.

The broader moral of the story revolves around aligning incentives, avoiding conflicts of interest and "separation of church and state"—separating those who are compensated to generate returns from those who assess whether or not those returns are valid.

The Lipper case did much to increase standards and promulgate best practices within the hedge fund community in the early 2000s, most notably in the area of valuation. People began to realize that when workers in a fund are given the option of valuing their own assets, like Strafaci was given, there will be nothing but their conscience stopping them from overvaluation. As such, the movement toward third-party administrators began.

A third-party administrator independently calculates the value of a fund, preventing people like Strafaci from getting away with overvaluations. This movement only increased when the slew of hedge fund frauds in the late 2000s were discovered to be overvaluing their assets. Today, you would be hard-pressed to find a hedge fund that does not have an independent administrator. That said, should you encounter such a fund, remember Edward Strafaci and run away.

* * *

"Is my money really all gone?" asks the client

"No, of course not." replies the advisor. "It's just with somebody else!"

—Anonymous Fraudster

HORSES, LIBRARIES AND HOCKEY: THE STORY OF WG TRADING

Stephen Walsh and Paul Greenwood were an interesting team. The two former minority owners of the New York Islanders hockey team ran WG Trading, a well-respected Wall Street trading firm. Either could have been confused for someone's sweet, old grandfather. Walsh, who was balding, wore out-of-style rimmed glasses, and had a collection of rare books, appeared to be the bookish grandpa. Greenwood, with his nearly full head of hair, knack for bowties and $2 million horse farm once owned by actor Paul Newman, seemed to be the cool and hip granddaddy. In reality, the two of them were a team of fraudsters who conned institutional investors, including charities and universities, out of more than $550 million.

Greenwood and Walsh gained a solid reputation on Wall Street in the 1980s when they created Shark, a computerized program helping traders find the right securities to buy. They sold Shark to Wang Laboratories and used the proceeds to buy shares in the New York Islanders hockey team.

In 1996, they began soliciting for a new fund, Westridge Capital Management, which traded through their own broker-dealer, the WG Trading Company. Their supposed strategy was an "equity index arbitrage," a strategy where one buys or sells an index futures contract[2] while also buying or selling

---

[2] Futures are financial contracts obligating the buyer to purchase an asset or the seller to sell an asset, at a pre-determined date and price in the future. Futures contracts may involve a physical commodity or a financial security.

stocks in that index. They claimed that it was a conservative strategy that consistently outperformed the S&P 500 index. While they did not attract a whole lot of investors, they attracted many large institutions who liked their reputation and supposedly conservative strategy. University of Pittsburgh invested $65 million, Carnegie Mellon $49 million, Sacramento Retirement System $90 million, and the Iowa Retirement Pension System a whopping $339 million. Many of them relied on the fact that Deloitte was auditing the company, though they were only auditing WG Trading Company, the broker-dealer, and not Westridge Capital Management.

The natural question is how they paid their investors. Instead of giving back all of the profits of their investments in cash, they chose to pay $667 million of it by issuing promissory notes through their subsidiary WG Trading Investors who, like Westridge, was not audited by Deloitte. The reason why they didn't pay in cash was twofold: they really weren't making as much money as they claimed and they were also diverting much of the money for their own use. They created documents to corroborate their professed trading and instead used the money to fund their own lavish lifestyles. According to FBI press releases, Walsh also used his money to "finance business ventures of his children" and pay millions in divorce settlements to his ex-wife, aside from building a $4 million home for himself and his current wife. Greenwood amassed a large collection of teddy bears, paid for a $3 million home for his ex-wife, and built a nearly $10 million home for *himself* and *his* current wife. The partners clearly had more than fraud in common.

With Deloitte checking off their annual audit of the WG Trading Company but paying no attention to Westridge or WG

Trading Investors, the scam continued until 2009 and WG Trading had solicited a total of $7.6 billion. But it was in 2009, in the aftermath of Bernie Madoff's hedge fund fraud, that people began to look at other hedge funds. The National Futures Association (NFA), a self-regulatory body that monitors futures traders, conducted an audit on all entities of WG, including WG Trading Investors. They found that while WG Trading Investors issued $667 million of promissory notes to their investors and claimed respectable returns, they only had $93 million in their accounts. They contacted Walsh and Greenwood, but the WG bigwigs refused to cooperate. As a result, the NFA suspended their membership and a domino effect followed. The SEC froze the assets and the FBI began an investigation.

It was soon discovered that the Walsh and Greenwood had taken over $553 million of their investors' money. The pair were both arrested, and Greenwood cooperated with authorities to testify against his partner. He received a reduced sentence of ten years in exchange for his testimony and agreed to pay $83 million from the money he had "personally obtained" from the fraud, aside from forfeiting $331 million to the government. (His sentence was later cut to five years.) Walsh was sentenced to twenty years and $51 million in payments. Deloitte had to face a suit brought by the Iowa pension fund but it was later dismissed because Deloitte only audited WG Trading Company and not the subsidiaries where the fraud happened, Westridge Capital and WG Trading Investors.

After the suit was dismissed, about 98 percent of the money was eventually recovered.

Key Takeaways

Walsh and Greenwood essentially used their hedge fund as their piggy bank. Much can be said about the need for a custodian to guard a hedge fund's assets and make sure they are used appropriately and we will address this later on in the Norshield case. WG Trading's lack of monthly reporting from a custodian should have been enough to scare away most investors.

What should have warded off the remaining victims was Walsh and Greenwood's utilization of promissory notes and the fact that only one of the three entities involved in the strategy was properly audited.

First, for a hedge fund to utilize promissory notes instead of holding partnership units with a net asset value is highly unusual. Unless there is a highly compelling reason for doing so (which there did not appear to be), it should have been an immediate red flag. Promissory notes are perfectly legitimate ways to pay investors, but are oftentimes used in Ponzi schemes, as they circumvent the need for an independent administrator and are usually privately negotiated, so verifying their value is often difficult.

Secondly, while hedge funds don't legally require an independent auditor like public corporations do, it certainly is best practice to have one. When a fund is issuing payments through promissory notes, which is an intensive accounting exercise, one should expect a proper audit and be intolerant of anything less. This is especially true when a fund has various arms and/or affiliates.

As we saw, while Deloitte conducted an audit on the broker-dealer arm of the WG Trading Company, they were not hired to do so on Westridge Capital, where Walsh and Greenwood siphoned most of the money away, or WG Trading Investors, from where the notes were issued. It is incumbent on the investor to ensure that every affiliate is included. Otherwise, one risks finding their notes being backed by nothing more than horses, bowties and teddy bears.

* * *

CHECKS AND BALANCES

ANTIGUA'S CD PLAYER: THE STORY OF SIR ALLEN STANFORD

Not many bodybuilders end up managing billions of dollars. But again, not many people had a life trajectory like Texan Robert Allen Stanford.

Stanford's beginnings were humble. He claimed that he was chopping wood by the age of thirteen and donating his earnings to a family whose house burned down. After receiving a finance degree at Baylor University, he founded a chain of health clubs in central Texas. The venture was a disaster. After descending into bankruptcy, Stanford hit a financial low (even flipping hamburgers to get by). That is, until his family business struck gold.

Gough quotes a *Forbes* report that Stanford, together with his father, purchased a slew of properties in the 1980s, when the Houston real estate market crashed, and made hundreds of millions when they proceeded to sell them off as the market recovered. Deciding to use his profits to get into money management, Stanford moved to the lightly regulated Caribbean island of Montserrat. There he founded Guardian International Bank.

Stanford's business plans were unusual to say the least. Operating as an offshore bank, he would not generate revenues by lending, as most normal banks do. Instead, he would aggressively sell Certificates of Deposits[3] (CDs) and invest them in a

---

[3] CDs are investment vehicles where one deposits money with a financial institution and has the right to withdraw that capital, plus a specified interest, at a fixed date in the future.

variety of stocks, hedge funds and commodities. Proclaiming himself as an investing genius, he guaranteed his investors interest of 7.5% in one year, a rate far above the market average. While many banks that sell CDs normally take the money given to them and lend it out at a higher rate, Stanford claimed that his investments far exceeded the returns that banks can achieve.

In reality, Stanford used the money to finance an array of deals, mostly relating to his own private businesses. As a result, when James Davis, Stanford's old college buddy, became the bank's Controller, he found the bank's assets to be worth half the recorded value on the financial statements.

Stanford relied on selling CDs to increase his cash position, generously rewarding salespeople who were more successful, and creating phony documents to assure his salespeople that his CDs were insured when, of course, they weren't. Charlesworth Hewlett, Stanford's accountant who ran a small office out of Antigua, another poorly regulated Caribbean island, was paid handsomely to help conceal the fraud. Allegedly, his total payments reached $3.4 million by the time Hewlett died in 2009. It is entirely possible that Stanford's Ponzi scheme was initially a temporary measure until his investments bore fruit, but they never did, so he continued cooking the books.

With countless cover ups, things began to unravel for Stanford. British regulatory authorities had decided to crack down on Montserrat, and, in 1990, they began asking many questions about the nature of Stanford's dealings. Among their many demands, the prosecution repeatedly insisted he get a more reputable auditor than Hewlett, whose tiny outfit (and questionable credibility) was hardly appropriate for any "legitimate" multi-million dollar operation. As the regulators cracked down further, Montserrat authorities threatened Stanford with revocation of his banking license. The sly Stanford was one step ahead. Instead of waiting for them to revoke it, he willingly gave it up and moved his operation to Hewlett's own island, Antigua.

Stanford was very lucky in his timing because Soufrière Hills, a dormant volcano on the southern half of the Montserrat, struck with a deadly force in the mid-1990s, forcing two-thirds of the local population to flee and the capital, Plymouth, to empty. Stanford was even luckier for his newfound ability to operate without bothersome regulators. He took full advantage of it.

As soon as he arrived in Antigua, Stanford renamed his company Stanford Financial Group and went on a buying spree to make local friends. Antigua turned out to be the perfect place, as it was an island that greatly needed help, and Stanford became their savior. He fished $50,000 from his pocket to buy the failing local bank, the Bank of Antigua, and gave the government $40 million in loans that he eventually forgave. In a matter of extreme "coincidence," Stanford soon received an Antiguan banking license to replace his Montserrat one and a residency permit. But having learned his lessons in Montserrat, Stanford didn't stop there.

As a beautiful Caribbean island with a destitute internal economy, Antigua relied largely on tourism to keep their poor from starving, and Stanford gave their tourist industry a welcome boost. He purchased large areas of land, in itself a great moneymaker for the locals, and instead of using them for his own businesses, he converted them into attractions—e.g. a horde of restaurants as well as a cricket stadium. He capped it all by building a brand-new hospital to service the island. He doled out tens of thousands to cover prime minister Lester Bird's American medical expenses and made generous contributions to local politicians. Thus, in the community and in all political spheres, he was heralded as a local hero and treated in kind.

After helping the government deal with Russian mob influences in the mid-1990s, Stanford was named chairman of the Antiguan Offshore Financial Sector Planning Committee. He was now charged with the responsibility of straightening out the Antiguan banking industry. Seeing this as an opportunity to expand his influence, he appointed his friends to all of the senior positions. When a new regulator—the International Financial Sector Authority—was established, Stanford somehow managed to become chairman of that as well, lavishing gifts upon his employees to earn their favor. And through it all, he kept on selling CDs, using fresh capital to repay previous investors in a full-blown Ponzi scheme.

In 2006, Stanford was knighted, enhancing his already robust social status. By 2008, he had sold $7.2 billion worth of CDs, with millions more on the horizon until the global financial crisis struck. While he claimed that Stanford Financial Group was performing well in spite of troubling markets, investors still hurried to redeem over $2 billion of CDs with few new investors walking through the door. Yet in his personal life, Stanford still spent money like water, throwing away $515,000 during one week in Las Vegas in January 2009 and lavishing gifts on the many women he romanced, including at least four secret wives.

Despite his precarious situation, Stanford made a bold claim he thought would get him out of trouble. He had recently purchased land in Antigua for a planned resort, which he hoped to sell from one company to another to eventually reach his goal of $3.2 billion. But with American authorities on his trail, Stanford never got the chance.

After a last-ditch attempt to escape the US on a private plane to Antigua failed, due to credit card problems, he was finally arrested by the US government. In 2012, Stanford was sentenced not only to 110 years in prison but he was also eventually ordered to pay more than $6 billion in restitution. While it is absolutely clear that Stanford lied to his investors about where the money really was, it is still unclear whether he intended for this to become a Ponzi scheme. He didn't simply use Peter's money to pay Paul; he actually did allocate money to his private investments and if they had gone well, he might have been able to pay out his CDs. In his first interview since being incarcerated, Stanford still insisted that he did nothing wrong and that the government was merely using him as a scapegoat. But for the many who lost millions to Stanford, his intentions didn't matter. He lied and put other people's money at risk. Every one of those 110 years is undeniably deserved.

Key Takeaways

So much was wrong with Stanford Financial Group. First, his much higher than average CD rate is the classic "too good to be true" warning, the takeaway which we will discuss in the Charles Ponzi case.

The fact that he chose his headquarters only in unregulated locations such as Montserrat and Antigua is also a red flag, one that we will deal with in the case of Martin Frankel.

Another significant takeaway here is the lack of an appropriate auditor for such a large organization, which we've already seen in the Equity Funding fraud.

But perhaps the most significant takeaway lies in the absence of governance and internal controls. At the outset, it appears that Stanford did not set out to conduct a Ponzi scheme. He simply wanted cash for his own investments and had they gone well, he would have been hailed as a hero. So how does one prevent a delusional director from using his company as a piggybank?

Typically, a board of directors with proper governance and internal control can ensure that a manager is running the company in the best interests of shareholders, not in his own best interests. If Stanford had an independent board of directors above him, he would not have been able to divert absurd sums of money for his own use. Unfortunately, there wasn't a shred of independent oversight around. Stanford's board was made up entirely of insiders, including his father and someone who remained on board for years after having a debilitating stroke. With no real governance, Stanford proceeded to "justify" his monumental deceits, to this very day believing that he did nothing wrong.

* * *

WHAT IS THE COST OF FRAUD TO THE ECONOMY?

Besides the pain of the victims, fraud has a much broader societal tax on the economy.

Capital markets hinge on trust. Every debt instrument is determined by the credit-worthiness of the borrowers and likelihood of getting repaid. Every fraud that reduces the trust of the market makes borrowing just a bit more expensive, makes access to capital a bit more elusive and slows the growth of the economy as a whole. In fact, even the equity of every public company is valued, in part, according to its weighted average cost of capital (WACC). In simple terms, how much it must pay for capital.

The less trustworthy we become, the higher the WACC, and the lower valued our companies become—driving down stock prices in the process.

There isn't a single corner of our society that isn't adversely affected by virtually every incidence of fraud.

THE TALENTED XANTHOUDAKIS WHO COULD MAKE MONEY DISAPPEAR

I f you were born late enough or have children of your own, you probably remember the TV show, *Arthur*. Based on the books by Marc Brown and currently the second-longest running show on PBS Kids, it features an annoyingly catchy theme song ("Believe in Yourself") and probably let the world know that the animal called an "aardvark" actually exists. But for all of the show's innocence and inspiration, the husband-and-wife team who produced *Arthur* weren't nearly as innocent or inspiring, and neither was their friend, John Xanthoudakis.

Xanthoudakis was born in Montreal to Greek immigrants and attended Concordia University to study engineering in the 1980s. While there, he developed an interest in finance, thinking that if he could create the right trading system, he would have a massive edge in trading. Upon graduating, he founded Ultron Technologies Corp. (perhaps inspired by the Stan Lee comic books of his childhood) and began trading with some success. But Xanthoudakis seemed to have a problem with adhering to rules and the Quebec Securities Commission noticed. First, they saw him selling securities without a prospectus and temporarily shut him down. Then he was caught for selling investments that weren't approved by the commission. Still thinking he had an edge, Xanthoudakis stayed in trading and established a hedge fund, Norshield Asset Management.

The fund received money from institutional investors, with retail monies going to Olympus United Funds Corporation and the institutional monies going to a Bahamian company, Olympus Univest. After that, though, the money was tunneled from one offshore account to another until it gathered into one large pool. From 1993 to 2007, Norshield raised $159 million from 1,900 retail investors and another $350 million from institutions.

That's when *Arthur* comes in. *Arthur*, along with *The Busy World of Richard Scarry, Zoboomafoo, Madeline* and *The Adventures of Paddington Bear,* were all produced or co-produced by Cinar Corporation, run by Ronald Weinberg and his wife Micheline Charest. Weinberg and Charest had originally met at a women's film festival in New Orleans. After working together on a few projects, they had decided to found Cinar (and later married). Having grown tired of being a NYC-based television distribution company, they decided to venture into their own productions in 1984 and moved to Montreal. First starting by producing English and French shows to suit Quebec audiences, they soon found great success in their productions and Cinar went public in 1993. By 1999, it had annual revenues of $150 million and a market cap of $1.5 billion.

Flush with money, Weinberg and Charest wanted to invest and turned to Xanthoudakis when Hasanain Panju, Cinar's CFO, came across one of Norshield's Bahamian funds, Globe-X. With Panju's help, they moved $108 million of Cinar's money into Globe-X without informing Cinar. In other words, Weinberg, Charest and Panju stole nearly $110 million from the company they founded.

Justice came quickly. That very same year, Cinar came under scrutiny for a completely unrelated phenomenon. They had been getting significant grants on the condition that they employ Canadian writers, but had actually been hiring American writers and keeping the money. Police began looking into Cinar's affairs and quickly found that they had just invested some $100 million with Norshield. Cinar's board was up in arms, demanding that the trio of Weinberg, Charest and Panju resign and that all of the money be returned. Reluctantly, Xanthoudakis struck a deal with Cinar's board promising to return all of the money; but after paying around two-thirds of the debt, Xanthoudakis claimed that he couldn't pay the rest.

Globe-X was forced into bankruptcy, but when bankruptcy officials started looking at Globe-X, they couldn't believe their eyes. Of the $108 million, only $21 million was invested, with the rest being transferred to other Globe-X- and Norshield-connected entities. Furthermore, they found that Cinar had given $7 million to cover a supposed Globe-X debt, only to have that money siphoned off to another Weinberg, Charest and Panju-controlled company.

A long investigation ensued. Charest died from surgery complications in 2004 and Norshield was shut down in 2005. Court-appointed receivers began looking into their assets and found a disappearing trail of money. With money constantly being shuffled between various Norshield entities, receivers found that money often disappeared when being funneled. Some money was also used to pay previous investors, like any old Ponzi scheme, but the most painful revelation was that receivers found a number of unexplained withdrawals, redemptions and mysterious third-party payments, with little contractual information about where the money was going. In one particularly egregious example, a Barbados bank subsumed under Norshield paid $60 million to an undocumented third party. And that was just one of many payments to a horde of undocumented recipients. Additionally, there were no audited records after 2003 and not a clue as to the whereabouts of all the money.

Of the $159 million taken from retail investors, receivers only found $31 million. In total, investors lost an estimated $482 million. Some thought that much of the money went to the Royal Bank of Canada (RBC), who was involved with Norshield, and suits were filed claiming that RBC had merely used Norshield as a front to get into hedge funds when they legally weren't able to operate one. Such claims did not have any factual base and even lawsuits against RBC for negligence and enabling the fraud were dismissed. Canadian author Bruce Livesey (*Thieves of Bay Street*) notes that to this day, the RCMP has yet to undergo a full operation looking into the missing money and it is suspected that much of the money went to Mafia families in Canada.

In 2010, the OSC charged Xanthoudakis and a fellow Norshield executive with making false statements, lacking significant documentation and dishonesty with investors. They were each slapped with $2.2 million in fines, in addition to the $295,000 cost of the OSC investigation and were both banned permanently from the securities industry. In 2011, Weinberg, Xanthoudakis, Panju and another accomplice, Lino Matteo, were all arrested and tried. After the longest-running jury trial in Canadian history, requiring two full years, a criminal trial finally concluded in 2016, and Weinberg was sentenced to nine years in prison. Xanthoudakis and Matteo were each sentenced to eight years. Panju, who cooperated with authorities and served as the Crown's witness on the case, received a mitigated four-year sentence in 2014 and was released on parole after two years.

With vast sums of money still missing, a Norshield victim named "Chris" set up a blog to keep the group updated and gather more information. Posts stopped in 2012, likely because the money will probably remain missing for quite some time.

Key Takeaways

In his book *Thieves of Bay Street*, Bruce Livesey uses Norshield to illustrate the dangers of the unregulated hedge fund industry. He goes as far as calling hedge funds "rogue forces within the shadow banking industry" that charge large fees for the privilege. While that is an extreme and unwarranted reaction, a more reasonable one may be to ensure that any hedge fund being considered for investment utilizes or employs the services of a credible independent custodian and truly provides the value the funds claim to offer, which, unfortunately, only a handful do.

A custodian is an independent entity that holds the assets on behalf of the owner instead of giving complete control to the hedge fund manager. After all, the only thing a hedge fund manager is supposed to do is figure out which investments to make. Other than that, there is no inherent value or reason for the fund to also hold the money. Moreover, if the manager has access to the assets, what's preventing the manager from claiming that they are investing the money when they really aren't? Or, even if they are investing money, what's preventing them from siphoning off some or most of the money to themselves or funding unexplained third-party payments? Who will step in and ask where the money is going to?

Norshield is the quintessential example of a hedge fund without an independent custodian. With all of the assets in-house, Xanthoudakis was able to move money as he pleased, and nobody was there to ask any harsh questions. A custodian would not have relinquished its clients' assets until knowing where the money was going and ensuring the security of investor capital.

* * *

WHAT IS MOST COMMON FORM OF INVESTMENT FRAUD?

Approximately 85% of all investment fraud cases are a function of asset misappropriation, with the person entrusted to guard the money simply misappropriating the capital and using it for their own purposes.

CALISTO TANZI'S SPOILED MILK: THE RISE AND FALL OF EUROPE'S ENRON

Calisto Tanzi was born in what some would call Culinary Central: northwestern Italy, a region that currently houses the EU's Food Safety Agency as well as the city of Parma, known for Parmesan cheeses and Parma ham. Born in 1938 in a village just outside of Parma, Calisto Tanzi had dreams of becoming an accountant. While he was still in college, his dreams were unexpectedly shattered with the passing of his father. Instead, at just twenty-two years old, he returned home to run the family business, which dealt with processed foods such as spiced meats and tomato purees.

Within two years of taking over, young Calisto decided that there was more money to be made in the dairy market and started the business from scratch by opening a pasteurization plant. He began selling milk, at first by going around door to door in the Parma area. Within a few years, he developed an ultra-heating system of pasteurization, allowing the milk to stay good and fresh for much longer. This was a major evolution in the process at the time. It didn't take long for his company to explode and the proceeds from his milk process were used to expand into other dairy product lines, including cream and yogurt, as well as a return to selling processed foods again. But the focus remained on dairy and the new dairy company was renamed Parmalat.

Tanzi expanded Parmalat outside Italy in the 1970s and by 1986, it was a global operation, producing over 600 million euros in revenues. He took Parmalat public in 1990, though the Tanzi family retained 52% control through another company, Coloniale SpA. Parmalat seemed to expand into other areas as well, including Parmatours, a tourist company ran by Calisto's daughter, Francesca. He also used 130 million euros of Parmalat money to buy Odeon TV, a local Italian syndication program.

Through it all, Tanzi seemed to have a large sense of duty. He bought Parma AC, the local football team when it was at the bottom of the league standings. He invested extraordinary amounts of money into it until Parma AC finally won two UEFA titles and one European Cup Winner's Cup. He helped support the local Verti festival and donated to help restorations at the local cathedral. In 1992, he was given an honorary degree in economics from Parma University to go along with a Knight of the Order of Labour Merit from the Italian republic. Tanzi seemed to be Italy's quintessential Renaissance man.

After going public, Parmalat began a succession of rapid expansions to the point of extreme excess. In 1991, they had 4,800 employees in six countries, and by 2003, they had 36,000 employees. Much of it was due to an incredible amount of spending in the dairy market, buying out local suppliers and opening up new factories. At one time they were selling 60% of the milk in New York City through various subsidiaries and opened almost twenty factories in Brazil while also acquiring a large local competitor, Batavia, for $160 million. By 2003, their expansion had led them to amass over 150 subsidiaries around the globe.

But behind the scenes, nothing was pretty. Along with the Tanzi family having majority control, the vast majority of board directors were Tanzi family affiliates that allowed Calisto to do whatever he pleased, whether it was sensible or a clearly colossal mistake. The rapid expansion, while increasing sales by the droves, did not necessarily increase profits, as the costs of expansion pretty much outweighed the gains. And then there were the special projects: his daughter's Parmatours, despite running nine beach resorts and four resorts in the Italian Alps, was a titanic failure. Yet Calisto kept on pulling money from Parmalat to keep the failing business afloat. His purchase of Odeon TV was equally disastrous. It went bankrupt after three years and was sold for a loss of €45 million. And for all its on-field success, Parma AC was a financial clusterfug, losing €77 million in 2002 alone.

How did nobody catch all this? The complicated company structure allowed Calisto to shift money from one subsidiary to another at will, with numerous offshore accounts involved.

In December 2002, Merrill Lynch downgraded the stock from "buy" to "sell" because of the complicated structure that it found to be unreadable. Other firms soon began to question the structure as well. From its high in April 2002, the stock fell forty percent by January 2003, so, that February, Tanzi set out to issue €300-500 million in bonds, but that made analysts even more suspicious. Why did Parmalat need to issue that much debt when, according to their financial statements, they were supposedly chock full with €3 billion in cash? Parmalat then canceled the bond issue and consequently remained short on cash. In December, they defaulted on bond payments of €150 million.

Tanzi downplayed it as a minor "liquidity problem," but the writing was on the wall. About a third of the board resigned and the new board voted to bring in savvy administrator Enrico Bondi to fix the company-wide mess. He brought in PriceWaterhouseCoopers to investigate and they found that while Parmalat had reported earnings ever since it went public, it had in fact sustained losses during twelve of those thirteen years. As it turned out, under Tanzi's orders, Parmalat recorded the assets and revenues from every sale twice on their books, after producing two invoices per every order (aka "double-billing scheme"). Additionally, Parmalat hid legions of debt through various schemes, such as recording €1 billion of debt as equity, recording €300 million in bank loans as intercompany loans, claiming €200 million in accounts payable were paid when, in fact, they were not. And most of all, writing off €3.3 billion in debt by saying they had repurchased debt securities. Many of these misstatements occurred on the books of the Cayman Islands-based Bonlat, one of Parmalat's many subsidiaries which claimed fictitious assets of almost nine billion euros made up of fraudulent transactions and claims of asset accounts that simply did not exist. By order of Parmalat's CFO, Bonlat's accounts were destroyed by an accountant as doomsday approached.

Additionally, PwC discovered that Tanzi had been skimming money from Parmalat to send to his daughter's Parmatours and the total transferred reached a whopping total of €926 billion.

Nine days after PwC began its audit, Parmalat filed for bankruptcy. In total, Parmalat owed €14.3 billion, making it Europe's largest bankruptcy ever, and earning Parmalat the nickname of "the European Enron." More than twenty people were charged by Italian prosecutors, including two of Parmalat's external auditors, and Tanzi was sentenced to a total of twenty-eight years in prison. Because he was almost seventy at the time, they let him serve the sentence in his own home in Parma.

Key Takeaways

While family-controlled companies are often charming, and board control by the family is fairly standard in Italy, poor governance practices and a lack of checks and balances also tends to become a gateway to frauds.

As we saw with Stanford, when CEOs like Tanzi stack boards with those who won't oppose whatever insane expenses they incur or the shareholder value they erode, it is the beginning of the end, culminating in either colossal failure, cover-up or both.

Tanzi conflated agendas and bastardized the mission of the company by directing the funds of its many shareholders into his daughter's hopeless enterprise. How could a world-class dairy justify buying media, touring and football organizations? Successful businessman-turned-president Donald Trump tried a similar formula of blending other interests outside his real estate and entertainment model such as Trump University, Trump Vodka, and Trump Airlines, which were wild-ass ideas with poor prospects for success. Hopefully, Trump and Tanzi can serve as salient reminders to steer clear of those who don't allow themselves a spirited challenge.

* * *

WHAT IS THE COSTLIEST FORM OF FRAUD?

While asset misappropriation is the most common form of fraud, in absolute dollars, over 90% of total value lost to fraud relates to corruption and financial statement manipulation. These tend to be much larger by incidence and affect groups rather than targeted individuals, as the masses are far less equipped to protect against corruption and financial statement manipulation.

AMERICA'S MOST NOTORIOUS MORAL WARRIOR: CHARLES KEATING AND THE SAVINGS & LOAN SCANDAL

Ronald Reagan was largely considered one of the most successful modern US presidents. His economic initiatives, termed "Reaganomics," helped improve the American economy by reducing inflation and creating an annual GDP growth of 3.4% and his foreign policy was credited for the collapse of the Soviet Union. His approval rating when he left office was a whopping 63%, second only to Bill Clinton's 66%. That said, his administration had its fair share of scandals. One of them was the Savings and Loan Crisis.

A Savings and Loan Association (S&L), also known as a thrift institution, is a company specializing in mortgage lending and savings deposits. Their industry skyrocketed following World War II with the "baby boom" and the encouragement of American suburbanization, with masses of families leaving urban areas and buying homes in the suburbs. By the time the '70s rolled around, the industry was slowing due to regulatory constraints, as rising interest rates and a slowing economy made it harder to qualify for mortgages and mortgages were the bread and butter of the S&L industry.

During the '70s, S&L companies managed to get creative enough to keep on going. While the volume of mortgages slowed, they maintained and even increased profitability by using innovative techniques to garner income, such as using interest-bearing checking accounts. In 1979, however, the industry received further blows as interest rates rose alongside inflation. S&Ls, which had $480 billion of their $600 billion in assets as fixed-rate mortgages locked in at much lower rates, paid the severe price. It soon was apparent that something needed to be done and the first thing to go was the regulations.

In 1980, President Jimmy Carter signed the Depository Institutions Deregulation and Monetary Control Act of 1980 (MCA) which allowed institutions to use any interest rate they chose and even allowed usury. But even that didn't help. Virtually every S&L was insolvent by 1981 and the industry was $150 billion in debt by mid-1982. To make things worse, the Federal Savings and Loan Insurance Corporation (FSLIC), the institution that acted as a safety net for the S&Ls by offering them deposit insurance, had only $6 billion in cash reserves.

And of course, any industry that's bankrupt readily admits it, right? Possibly . . . in Lalaland.

The industry wasn't interested in admitting its own insolvency for obvious reasons. The Reagan administration wasn't interested in admitting it either, as the $150 billion of added debt would prevent them from implementing Reagan's 1981 tax cuts. Neither the Democrats nor the Republicans in Congress were keen on admitting to it, as programs resulting from the S&L industry were very popular among voters. After all, who doesn't want to buy a house? And to buy a house, you need the S&Ls. So the Bank Board, headed by the Reagan-appointed Richard Pratt, allowed its own set of loose reporting standards called the RAP to trump the normally required Generally Accepted Accounting Principles (GAAP).

Continuing with the legacy of Jimmy Carter, Congress opted for the Garn-St Germain Depository Institutions Act of 1982. The act did some good by allowing the S&L industry to use adjustable-rate mortgages to prevent inflation from affecting them but it also deregulated the industry and expanded its lending abilities. The bill passed in an overwhelming 272-91 majority in the House and optimists thought that this would help the S&L industry "grow" out of their problems. Into this mess stepped Charles Keating.

Keating, a former champion swimmer at the University of Cincinnati and a lawyer by training, first gained national fame as an anti-porn activist from the late '50s through the early '70s and was even appointed by President Nixon to the President's Commission on Obscenity and Pornography in 1969. During that same period, he teamed up with a former law client, Carl Lidner, Jr., to found American Financial Corporation, a holding company that contained many of Lidner's various businesses. While he was officially just one member on the board of directors and still practiced as a lawyer, Keating became the unofficial face of the company until he finally left law in 1972 to join the now-$1 billion company as executive vice president.

It didn't take long for Keating's reputation to spread and he was known to be aggressive and arrogant. While involved with *The Cincinnati Enquirer*, the only local morning paper, he even pressured the editors to cover his children's high school sports games.

In 1975 and 1976, many stockholders filed lawsuits against American Financial and an SEC investigation charged Keating,

Lidner and others for defrauding investors and submitting false reports. Keating left American Financial in 1976 and moved to Phoenix, Arizona to run American Continental Homes, a hopelessly insolvent homebuilder that he received as part of his compensation for leaving American Financial. Even though common belief was that he was chiefly responsible for the questionable dealings of American Financial and the SEC case was still ongoing, he was able to start anew in Arizona on somewhat of a clean slate.

As the chairman and controlling officer, he helped turn American Continental Homes around by adding various divisions and bringing a strong work ethic and leadership to its environment, eventually renaming it American Continental Corporation. The SEC case settled in 1979 with a mere consent order to not commit fraud again and Keating began cozying up to Arizona politicians. After Reagan won the 1980 election, he was even suggested as a candidate to serve as US ambassador to the Bahamas, only to be turned down when his SEC run-in was brought up.

ACC soon had 2500 employees and was the largest homebuilder in Phoenix and Denver. While Keating's aggressiveness was hated outside his own company, his workers liked him due to his leadership abilities. When he demanded longer hours, Keating provided his workers with incentives and bonuses. But even as American Continental's profits numbered in the millions and its assets reached $6 billion, the ever-aggressive Keating was not satisfied. He soon saw his opportunity in the moribund S&L industry.

In 1984, ACC used $50 million financed by Michael Milken's junk-bond trading operation to purchase Lincoln

Savings and Loan Association, an S&L, which was then insolvent to the tune of $100 million. He fired its management and with regulations no longer in his way, he set out on what some called "aggressive expansion."

Going on a spree of land buying and investing in high-yield junk bonds among other questionable investments, Keating increased Lincoln's assets over the next four years from $1.1 billion to $5.5 billion, at least on paper. He was far from the only person to do this, as the entire S&L industry was taking advantage of the loose regulations to act this way, but he did it with reckless abandon. By 1985, the Federal Home Loan Bank Board (FHLBB) began to worry that all of these risky investments would end up costing the government insurance funds and formed a policy that prevented S&Ls from putting more than 10% of their assets in "direct investments." Naturally, Lincoln Savings caught their eye and a 1986 FHLBB investigation found that, contrary to Keating's claims, Lincoln had $135 million in unreported assets and their investments were over $600 million above the 10% limit.

Keating pulled every trick from the book in response. He claimed the FHLBB were "homos" who were targeting him because of his strong moral views. He tried hiring away FHLBB employees and their wives, and even recruited noted economist Alan Greenspan to conduct a study proving that direct investments posed no great danger. But these ploys all stunk of desperation and a government takeover of Lincoln was looming over Keating's head. So, Keating turned to his political friends for help. With some smooth talking and the assistance of five senators who became known as the "Keating Five," one of which was 2008 Presidential hopeful John McCain, Keating managed to get a memorandum of understanding from the FHLBB and was allowed to continue his ownership of Lincoln Savings and American Continental.

He proceeded to continue his old act of hiding losses, paying himself a massive salary as he propped up assets with questionable investments and gathered together fifty-four companies in an entirely confusing conglomerate. In 1988, he made his biggest investment yet, constructing a $300 million hotel in the Phoenix area and then a 20,000-acre development in Goodyear, Arizona that was supposed to eventually house 200,000 people. But even as Lincoln stayed busy, Keating kept on diverting much of its funding back to American Continental where they were used in a mixture of Keating-style investments and personal expenses. Furthermore, as American Continental began failing, Keating turned to his Lincoln investors, swaying them to exchange their federally insured deposits for high-yield American Continental bonds. It was a scam that Federal Deposit Insurance Corporation (FDIC) chair L. William Seidman would later call "one of the most heartless and cruel frauds in modern memory."

Time eventually caught up with Keating and all of his political allies couldn't help. In April of 1989, Lincoln was seized by the FHLBB as American Continental finally went bankrupt. 23,000 bondholders were left with bonds that weren't worth the paper they were written on. Bondholders lost nearly $300 million and the government had to pay $3.4 billion for Lincoln. Keating was charged with $1.1 billion racketeering fraud. Between state and federal convictions, Keating was sentenced to twelve-and-a-half years in prison and was ordered to pay $122 million in restitution to the government. He was released after four and a half and went on to live a quiet life as a business consultant and refused to comment when the Keating Five was raised during John McCain's presidential bid. Always making sure to remain in good physical shape, he lived to be ninety, when he died in an Arizona hospital.

Key Takeaways

Keating was one of many S&L executives to take advantage of the loosened industry regulation; other notable cases including Hal Greenwood's Midwest Savings and Loan and Silverado Savings and Loan, each of which needed a bailout of over $1 billion. As the government and industry began to recognize the insolvency, it came to light that 1,043 out of the 3,234 savings and loans associations were failing.

William Black, a former FHLBB litigation director who played a pivotal role in exposing Congressional fraud during the S&L crisis, defined the frauds committed by Keating and others as "control fraud." He noted that while companies have all forms of controls instituted to prevent thieves, the CEO is beyond all of them and can take full advantage of his/her position. He can find people who will accept dubious accounting practices, allowing him to overvalue his assets and create transactions to fabricate income and hide losses.

Control fraud can only be avoided by ensuring that there are external checks and balances, with no one person having control over all elements of financial management. Avoidance also requires having a robust board of directors that sets and enforces procedures for cash management, disbursements, conflicts of interest policies, and related-party transactions. And the best protection of all, as we will focus upon at length in the section on Quality of People, is ensuring the most-senior people involved have impeccable integrity. Notwithstanding his numerous talents, impeccable integrity is one thing Keating certainly did not have.

* * *

WHAT IS THE AVERAGE LOSS FROM FRAUD?

A 2016 study conducted by the Association of Certified Fraud Examiners on the prevalence and impact of fraud found a median loss of approximately $150,000 per case. In instances where the perpetrators held positions of greater authority, however, the median loss increased to approximately $500,000 per case.

From the estimated $3.7 trillion USD that's lost to fraud, approximately 22% of cases involve losses of more than a million dollars.

WANT TO MAKE IT BIG?
START A CHARITY!

The term "charity fraud" is seemingly a paradox of epic proportions. After all, fraud is taking other people's money for yourself while charity is giving your money to others, right? Not according to James Reynolds, Sr.

A heavy-set man, Jim Reynolds originally worked at the American Cancer Society, running their office in Knox County, Tennessee. According to *The Atlantic*, he was fired in 1984 for stealing a donated vintage 1968 Ford Mustang that was meant to be auctioned and for overall "sloppy record keeping." Apparently, a man without shame, Reynolds founded a new cancer-related charity in 1987 with a remarkably similar name, the Cancer Fund of America (CFA).

Supposedly a charity helping families dealing with cancer, CFA's offices looked pleasant enough. Located in Knoxville but still surrounded by greenery, a bright blue awning hanging over the front pictured a rising sun over an American map. The motto on the awning, "Helping Today for a Brighter Tomorrow," eventually made it to CFA's Facebook page in the twenty-first century.

Seeing increasing success, CFA spread its wings to set up three affiliates: Cancer Support Services for families, Children's Cancer Fund of America for children, and the Breast Cancer Society for women. "Coincidentally," two of these three were headed by Reynolds' (later-ex) wife Rose Perkins and his son James II, with the third being headed by a friend, Kyle Effler.

Other executive positions were filled by (often unqualified) family and friends from their local Mormon church.

The absence of qualifications didn't prevent the four charities from raising an ever-growing pool of money. They used initial donations to fund a boiler room of telemarketers. In the words of *The Atlantic,* the telemarketers sent out "solicitations designed to tug at the heartstrings" and signed by the supposed benefactors. The telemarketers then took as much as 80% of the proceeds on a regular basis, and sometimes as much as 95%. Most of the remaining money was dispensed through generous bonuses to Reynolds and his cronies, and used for Disney World trips, college tuitions, Caribbean cruises and other luxuries. A minute amount was delivered to the actual charity.

According to the *New York Times,* their packages to cancer patients consisted of plastic cutlery and Little Debbie snack cakes. Carol Smith, whose dying husband received a CFA package, remembers throwing it out when it arrived after her husband felt as if he had been "slapped in the face." In some cases, the CFA got too lazy to send it to cancer patients and sent packages instead to the local youth soccer group and the Knoxville Firefighters Association.

Nonetheless, overvaluing their own packages and recording charitable acts that they never did, the books made it seem as if CFA was actually doing what they were supposed to be doing and they ran largely unhindered for over twenty years. Yes, there were some hiccups along the way, with six states fining them a total of $525,000 for various violations, including lying to donors, but between 2008 and 2012 alone, they raised a total of $187 million.

The public first began to see CFA's true colors in 2013. That year, the *Tampa Bay Times* combined with the Center for Investigative Reporting looked into bad charities, a project that was later joined by the US cable network CNN. With the headline "How One Family Turned your Goodwill into their Livelihood," reporters Kris Hundley and Kendell Taggart detailed the true goings-on at CFA, including how less than two cents of every dollar went to charity. They also exposed that in the previous decade, $80 million of the CFA's charity dollars went to telemarketers, $5 million to Reynolds family members and less than $1 million to cancer patients. They also found that in CFA's early years, Reynolds had filled his packages by convincing local businesses to donate everything they didn't need, all the while splitting the charity proceeds with the telemarketers. CFA became #2 on the joint project's final list of America's 50 Worst Charities, only behind Florida's KidsWish Foundation (more on that later).

The Federal Trade Commission, working with all fifty states, finally took action in 2015. Calling it "one of the largest actions brought to date by enforcers against charity fraud," the FTC calculated that millions of donors gave on average $20, reaching the aforementioned $187 million in just four years. South Carolina's Secretary of State noted with irony that while some charities send dying patients to Disney World, the Reynolds family used dying patients to get themselves to Disney World.

At the end, only an estimated 3% went toward the charity's actual purpose and with the money already spent, none of it was likely recoverable. In the meantime, two of the charities headed by Reynolds' ex-wife and son were to close their doors after reaching a settlement. CFA and Reynolds, Sr., though, the main actors, continued their fight, finally agreeing to shut down in February 2016.

According to ABC News, the Breast Cancer Foundation posted the following on their website: "While the organization, its officers and directors have not been found guilty of any allegations of wrong doing, and the government has not proven otherwise, our Board of Directors has decided that it does not help those who we seek to serve, and those who remain in need, for us to engage in a highly publicized, expensive, and distracting legal battle around our fundraising practices."

Talk about trained liars, never stopping to spin the charitable story for their own benefit.

Key Takeaways

Despite being the most brazen charity fraud in recent memory, CFA didn't even make it to the top of the *Tampa Bay Times/* Center for Investigative Reporting's list. KidsWish, which claims to fulfill the wishes of dying patients, like the better-known Make-A-Wish Foundation, occupied that. They used similar practices to CFA, hiring telemarketers, paying large salaries, and putting family members into board positions with overly generous salaries—even past retirement. While not as brazen as CFA, only 2.5% percent of the donated money made its way to charity, and when finally forced to face the music, KidsWish hired a crisis management specialist to help the charity moving forward. The common denominator between these two charities is that they both mimicked respected charitable organizations, and chose very similar names, thereby leveraging undue familiarity and credibility for their faux charities.

The more salient point is that donors are no different than investors–investing with the intent of receiving a social, rather than a financial, return. They are equally reliant on the stewardship of people and institutions, who are positioned to offer them the best return on investment. And just as in any other fraud, CFA offered similar red flags and warning signs. They inappropriately leveraged the credibility of other organizations; the principals had a seedy past, the governance and unqualified insiders, high-flying lifestyles and the brazen disregard for high expenditures or the capital of their "investors."

The closing message is that money is fungible and whether it is used for a social or financial investment, the same best practices need to be expected and demanded, lest you want to fund the cruises of those that have no respect for you or the value of your hard-earned capital.

* * *

"GIVE, AND I SHALL TAKETH FROM YOU": THE LIES OF GERALD "DOUBLE YOUR MONEY" PAYNE

People tend to respect their pastors. Unless their pastor happens to be Gerald Payne. Payne, a Florida contractor who spent time in jail for lying to a jury in 1979, decided to become a preacher in the 1980s. The problem was that Payne didn't find the preacher pay to be suitable so he conveniently decided to nix the commandment of "Thou shall not steal." Thus, in 1988, Greater Ministries International (GMI) was formed.

On the surface, GMI was a church, one that cared for the homeless and needy. Sounds wonderful, no? But as Payne and co-founder Haywood Hall touted, GMI was no simple church. It was a church that had investments in precious metals and if you invested in it, you would soon see your money double, triple and even quadruple. Payne named their main program the "Double Your Money Gift Exchange." He encouraged people to empty their life savings into this once-in-a-lifetime opportunity and enshrined the enterprise with religious-laden messages, quoting passages such as, "Give, and it shall be given unto you" (Luke 6:38).

Payne and Hall targeted the fundamentalist Christian community. They recruited other pastors who were known elders, paying 5% commission for every recruit, and aggressively distributed leaflets gushing with biblical scripture and anti-government messages.

Success came quickly. GMI seminars became standing room only. Many were convinced and invested tens of thousands— in some cases, millions—of dollars. Of course, in traditional Ponzi-scheme fashion, GMI used money from subsequent investors to pay out the previous investors. GMI was meticulous about paying out "gains" on time, and the investor base continued to grow, with members of the fundamentalist Christian community referring their friends and families to join this miraculous venture.

GMI continued unhindered for many years, as Payne was always conscious of depositing less than $10,000 at any given time to avoid reporting requirements. While word did spread like wildfire within the fundamentalist community, the world at large had no knowledge of GMI because its client base was incredibly insulated, distrusting of the government and the vast majority of media outlets. But by the late 1990s, the world was beginning to catch on.

Florida regulators made efforts to shut down GMI, but the courts ruled that it was not subject to state jurisdiction. GMI also changed its name to Faith Promises and stopped claiming explicitly that it would deliver high returns. Federal agencies got involved but their progress was extremely slow. A number of newspapers alleged that GMI was a fraud, and GMI filed a libel suit against three of them for a total of $10 billion. Appealing to their base, GMI principals claimed that the media was waging a war against Christianity.

Slowly, however, cracks began to show. GMI elder Patrick Henry Talbert was arrested in November 1997 for, in a completely separate incident, defrauding eleven elderly Floridian women of $256,000. He was convicted by next April. Former GMI employee Jonathan Strawder was arrested for a pyramid scheme similar to GMI's, named Sovereign Ministries, and was sentenced to five years in June 1998. By then, even some extreme Christian publications began doubting GMI.

The hammer fell on Payne in the summer of 1998, albeit in a completely fluky fashion. By sheer coincidence, the state of Colorado shut down Best Bank, the bank where Payne had been storing much of his money. Payne soon found himself unable to pay off his investors and began using gold certificates as payment. Finally, on March 13, 1999, federal regulators concluded their four-year-long investigation and charged Gerald Payne, his wife Betty, Don Hall and many others on various counts of fraud.

At the day's end, GMI had stolen from 18,000 people and siphoned away between $450-500 million. Early investors who received payments did not lose as much, but in total, an estimated $174 million was lost, over half coming from the state containing the highest combined Amish and Mennonite population, Pennsylvania.

Key Takeaways

The most salient takeaway from the Payne case is that best practice investing and personal passions or religion rarely mix. Whether it is fundamentalist Christians or any of the other group, affinity fraud, as it is often called, is concentrated on tight-knit community, where trust is implicit. People let their guards down when spirituality is involved, and they become ripe targets for fraud. That is why Payne only accepted Christian investors. For any fraud operator, it is much easier to deflect proper due diligence by claiming that critics are insufficiently pious or by questioning their religious loyalties, than it is to deal with the difficult due diligence questions at hand. For that reason, according to the North American Securities Administrators Association (NASAA), more than 30,000 Americans lose over $600 million per year to frauds that use God as the lure.

Another key takeaway is the reminder that the most important due diligence question we can ask is, "Who are we doing business with?" or "What is the quality of the people involved?" In Payne's case, there was a perfectly visible track record. Payne had spent some time in jail for lying to a jury. His partner, James Maher, was put on probation for operating a pyramid scheme for the exact crime that Payne and Maher committed together at Greater Ministries International. When Payne wanted to go overseas, he turned to Niko Shefer, a South African who had served six years in prison for bank fraud. And another one of Payne's partners was Patrick Talbert, who was twice sued by people who accused him of swindling them. And then there was Charles Eidson, the trusted legal advisor to Greater Ministries, who never actually went to law school or received a legal license. Furthermore, Eidson was previously arrested on mail fraud and other federal charges, including lying to customers in a previous business, illegally practicing law, and founding a virulently anti-Semitic organization.

An unbiased observer who met this cast of characters would (and should) run as far as possible in the opposite direction. That is why understanding who you're in business with is the first and most important question of any due diligence process.

Another fundamental principle of any due diligence process, in any investment, is the ability to understand how exactly money is made and whether the associated returns make sense. Payne was a master at giving vague and non-specific answers. He claimed to be investing in gold or silver mines and high-interest foreign debt but could never be pinned down on the details. Of course, Payne's claims that investors would get their money doubled, tripled, and even quadrupled in less than two years was virtually unprecedented, and should have been the first and most obvious red flag for GMI investors.

* * *

COMPLIANCE & REGULATION

RUDY KURNIAWAN VS. BILL KOCH: GUESS WHO IS STILL STANDING?

There are many levels of wine connoisseurship. Some people know a little. Some know a lot. Some pretend they know a lot. And then there's Rudy Kurniawan.

A small, wiry man of Indonesian background with an easy sense of humor, nobody quite knew where Rudy came from. His dress was casual, atypical for people who usually attended ritzy wine auctions, but Rudy let his actions do all the talking. Claiming that he only got into fine wine after trying a bottle at a restaurant in 2000, he began bidding compulsively at various West Coast auctions, doling out thousands of dollars night after night and even outbidding billionaire wine collectors like Bill Koch. An *LA Times* journalist reported that one Saturday afternoon at Christie's Beverly Hills auction, Rudy spent an estimated $500,000, including $75,000 on a single case of twenty-four half-bottles of 1947 Chateau Cheval Blanc. Other reports estimated that, at times, he spent a million per month.

Where did Rudy get his money? Unclear. He claimed that it came from family businesses overseas but refused to give details, saying that he was part of a tight-knit family that didn't want too much publicity. Nonetheless, with his easy nature and seemingly unlimited supply of good wine, he quickly attracted a large group of like-minded friends, and was a wine party regular. Rudy was far from stingy. His best wines were shared with friends.

Throughout it all, one thing that amazed people more than his vastly growing wine cellar was his impeccable taste. Time after time, Rudy could sample all different types of wines and somehow know each one, even blindfolded. He became well known among elite circles, befriending *Rush Hour* producer Arthur Sarkissian, Univision CFO Andrew Hobson, Hollywood producer Jef Levy and the agent for Will Ferrell and Larry David. To top it off, he became buddies with legendary Chinese actor, Jackie Chan. So much so that at a lavish birthday party for Rudy's mother, Chan stood on a chair and announced: "Rudy, you are the best!"

Not coincidentally, as Rudy went, so went the market. Constant bidding wars that he always won drove up the wine prices and every wine collector across America knew Rudy. Between 2001 and 2006, the wine market went up 62% and in 2015 alone, the market for old wine rose 31%, with a total of $166 million being spent. Taking advantage of the now sky-high prices, Rudy formed a team with John Kapon, an energetic young auctioneer in Manhattan, who headed the auction of well-known wine store Acker Merrall. In January 2006, Kapon conducted an auction of Kurniawan's wine entitled "the Cellar" and sold 1700 lots for $10.6 million. Later that year, he held another auction for Kurniawan that generated $24.4 million. Business was booming.

But it was French winemaker Laurent Ponsont, producer of Domaine Ponsont, who first noticed something was wrong when someone asked him about a wine of his purchased from Rudy. The wines were dated to the '60s and '70s. The problem was that Ponsont only began producing that wine in 1982.

Ponsont flew to America to meet Rudy, where Ponsont calmly explained how the wines must have been frauds. Rudy apologized profusely, saying that he has so much wine to keep track of and that he received the wine from a Mr. Pak Hendra and gave Ponsont two phone numbers. Ponsont was not sure whether Rudy was "predator or victim," but he still showed up at the next Acker Merrill auction midway and demanded that his wines be withdrawn. Kapon complied and even refunded some of Rudy's wines that had been sold, leaving both Acker Merrall and Rudy with a slew of negative publicity.

In the following years, Rudy still sold privately but had a hard time organizing auctions due to the Acker Merrall fiasco. But that proved to be the least of his problems as Ponsont was continuing his investigation. He began by checking the authenticity of the numbers Rudy had given him. One turned out to be the phone number of an Indonesian airline company and the other led nowhere. He also found that "Pak Hendra" was likely made up, as "Pak" meant Mr. in Indonesian and "Hendra" was the Indonesian equivalent of "Smith." But Ponsont didn't cause nearly the amount of problems as Bill Koch.

An avid collector of many things, Koch made wine one of his collecting passions and had a royal-sized cellar of his own, even doling out $100,000 dollars apiece for four bottles that he thought belonged to Thomas Jefferson from a German collector. After realizing that they were fakes, he sued the collector and started an intense campaign against fake wines. He hired private investigator Brad Goldberg; very soon, they focused their attentions on their bidding competitor Rudy. Not only because he was single-handedly driving up prices; Koch had also bought

Rudy's bottles from him through Acker Merrall which he later discovered to be frauds.

In September 2009, Koch's team concluded their investigations by suing Rudy and claiming that his real name was Zheng Wang Huang and that he owed about $8 million in fees to Acker, which he had yet to pay along with $3 million to a large New York bank.

Three months later, FBI agent James Wynne contacted Ponsont and began building a case. They discovered Rudy was an illegal alien who had been ordered to leave the States in 2003 but had not done so. After combing through his cash accounts, Wynne found that despite all his claimed wealth, Rudy was constantly short on money and short by a lot. Wynne found a slew of private emails in which Rudy begged for money, including one desperate beg in 2007 despite having just recently sold $35 million worth of wine through Acker months before. He also found that Rudy had illegally pledged eighteen pieces of art as collateral for his debts. Further digging showed that Rudy's maternal uncles were Hendra Rahardja and Eddy Tansil, two of the biggest fraudsters in Indonesian history, each of whom scammed victims out of more than $500 million apiece without much ever being recovered. More documents showed Rudy wiring as much as $17 million abroad to his family members in 2007. It didn't take a genius to figure that his relatives had fronted the original buying money to Rudy, though Wynne never found evidence for that.

The police showed up at Rudy's home in March 2012 and found piles of empty bottles and mounds of wine labels and seals. Even more incriminating, some wine bottles were floating in the sink after having their previous labels torn off. Bottles upon bottles had Rudy's private notes on them, many of them explicitly talking about combining different wine bottles together. In short, Rudy's bottles were fakes.

Rudy was eventually sentenced to ten years in prison and $28.4 million in restitution payments. All of his located bottles were tested to see if they were fraudulent. Many were real, but the fakes were sent to a dump in Texas. To this day, it's widely believed that Rudy must have had accomplices—likely his criminal family abroad—both to give him money to purchase wine, as well as someone else to help him bottle the fakes. Creating over 15,000 fake bottles alone would seem simply impossible. To this day, nobody else has been tried and it's estimated that at least 10,000 of Rudy's bottles are still out there on the market, waiting for the opportunity to dupe some more buyers.

Key Takeaways

Among Rudy's innovations was his ability to execute a remarkably "long con." He had developed a palate that was unmatched and a knowledge base that was extraordinary even within connoisseur circles. Long after the dust settled, his friends still couldn't believe that the fraud was actually true, as the relationships he built, the networks he penetrated and the reputation he established within auction houses was nothing short of legendary. His talents were enough to stand on their own merits, even if no fraud was ever executed.

The Kurniawan case is a case study of just how painfully effective a fraudster can be when there is a long runway and unknown parties in the background bankrolling the execution of the fraud or subsidizing its related activities. It's a reminder that even the savviest among us can duped.

These cons are further exacerbated in transactional scenarios that have three additional components:

- Where trusted intermediaries, such as a prestigious auction house, provide a cloak of legitimacy where none might be warranted.
- In asset classes or strategies that are largely unregulated by any governing body. While wine may be a wonderful diversifier, unregulated businesses tend to invite the foxes into the henhouse.
- When the backgrounds of the people you're dealing with are unknown.

The big question that no one has been able to answer about Rudy is "where did he come from?" No one could offer any other answer but that he came from a wealthy foreign family. His lifestyle certainly suggested it, but there was no one who could corroborate it. Kurniawan's victims learned that people, just like wine, cannot be trusted until their provenance has been established.

* * *

There is sufficiency in this world for man's need, but not for man's greed

—Mahatma Gandhi

SOVEREIGN PROMISES: SIR GREGOR MACGREGOR & THE DOMINION OF MELCHIZEDEK

Sir Gregor MacGregor is widely recognized as the creator of the "fake country" scam. Formerly a British general in Latin America, in 1822 the Scotsman MacGregor returned to England and began selling bonds and tracts of real estate in the country of Poyais. Claiming to be the "Cazique"—a local leader in Latin America—of Poyais, MacGregor started a publicity campaign, highlighting the marvels of Poyais, its astonishing infrastructure, the friendliness of its pro-British inhabitants and the opportunities for riches it presented. He established Poyaisian embassies in London, Edinburgh and Glasgow. He hired publicists and engaged journalists to drone on about its reliably magnificent weather patterns, its attractive topographic features and to aggressively promote a book on the country written by Captain Thomas Strangeways. Of course, he neglected to disclose that he authored the book under an alias, concocted its flag, currency, constitution, coat of arms and every other minute detail of this nation.

Eventually, Poyais penetrated England's common consciousness.[4] MacGregor proceeded to issue approximately £1.3 million worth (the equivalent of over $2 billion today) of Poyaisian bonds to investors; at the same time, he sold an

---

[4] MacGregor's story was so compelling and believable that other fraudsters soon set up competing offices and sales efforts offering Poyaisian land debentures and certificates, taking on MacGregor at his own game.

undetermined number of acres to 500 people. Seven shiploads of people prepared to serve as the colonists of Poyais, and on September 10, 1822, the first ship of Poyais pioneers left everything behind to pursue their golden prospects in the land of Poyais. Of course, instead of finding the land of opportunity, they found a mosquito-infested barren forest and the majority of these pioneering colonists died of malaria and yellow fever. Fewer than fifty survived.

When word of MacGregor's scheme reached London, he was arrested. Before trial, however, he escaped to Paris, where he attempted to recreate the legend of Poyais. He wasn't nearly as successful, and was arrested again. After being acquitted, he spent another ten years attempting to pull off smaller Poyais-related frauds. After those had fully run their course, he settled in Venezuela, where he was welcomed back as a war hero and eventually buried with military honors.

As is oftentimes the case, other fraudsters saw the success of MacGregor's scam and decided to follow suit. In today's global world, where one can use Google Earth to see any place on Earth, one would think that such a scam would be hard to pull off. Unsurprisingly, gullibility still prevails. In fact, scammers have even used the internet to further such scams. One classic example is the Dominion of Melchizedek.

A 1991 *Forbes* article featured the story of convicted fraudster, Mark Pedley. Pedley had been convicted of mail and interstate fraud in 1983 for selling land he didn't own in a Sacramento suburb, receiving three years imprisonment. He was convicted again in 1986, this time by a federal court in Boston, for a six-million-dollar peso conversion scam he conducted in 1982 and 1983. He was sentenced to eight years in prison and a $25,000 fine. But the public did not know this in 1990; when Mark was paroled again, he changed his name to Branch Vinedresser and founded the religiously-inspired Dominion of Melchizedek (DoM).

The *Dallas Observer* quoted Pedley, describing DoM as an "ecclesiastical and constitutional sovereignty" founded on "the principles of the Melchizedek Bible," a revamped Christian Bible authored by Mark's father David. The elder Pedley was also a convicted fraudster who had supposedly died in a Mexican prison in 1987 (though the *Washington Post* reported that the Pedley family refused to allow FBI agents to fingerprint the corpse and agents believe that the death was probably faked).

According to Robert Tillman's *Global Pirates: Frauds in the Offshore Insurance Industry,* Pedley then set out to give his country financial legitimacy and created a currency called "Equicurrency." He had Equicurrency listed in a prominent France-based newspaper, the *International Herald Tribune,* claiming a total value of $10 billion. He also paid to be listed in Bloomberg's databases. He filed an 8-k for Currentsea, a penny-stock company he acquired, claiming ownership of 10% of the world's oceans and a resulting market cap of $500 million. In truth, it was only worth $386. After the aforementioned *Forbes* article exposed the man behind the Melchizedek mask, Pedley was quickly put back into prison to finish his sentence, as Melchizedek was deemed a violation his parole. Another stint in prison did nothing to deter Pedley.

As the internet emerged in the early 1990s, he formed an official website, www.melchizedek.com, where he detailed the "wonders" and "principles" of his "country." He installed his wife, Pearlasia Gamboa (whose own dubious businesses were banned from California and Indiana), as the country's president and he assumed the role of vice president. He first claimed the Malpelo Island, a barren rocky island 500 kilometers off the coast of Colombia, but Colombia quickly asserted that it had claim to the island and even kept a small army outpost there. DoM then moved to another Pacific island named "Karitane," but French Polynesian authorities were quick to point out that the only land near "Karitane" was nine meters under the ocean's surface. No longer interested in moving, DoM then claimed that Branch Vinedresser acquired a lease until 2049 on the uninhabited Pacific coral island of Taongi, part of the Marshall Islands.

But even as the logistical elements of Melchizedek were reminiscent of a musical chairs game, their financial dealings were actually quite deadly. Before his arrest in 1991, Pedley founded a number of "banks" in Washington, D.C., where the word "bank" can be used even by a company that isn't an actual bank. While those were shut down before they could do much damage, DoM began setting up fraudulent banks all over the world, chartering them in Melchizedek. One such bank, the Caribbean-based Credit Bank International run by Roger Rosemont, convinced 1400 investors to invest $4 million in a Ponzi scheme before the SEC stepped in and announced: "Credit Bank is not a bank; Melchizedek is not a country and Rosemont is not an ambassador." To combat this, Pedley/Vinedresser (who at some point switched his name to David Korem) claimed that fraudulent bankers like Rosemont did not represent Melchizedek and told the *Wall Street Journal* that "every country has naughty banks."

While Pedley now sported a foot-long beard and declared war on France for its nuclear testing in the Pacific, Melchizedek's web of fraud stretched very far. Aside from selling over 300 banking licenses for more than $10,000 each along with useless government bonds, they also had agents selling DoM passports in the Far East, claiming that they were legitimate travel documents. An entire network of DoM agents traveled the world selling useless documents to naïve buyers, so much so that *Offshore Alert* (the magazine that brought down Marc Harris) compiled a list of Melchizedek officials to look out for and posted it on their website.

Thirty-one-year-old Jeff Reynolds, a previously convicted Dallas fraudster, based his "California Pacific" company in Melchizedek and appointed himself the Secretary of Commerce of Melchizedek. In a crime that even surpassed Pedley's, Reynolds proceeded to sell $47 million worth of fraudulent insurance policies before being brought in on twenty federal fraud charges.

Pedley kept at his earlier penny stock promotions, with him and his wife Pearlasia promoting a fraudulent penny stock ZNext. While Pearlasia didn't show up to court and was banned from selling penny stocks, Pedley was actually charged criminally for his role and in 2011 was sentenced to two years in prison.

But even another prison sentence didn't keep Melchizedek at bay. To this date, the Melchizedek website is still operating, albeit in more muted form. If you choose to visit it, you will be greeted by warm messages of unity, peace and philanthropy. The topography of the island of Taongi is described in detail, as are numerous claims of international recognition and details about the government structure that contains an executive, legislative, and judicial branch (sound familiar?).

In what was possibly a Freudian slip, the site says that all members of Melchizedek are literate. Since those members refer only to Pedley, his wife, and other DoM officials, that statement might just be the only shred of truth on the site.

Key Takeaways

As Tillman notes in his aforementioned *Global Pirates*, DoM has "revolutionized" the fraud industry and inspired copycat fake countries, including the Principality of New Utopia and the Kingdom of Enen Kio.

The lessons from Melchizedek are similar to other previously mentioned frauds. As is the case by the Eiffel Tower and Brooklyn Bridge, don't trust simple documents without doing your due diligence. Do a background check and always be wary of paying upfront fees for dubious or unconfirmed claims.

However, there is another unique takeaway from Melchizedek and that is the limitations of regulation. As we will see in the next case, regulators can only be as good as the space they cover. What frauds like Poyais and the Dominion of Melchizedek remind us is that fraud can easily find a home in the crevices between.

Pedley and his cronies were able to continuously dupe investors with their financial products issued and banks chartered in Melchizedek, a place that only existed in cyberspace, far from the reaches of the SEC or any governing body. They have no physical existence and are de facto beyond jurisdiction. All the SEC can do is declare that DoM doesn't exist, nothing more. The fact that in 2019 the Melchizedek website is still up and running attests to this.

* * *

WHERE ARE THE AUTHORITIES AND LAW ENFORCEMENT IN PROTECTING AGAINST FRAUD?

It's the unfortunate reality that private investors cannot rely on authorities or law enforcement to protect them from the grips of a scam. Authorities either do not show up in time or prove to be ineffectual when they get there. The fact that the SEC knew about Madoff for at least five years without doing one iota about it (and that the victims of fraud cannot legally sue the SEC) should serve as a painful reminder to investors that the onus of protection rests on our very own shoulders.

It has been sarcastically said that "fraud under $100 million is legal in America." The quip is due to the sad fact that regulators and authorities are inundated, having far less resources than they need to investigate or pursue every potential fraud. Instead, they pursue those that make (or are likely to make) headlines in the media. And since small frauds under $100 million or so aren't sexy or dramatic enough for the media, they prove to be less interesting to the authorities as well.

MARTIN FRANKEL: THE ANXIOUS NERD WHO FORCED A GLOBAL MANHUNT

I f you would have gone back to the 1960s and met Marty Frankel in his Toledo high school, you would likely think that this nerdy teenager would become a rocket scientist or astrophysicist. Definitely not a world-famous fraudster who would lead the police on a cross-country manhunt.

An anxiety-riddled kid whose wiry look and penchant for babbling garnered constant comparisons to Woody Allen, Frankel only became interested in finance when he wanted to find something on which to test his astrology predictions. But that interest soon grew and—after dropping out of college because exams made him too anxious—Frankel opened a trading account and received a broker's license. After being hired and quickly fired by a local Toledo brokerage, Frankel set up his own operation in his rented apartment. He incorporated it as Winthrop Capital using a false name, James Spencer, an act that would later become his specialty. But Frankel found trading difficult, as his anxiety made him too nervous to potentially lose money, so he traveled to Florida hoping the change of scenery would help.

He quickly gathered over a million in assets from wealthy investors for The Frankel Fund, but his trades were unsuccessful, and he used investor money as his own to cover his rent along with other assorted expenses. After a variety of fraudulent enterprises through an assortment of entities, the SEC began investigating him in 1989. By 1992, they had seen enough to ban him from securities trading for life. But Frankel was prepared for this with other plans.

In 1991, he had formed Thunor Trust,[5] with the intent of buying up many small (and mostly failing) insurance companies that operated in rural Southern states. Headquartering in Tennessee, Frankel targeted companies in states with poor insurance regulations (insurers were regulated by states rather than the SEC), the most notable one being Tennessee itself. He applied in Tennessee for a securities license under the company name, Liberty National Securities, and for the approval of insurance regulators under the name Thunor Trust. He avoided using his own name to avoid connections with the then-ongoing SEC investigation of "Martin Frankel."

Appointing Tennessean John Hackney as the face of the trust, he proceeded to buy up his targeted failing insurance companies for a total of $71 million. When the insurers asked where the money was coming from, Hackney replied that it was from "wealthy families from up North" who "don't want their names revealed." Thunor Trust told the insurers that they were investing their money at a 20% clip through (Frankel's own) Liberty National brokerage, where Frankel was instead diverting most of the funds from the brokerage to his private accounts. By having insurance companies "investing" with him, Frankel

---

[5] Ironically, in Germanic mythology, Thunor was recognized for bludgeoning people with a fiery axe or hammer, often referred to as Thor, the God of thunder and lightning.

was able to effectively buy these insurance companies with their own money and use the rest for his personal pleasures.

In short order, Frankel built two mansions in Greenwich, Connecticut, with one of them being a large security-heavy estate with gun-carrying guards and six-foot metal fences to assuage his safety anxieties. Like he did in his younger years, he used his house as his headquarters and filled it with so much security that nearly everyone in the neighborhood began conveniently avoiding his place. Whenever he did meet his neighbors, he would tell them that his name was Michael King, babbling about how he was among *Fortune*'s 400 wealthiest men in the world. He bought $1.8 million worth of luxury cars to fill his garage, spent untold dollars on around-the-clock chefs, and was known for using expensive bars of soap only once before disposing of them.

As the internet became popular, he lived up to his creepy exterior and began trolling the internet for women and placing ads looking for dates. Soon enough, hordes of women could be seen entering and leaving his mansion with an entourage of bodyguards. Using a range of aliases including David Rosse, Eric Stephens, and Robert Guyer, he convinced Prudential to trade securities for Thunor's insurers and Ernst and Young to sign off on one of his deals, even convincing well-known legal and lobbying firm Akin Gump to represent him. He used the insurer's money to trade at unusually high volumes, and all sorts of dealmakers joined the many women as mansion visitors.

In 1998, looking for further credibility, Frankel formed a Catholic charity, St. Francis of Assisi Foundation, with the stated goal of alleviating the suffering of the poor, for which its namesake was known. Of course, the BVI-based foundation, which Frankel used for other business transactions, was also a front to bilk the Church out of the $55 million he had promised them. Frankel was managing over $335 million by 1999, while having siphoned away more than $200 million for himself on lavish living, along with cash stashed in a variety of Swiss accounts.

Of course, it didn't last forever. By late 1998, Tennessee authorities began asking why so much of these insurance companies' capital was placed in one spot, and why there was such aggressive trading turnover in the accounts. In March 1999, a Mississippi regulator stumbled upon the fact that numerous insurance companies were giving money to the now Connecticut-based Liberty National Securities while paying minimal commissions and began investigating. At the same time, people in his Greenwich neighborhood were starting to get nervous. His constant flow of visitors disrupted the neighborhood; whenever the man they knew as Mike King ventured out of the house, he rambled about one strange anxiety after the next. He first rambled about the need to install bulletproof glass and to up his own security. His tall tales about his business ventures were hard to believe and when he made an effort to buy up another house on the block, one curious neighbor hired private investigator Michael Henehan to look into him.

Henehan immediately found out "Mike King's" true name and that Frankel's Liberty National was trading securities when Frankel himself was banned from doing so. He met with the local Attorney General as well as a zoning officer, and when that officer sent a letter to Frankel addressed to "Martin Frankel" instead of "Mike King," the already anxious Frankel was now petrified. When the Missouri regulators finished their investigation and told Frankel that Liberty National would have to return money to the insurers, he knew it was time to act.

Frankel left town but not before ordering an assistant to burn all evidence at his Greenwich mansion. In a comical twist of events, the fire set off the smoke alarm and brought authorities to his mansion, where a stockpile of incriminating documents were waiting for them. By the time they were ready to act, Frankel had already left the country using one of his many aliases and a worldwide manhunt began.

Equipped with numerous passports and identities, Frankel didn't even bother with wigs or disguises. He made his way through Europe freely until he was finally found in a German motel in September 1999 with diamonds worth $8 million on hand. He was first imprisoned in Germany for a few years for not reporting the diamonds for taxes but was then sent back to the United States to face his trial. The 2004 verdict concluded that his $110 million in personal assets and cash would be used to pay part of the losses. Due to Frankel's cooperation with authorities to recover some of the missing money, his jail sentence was reduced to sixteen years and eight months. John Hackney, who eventually admitted to receiving $7 million from Frankel to participate in the scam, received four years in prison and was also forced to pay restitution.

Key Takeaways

Frankel's ingenuity came from the recognition that small, failing insurance companies were ripe for the embezzler's picking. Virtually every insurance company that's still operating has a regulatory requirement to maintain a healthy cash reserve, usually 8-12% of its capital base. On top of which, insurers tend to have sizable pools of investments from the premiums they collect, and additional pools of capital to invest from the investment products they sell to customers (e.g. annuities). For Frankel, failing insurance companies signaled the ability to plunder some cushy coffers, with pitiful governance, in poorly-regulated states, and (most importantly) with sensible rationale for failure when the company eventually collapses. The perfect target.

For those purchasing insurance policies, the obvious takeaway is ensuring the ongoing viability of their counterparties. Insurance is often purchased to prepare for the worst-case scenario. By partnering with insurers that aren't robust, or that have operational difficulties, the likelihood of avoiding the "worst-case-scenario" is hardly mitigated.

When investors loan out capital, and certainly if they consider insurance-linked investments, how that capital is deployed or invested should be of the utmost concern to the lender or investor. If one cannot get assurances, avoid the loan or investment at all costs.

Lastly, the most critical takeaway is knowing who you are dealing with, what their motivations might be, and what conflicts of interest it presents. Frankel went to great lengths to ensure his involvement in both companies was unknown, allowing the fox to guard the henhouse. If everyone knew that both Thunor Trust and Liberty National brokerage were owned and controlled by the same person, no rational person would agree to invest capital with them, as the conflict of interest would be too great for anyone to bear.

In today's age of information, accepting the anonymity of any counterparty or trustee is both unnecessary and unacceptable, unless you'd be happy to have someone living the high life at your expense.

* * *

WHY IS TRACKING DOWN FRAUDSTERS SO DIFFICULT?

The irony is that while many individuals who were defrauded do not report the fraud, simultaneously, many investors who legitimately lost money through poor investment decisions believe that they were defrauded.

The data suggests that approximately 50% of those who report investment fraud are reporting in error. In other words, they believe they were defrauded, when in fact they merely lost money in a bad investment.

Unlike other frauds (e.g. credit card fraud or identity theft), there is often a fair bit of ambiguity with investments and it can be difficult to determine whether victims were deliberately defrauded or if they were simply involved in a reckless investment with an inferior partner.

LOOK OUT FOR THE REPEAT ANTICS OF ROC HATFIELD

Roc Hatfield is definitely unique. Unlike the other charlatans who committed fraud while operating within the bands of capital markets, as either a registered broker, advisor or money manager, Hatfield had no need for this formality. He was not registered to sell securities with the SEC, the agency whose primary responsibility is to protect investors. And, in part, not being registered is what allowed Hatfield to lay his traps.

Starting in 1986, Hatfield began advertising the Centuri Mining Corp within the pages of the *Wall Street Journal*. Of course, he made no mention of the fact that the securities were not registered. He seduced investors with the mouthwatering tale of Centuri's possession of $225 million in gold deposits on Colombia's Nechi River. Needless to say, these deposits were a figment of Hatfield's imagination. But once word of this dazzling opportunity started to spread, the SEC quickly shut down the operation and warned Hatfield not to do it again.

Hatfield was back in the market in 1993, this time as the CEO of Marada Capital Inc., a brokerage firm that (once again) was not registered with SEC. Hatfield built a "boiler room" and hired telemarketers who he rebranded as "brokers." Offering extraordinarily high commissions of 40%, he began selling its (worthless) stock to unwitting investors, claiming that Marada Global Corp had exclusive agreements with Caribbean islands to develop an airline, casinos and hotels. Marada even claimed that it would apply to be publicly listed and traded on NASDAQ. All of its claims were bogus.

In 1994, the SEC shut him down again, and once again warned him never to repeat. This time, however, they barred him from ever trading securities, which of course he never legally traded in the first place. If that wasn't enough, a California court sentenced him to two years in prison for criminal fraud and unlawful sale of securities, among other charges.

Like a snake that can't alter its slither, Hatfield was back at it in 2002. This time he was selling notes paying high levels of interest from Global Diamond Fund Inc. (GDF). This investment was supposedly secured by South African diamond operations and jewels. Again, the SEC shut him down and has been in pursuit of Hatfield ever since. In true Hatfield fashion, he has not complied with court orders and has been repeatedly held in civil contempt.

Key Takeaways

There are three main lessons Roc Hatfield offered us. For starters, a basic background check on the principals of any financial organization is an absolute must. It doesn't cost much, and for any sizeable investment it is a rounding error of an expense but has the potential to save your hide down the road. And even if someone wants to be penny-wise and pound-foolish, the SEC has a free resource on its website where you can check to see who has had previous run-ins with the SEC. There may have been excuses in the pre-internet age but not today.

In Hatfield's case, not only did he have a track record, but his partner in crime and "chief diamond buyer" at GDF, Jack Paulsen, was also a repeat securities' law violator.

Secondly, the value of someone's social media presence as a litmus test of legitimacy is next to nil. If you google the name "Roc Hatfield," the results will look impressive. The brown-moustached Mr. Hatfield is apparently an author of numerous books and an artist with a 2008 album titled *Edge of Paradise* aside from other musical ventures. He has tens of thousands of followers on Twitter and even more Facebook likes. With his history of frauds, it's likely that his social media following is also somewhat contrived.

Lastly, it is prudent to adopt a simple rule of thumb: never invest with anyone who is not properly registered. Neither Hatfield's Centuri securities, nor his Marada brokerage firm, nor his Global Diamond Fund were registered. While the cost of compliance is getting increasingly high, registration is the law and for the benefit of the investor. It demands that registrants maintain a minimum standard of disclosure and fairness in all their dealings. Any non-registered investment firm selling securities isn't only contravening the law, it is also demonstrating blatant disregard for the protection of its investors.

While these non-registered firms may fly beneath the regulators' radar, the red flag it raises is so easy to spot. Had Hatfield's investors merely inquired about this registration, they could have kept their hard-earned wealth out of his fraudulent clutches.

* * *

HOW MANY SWINDLERS GET AWAY WITH IT?

Sadly, far too many. As we saw, only twelve percent of investment fraud victims report it. Of those that report it, only fifty-one percent of all perpetrators are prosecuted. And of those that were prosecuted, only thirty-one percent were incarcerated.

Often, there is a jurisdiction-related complication or some other technicality limiting the reach of authorities. The disappointing reality is that most perpetrators continue living life just as they did before their scams were brought to light, without justice having been served.

THE RISE AND FALL OF PANAMA'S ESCAPE ARTIST: MARC HARRIS

Long before the Panama Papers scandal, the guy to know for all your tax evasion needs was Marc Harris and the company to call was his eponymous Harris Organization.

Harris, an immaculately groomed American-educated accountant, claimed to have left the United States near 1990 due to persecution from the IRS. After renouncing his American citizenship, he became a citizen of Panama and purchased the Trust Services firm from Robin Bailey and Derek Sambrook, only to have them buy it back when they were dissatisfied with his trading. So Mr. Harris turned to the latest technological advance, the internet.

Using the domain names of marc-harris.com and escapeartist.com, Harris founded the Harris Organization, doing just about everything an offshore company can do, such as setting up offshore banks and administering offshore trusts, insurance or annuity companies. From trust company formation to a variety of tax-avoidance programs, dubbed the "Harris Matrix," Harris was the one-stop shop for offshore services. And all of it for half to a third of the regular going rate. With an address in Panama but incorporated in the Virgin Islands, the Harris Organization supposedly saw immediate success. By 1998, Harris claimed to have over $1 billion under management and over $35 million in capital. It boasted 150 employees and was among the largest offshore providers in the world.

But even as more and more US investors flocked toward Harris, doubters arose as well. Jim Bennet, a Texas attorney who met with Harris in London, was spoon-fed the wonders of the Harris Organization but decided to recruit *OffshoreAlert* editor David Marchant to investigate before making a trip to Panama. Marchant, a British offshore investigator who founded *OffshoreAlert* in 1997 for the purpose of exposing international financial crime, rolled up his sleeves and got to work. The results were nothing short of astounding.

Marchant published his findings in his March 31, 1998 edition of *OffshoreAlert* and they were not pretty. Harris did not have the $1 billion in assets that he claimed. He had $40 million, quite miniscule for a large organization with 150 employees. Furthermore, Marchant found that while Harris claimed to be a qualified CPA, in fact, he only had his license for three or four years before it was suspended in Florida. The reason: exhibiting incompetence and negligence in auditing a mutual fund without disclosing operating affiliates, accurate cost and market value of marketable securities, and the minor detail that he personally ran and owned the mutual fund. Worst of all were the actual affairs of the Harris Organization.

According to Marchant, the Harris Organization was "one of the biggest offshore scams of all time" and "is being run as a massive Ponzi scheme in which clients are being defrauded out of millions of dollars." He reported further that the "situation is so serious that The Harris Organization . . . is hopelessly insolvent, with net liabilities of at least $25 million, according to sources knowledgeable of the group's financial affairs." Other results were that Harris doled out massive bonuses and commissions to himself and his cronies, borrowed client money without permission, fabricated and marked up assets, and may have been dealing with proceeds from drug trafficking and other illegal activities. The bottom line: Harris was a fraud.

Within a month, multiple clients took heed of Marchant's warnings and closed their accounts, but Harris did not falter. He filed a libel suit against Marchant for $30 million. In 2000, the court eventually ruled that Marchant had substantial basis for his claims and dismissed the suit entirely.

His reputation largely in shambles, Harris remained in Panama until 2002. Increased Panamanian regulations forced him to move to Nicaragua but after being expelled from Nicaragua, he was finally arrested in June 2003. He was ordered to pay over $26 million in restitution and sentenced to seventeen years in prison. Marchant, on the other hand, has continued his career as an investigative journalist, and as of 2009, the *Wall Street Journal* reported that eleven people have been charged because of his findings. But with Harris' restitution likely never to be paid, one could hardly call this a "happily ever after."

Key Takeaways

It's very easy for fraudsters to operate in a domain that's murky or difficult to understand. Harris had many of his entities domiciled in small jurisdictions like Nevis, an island with 10,000 people, light regulations and neither the will nor the ability to do anything about known instances of fraud. Offshore entities can rarely be relied on to protect investors, so unless all the other ducks line up and the party you're dealing with is confirmed to be 100% legitimate (with no other red flags) it's safer to simply walk away.

When hiring anyone to do a job that is even mildly complex, and certainly one that involves the custody of capital, one needs to be certain that the professionals involved are all licensed or sanctioned by some credible authoritative body. It is remarkable that Harris provided a range of services in his organization but didn't have a single license. There are plenty of offshore funds that can offer legitimate benefits, which are properly licensed and regulated; use them (after checking Marchant's newsletter first, of course).

Another red flag was Harris' gross undercharging, far below industry standards. Harris was charging less than his competitors were by over 80%. Seasoned lawyers and accountants in the industry claimed that it was simply impossible, even with cheap offshore labor. This undercharging was a red flag in other instances of fraud. For example, Madoff was the only hedge manager that did not have a management fee, while his feeder funds often charged 1% management fee and 20% of the "profits." Such extreme undercharging makes no rational sense, and no credible investment manager with a consistent track record would even consider it.

One a final note of caution: companies and investment opportunities that are entirely tax-premised need to be approached with extreme thoughtfulness, and in most instances avoided. Frequently, the manufacturers of aggressive tax solutions are pushing the envelope and developing crafty vehicles or entirely fictitious solutions that enrich themselves rather than those who buy into it. And when tax authorities challenge it or the court rules against the tax benefit, the manufacturer is nowhere to be found and investors are often left with both the bill and the aggravation.

* * *

ARE THERE ANY SHARED PSYCHOLOGICAL TRAITS AMONG CON ARTISTS?

According to Maria Konnikova, in her book, The Confidence Game, there are generally three traits that epitomize seasoned swindlers, namely: psychopathy, narcissism and Machiavellianism (21-25).

Psychopathy refers to a psychological disposition characterized by the absence of empathy for others or any feelings of guilt and remorse.

Narcissism involves a highly inflated sense of self-worth and entitlement. That expresses itself in the individual willing to do anything to maintain the image (usually, the illusion) of grandiosity.

Konnikova defines Machiavellianism as the ability "manipulate or exploit" others to serve one's own selfish purposes. This typically involves a fair bit of lying and convincingly deceiving others.

The combination of these three traits has been visible among many of the fraudsters featured in this book and should serve as a red flag in identifying other shady characters in the future.

YBM MAGNEX: THE STORY OF THE BRAINY DON WHO LOVED CANADA

Semion Mogilevich is a unique mixture of brains and brawn. Born in Ukraine and educated at the University of Lviv, Mogilevich speaks many languages and has passports for numerous countries. But with a neatly trimmed moustache very reminiscent of Vito Corleone, the FBI considers Mogilevich to be one of the most dangerous mobsters alive, giving him a six-year spot on their Top 10 Wanted List before extradition problems forced them to remove him. He started off with small crimes, leading to two stints in prison, meeting mobsters there and receiving his education in organized crime. Building his own empire, Mogilevich is believed to live in Moscow with his wife and three children and has garnered the nickname "the Brainy Don" for his incredible business acumen. There was no clearer example of this acumen, combined with outright fraud, than in the case of YBM Magnex.

It started in the 1990s, when Mogilevich was making boatloads of money through prostitution rings and weapons smuggling. The problem was finding a place to keep the cash. He stored the first $50 million of his proceeds in a London law firm while posing as a businessman. However, the façade was over when London police came knocking and quickly confiscated $2 million of it. No worries. Mogilevich had already started a Plan B, founding Hungarian industrial magnet manufacturer called YBM Magnex. Of course, the company was a farce, with Mogilevich's cronies holding key positions and Mogilevich bribing lawyers and accountants to make sure his name wasn't directly linked to the company.

He set up offices in Newtown, Pennsylvania and registered another shell company called Pratecs in Alberta, Canada, where shell companies are known to gain access to the stock exchange without much oversight. But even Alberta regulators got nervous when British authorities commenced legal action against Mogilevich for his money laundering scheme, and they temporarily halted Pratecs' trading. When Russian authorities refused to cooperate with the British, the case collapsed and Pratecs was able to resume trading.

In March 1996, Mogilevich had YBM listed on the Toronto Stock Exchange, with him and five associates controlling almost one-third of its shares. Much like Bre-X, YBM issued press releases detailing how profitable it was and even enlisted former Ontario premier David Peterson and Marathon Securities director Owen Mitchell to serve on its board of directors. Mitchell had invested in YBM himself and First Marathon became YBM's underwriter.[6] YBM first recruited Coopers and Lybrand, which later merged to become PwC, to serve as its auditors and then enlisted Deloitte and Touche when Coopers refused to sign off on the audits. Deloitte also refused to sign off on the audits, but by then it didn't really matter. YBM was soaring.

With its press releases and perceived legitimacy due to Mitchell and Peterson's involvement, YBM's shares had risen greatly from the ten-cent price it had started with. All the while, the FBI and Canadian Mounties had been closely watch-

---

[6] In this case, underwriting refers to the role of an investment bank to raise capital for corporations.

ing YBM, knowing that YBM was about to issue a prospectus to raise capital in 1997. The FBI even asked the Mounties to inform the Ontario Securities Commission (OSC) that YBM was likely a front for the Russian mob, but without any concrete proof, the OSC dismissed the concerns.

While YBM was temporarily allowed to continue, in the months that followed the OSC grew increasingly concerned, particularly when French officials warned the Toronto Stock Exchange (TSX) that YBM claimed profits without having any known sales in Europe, along with a confirmation that it "was obviously a front for money laundering." Fresh with the memory of the $6 billion of losses to Bre-X, TSX officials contacted the OSC with a strong warning that YBM could end up being "worse than Bre-X." Yet, when Deloitte produced a fairly clean audit (notwithstanding it's identification of "certain irregularities"), the OSC surprisingly allowed the prospectus to go forward.

YBM quickly raised $100 million, witnessed its stock price soar to $20 and reached a market value of $1 billion. YBM tried to get listed on the New York Stock Exchange (NYSE) in 1997 and failed. Yet, with its shares trading so well on the TSX, all of those involved must have been pleased.

But it all unraveled quickly. Deloitte saw concerns while doing the audit on 1997's financial statements and refused to complete the 1997 audit. Stock prices began to fall and things got worse (or better) when the FBI raided YBM's headquarters in 1998 and found a bunch of documents but no trace of magnets. At last, the OSC put a halt to YBM trading, but many brokers kept on trading on behalf of their Russian clients.

One egregious example was Griffiths McBurney, who kept on trading nine months after the trading halt, at times transacting as much as $27 million worth of shares (providing them with $400,000 in commissions) on a single day.

The OSC began pursuing YBM executives and underwriters for failing to disclose that Deloitte refused to complete their 1997 audit. With a three-year trial ending in 2003, company executives ended up paying $1.2 million in fines, with some being banned from public securities for life. While Mogilevich and three other cronies were indicted, only the crony who was then in America running the business (a fellow named Jacob Bogatin) was arrested. The other three were safe in Russia. At the end, it's estimated that $825 million was put into YBM with only $120 million being returned. Mogilevich personally netted at least $18 million without ever stepping foot on Canadian soil.

Postscript: *After American investigative reporter, Robert I. Friedman, wrote a detailed story on Mogilevich's crime dealings, he had a $100,000 price put on his head by Mogilevich. While my head is not worth nearly that much, if you elect to sell me out, all I ask, dear reader, is that you please split the profits with my wife and children.*

Key Takeways

Pat Huddleston compiles three main takeaways on this case. The first is the change in auditors, a red flag for all varieties of fraud, especially when done by a public company. It costs money to change accountants and if a company is doing that, there has to be a highly compelling reason for it.

He also notes that, like in the earlier case of Bre-X Minerals, YBM pumped up their shares with golden-looking press releases, which are as easy to concoct as preparing pasta. (In case you don't know yourself, simply boil water in a pot and drop the pasta in. It's that simple.)

But the main takeaway noted by Huddleston lies in the differences between American and Canadian exchanges. As incompetent as people claim the SEC is, it is at least a national organization with jurisdiction throughout America. Canadian securities regulators, on the other hand, are divided by province, with each Canadian province having its own securities commission. This leads to breaks in communication and invites more pump-and-dump charlatans or even pure speculators to target Canadian exchanges over American ones. The fact that YBM was based in America but still chose to trade on Canadian exchanges is extremely telling on its own. Why go abroad when you have a stock exchange in your backyard? Moreover, while YBM was able to gain a listing on the TSX, it was not able to gain a listing on the NYSE. Any time that someone is discredited in their own neighborhood, but heralded in a foreign domain, it's prudent to ask what the locals know that the foreigners are missing.

These are red flags that corporate investors should not ignore. Even if former premier David Peterson happens to be on the board.

* * *

It's discouraging to think how many people are shocked by honesty and how few by deceit

—Noel Coward

Half the work that is done in this world is to make things appear what they are not

—Beadle, E. R.

QUALITY OF PEOPLE

RICHARD WHITNEY: THE DARK KNIGHT OF WALL STREET

Have you ever encountered someone who appeared virtually invincible? Perhaps it's a celebrity, a beloved community or religious leader, or just an industry guru so well respected and admired that nobody saw it coming. That's precisely what Wall Street witnessed in the 1930s when they discovered the truth about Richard Whitney.

Born in Boston into the prominent Whitney family, descending from the early settlers of Massachusetts called the Pilgrim Fathers, young Richard was surrounded by aristocracy. His father, George Sr., was the president of the North National Union Bank and his uncle sat on the board of J.P Morgan and Co. A teenaged Richard was sent after his older brother, George Jr., to Groton School, a private and ultra-exclusive Episcopal boarding school where Richard was captain of the baseball team. From there he went to Harvard, where he became a member of the elite Porcellian Club and a member of the crew team.

After Harvard, the Whitney brothers found themselves in New York City. Richard joined Cummings and Marckwald, a bond brokerage firm. By then, George had already found work at J.P. Morgan and Co. and was rising up their corporate ladder. Not to be outdone, Richard enlisted the assistance of his uncle and brother, along with a loan from his family, to buy himself a seat on the New York Stock Exchange (NYSE) at the tender age of twenty-three.

In 1916, Whitney married Gertrude Sheldon Sands, a widow of equal pedigree. Her first husband was a stepson of William Kissam Vanderbilt, a famous railroad manager and a member of the Vanderbilt family, and her father had served as the president of the Union League Club, an elite New York private club. Shortly after his wedding, Cummings and Marckwald became Richard Whitney and Co.

Whitney lived on the East Side and purchased an estate in rural New Jersey. With the help of George Jr., he became J.P. Morgan's main broker and Richard Whitney and Co. promised to be an astounding success.

Whitney's social standing was equally impressive. He was among the elites of New York City and was appointed as the treasurer of the highly exclusive New York Yacht Club. He was soon elected onto the Board of Governors of the New York Stock Exchange, where he quickly rose in the ranks to become its vice president. He remained in that position until the crash of 1929, an event that would elevate Whitney from an illustrious member of high society to the financial legend that salvaged the market.

The crash of 1929 occurred in stages. First, the bull market of the Roaring '20s peaked in early September of 1929. Subsequently, London markets crashed on September 20 when top British investors were imprisoned for fraudulent activities, causing a small worldwide downturn. And finally, after about a month of volatile markets coupled with periods of heavy trading, the New York Stock Exchange opened on October 24 to very heavy trading. After reaching record highs, the market plunged by 11%. Since prices collapsed so quickly, the ticker tape couldn't be properly updated, which only added to the panic. With chaos ruling the trading floor, several of New York's leading bankers gathered at J.P. Morgan's offices to devise a solution.

Their decision was quick. They would use the proven tactic that had stopped past crashes. They would form a pool of money to invest in safe blue-chip stocks in the hope that it would stabilize the market. This tactic helped stop the Panic of 1907 and so Wall Street's leading bankers gathered around $130 million to invest. With the president of the Stock Exchange vacationing in Hawaii, they chose Vice President Whitney to be their agent.

At around 1:30 p.m., the well-dressed Whitney strolled casually across the stock market floor toward the spot where U.S. Steel was trading. Making what *New York Times* journalist Albin Krebs described as "the most famous single stock order in stock market history," he used the pooled money to bid 10,000 U.S. Steel shares for $205 each, a blue-chip stock which was then trading for under $200 a share. Using the remains of his plentiful cash pool, he proceeded to make other purchases of major companies, including AT&T, General Electric, and Anaconda. To the relief of Wall Street, the strategy worked; the Dow Jones rose to close the day and its decline was halted. When the hysteria settled, the fact that Whitney had been bidding with other people's money and was merely an agent was forgotten. He became known to investors as the savior of the NYSE, the "White Knight of Wall Street." Even when the markets eventually crashed just days later on Black Tuesday, Whitney's heroics lived on. And in 1930, he was appointed president of the NYSE.

For five years, Whitney remained very active in his role as president. He fought President Franklin D. Roosevelt's efforts to reform Wall Street during the Great Depression and lectured senators on how Wall Street was impeccable as it was, claiming that regulations would only ruin it. Eventually, though, Whitney left the NYSE and Roosevelt's regulations passed.

Despite all his success, Whitney had his doubters. Unfortunately, they kept their doubts to themselves, as anyone who questioned the president of the NYSE was basically ignored. Nonetheless, in the background, rumors spread through Wall Street that Whitney's firm was going under and those rumors were actually true. Unbeknownst to the public, the heroic Whitney was a true case of Dr. Jekyll and Mr. Hyde. On the outside, hero and financial genius. On the inside, a reckless investor with no capacity to manage his own affairs.

Over his years at Richard Whitney and Co., Whitney invested very poorly, covering up his losses in highly speculative ventures by borrowing money from his endless list of rich relatives and elite friends. He lived a lavish life while running an insolvent firm. Even as he was borrowing more to cover his losses, his investing habits did not improve. Soon enough, Whitney faced a dilemma: borrowing was no longer sufficient to keep his firm afloat.

In 1936, Whitney did the unthinkable. He violated his fiduciary duties and raided the funds left in his stewardship. He started with the New York Yacht Club (NYYC), where he was now trustee, treasurer and broker, siphoning off $150,000 to pledge as collateral for a personal bank loan. About a year later, he did the same with the Stock Exchange

Gratuity Fund, an insurance fund formed to ensure support for the families of deceased Exchange members, where Whitney was also both broker and trustee. This time though, he upped the ante, taking over $650,000 worth of bonds and over $200,000 in cash, totaling more than $15 million in 2018 dollars. He even embezzled money from his father-in-law's estate. Yikes.

If Whitney had his way, who knows if he would have ever gotten caught. The few rumors and doubters weren't enough to stop him. But it was ultimately Roosevelt's regulations that exposed him.

The SEC had forced the stock exchange to accept some self-regulatory measures and they soon requested an audit of Richard Whitney and Co. The audits revealed the true nature of Whitney's firm and on the morning of March 8, the announcement was made in the New York Stock Exchange that his brokerage was insolvent. When the final conclusions were made public, Wall Street was shocked to learn that Whitney had embezzled more than $30 million from an assortment of family, friends and organizations, to which he still owed almost $7 million after declaring bankruptcy.

He was sentenced for up to ten years at Sing Sing prison, but given a shorter prison stay due to his cooperation with authorities and was released in 1941 due to exemplary behavior. His brother George stood by him and helped repay his debts, as did his wife Gertrude, who seemed to forgive the fact that he stole from her own father and sold off their house to help raise money. Whitney settled in as a treasurer of a dairy farm, along with other smaller business ventures, and eventually died in 1974. He was eighty-six years old.

Key Takeaways

There were many things wrong with the Whitney case. The most obvious was Whitney's position as both agent and principal, serving as both the broker and trustee for the institutions who deposited assets in his care. That gave him the ability to use the assets at his own discretion without the slightest hint of oversight.

However, the main lesson that Whitney has become associated with is to not let a person's reputation derail the process of proper due diligence and governance best practices. Few people had a better reputation and more credibility than Whitney, "the White Knight of Wall Street." This allowed him to continue embezzling without anyone giving thought to whether Richard Whitney and Co. was actually successful, forcing any second-guessers to swallow their tongues. The fact that his main success on Black Thursday involved money that wasn't even his only added insult to injury. In this regard, Whitney has been compared to Bernie Madoff, whose pedigree as the chairman of the NASDAQ allowed him to run an unquestioned Ponzi scheme for decades.

Investors should remember that you never know which Dr. Jekyll is hiding a Mr. Hyde, and no person, regardless of their pedigree or reputation should be given carte blanche.

* * *

Deception is one of the quickest ways to gain little things and lose big things

—Thomas Sowell

MARTHA'S RUSH TO THE DOOR: A CASE STUDY IN INSIDER SELLING

Martha Stewart's insider trading scandal was big news in the early 2000s. Her six-month extended trial garnered much publicity, so much so that her press conference where she announced that she would commence her jail sentence was aired live on national TV. The details of the case, however, along with the decades of financial chicanery that accompanied them, were far less known.

The '80s were well known as an intense time for corporate greed and ImClone Systems was no exception. Founded in 1984 by Ohio State graduate and medical researcher Dr. Sam Waksal, ImClone devoted itself to the noble cause of developing cancer cures. However, Sam proved to be anything but noble.

Waksal's educational history was dubious. Despite having a top-flight CV, with stints at Stanford, Tufts University and the well-regarded National Cancer Institute, he was found to have fabricated lab results at Tufts and lied about the sources of antibodies at Stanford (and was subsequently asked to leave). His time at the Cancer Institute also raised questions, as his lab contributions somehow became contaminated when it was time to turn in his results and his fellowship was not renewed. Such behavior continued at ImClone. In 1986, Waksal forged the signature of company general counsel John Landes. While the company knew about it and officially launched an internal investigation, they never concluded or reported anything. Landes himself would later testify in Congress that he had thought it wasn't a big deal, to which Pennsylvania rep and sub-committee Chairman Jim Greenwood responded: "My children know better than that, Mr. Landes."

After going public in 1991 at $14 a share, it took Imclone almost ten years to finally cash in. In 2001, it filed its first Biologics License Application, after spending a while acquiring the rights to and subsequently developing Erbitux, an inhibitor used in the treatment of colon cancer, head and neck cancer and certain lung cancers. Imclone's stock rose to over $70 per share and major pharmaceutical company Bristol-Myers Squibb acquired a 40% stake in Imclone for $2 billion. But concerns about the clinical trials led the FDA to reject the drug and it officially informed Waksal of the rejection on Christmas Day 2001.

Waksal began drafting a press release scheduled for December 28, giving him three days of insider knowledge before the public knew about the rejection. Waksal had accumulated $75 million of personal debt to fund a lavish Manhattan life-style, a fancy home in Soho and celebrity-studded parties he had become accustomed to throwing. He had pledged stock war-rants as collateral for the debt, and their downfall would mean his bankruptcy. Knowing that he couldn't sell his shares without alerting the SEC, he transferred almost 80,000 ImClone shares, worth $5 million, to his daughter Aliza. He did it through Merril Lynch broker Peter Bacanovic and directed his family to begin selling. They did so, as did company executives. Aliza sold $2.5 million worth; Sam's father Jack sold $8.1 million worth; vice president of marketing and sales Ronald Martell sold $2.1 million worth and John Landes had already sold $2.5 million worth earlier in December.

Bacanovic in turn ordered his assistant Douglas Faneuil to "call Martha," who was traveling at the time but managed to sell $230,000 worth of shares through Bacanovic on December 27. When the news went public that the FDA rejected Erbitux, shares plummeted, and Stewart successfully avoided a $45,673 loss with her early sale. Of course, that represented less than .03 percent of her assets, but size didn't matter. It was still insider trading.

An internal auditor at Merrill Lynch, Brian Schimpfhauser, noted the suspicious activity surrounding Bacanovic and alerted the authorities. Douglas Faneuil, Bacanovic's assistant, later came forward to fill in the missing details in exchange for immunity. Waksal's guilt was clear as day but Stewart tried wiggling out of it, first by saying that she had previously ordered Bacanovic to sell the stock if it ever rose above $60, which it happened to have done due to the Erbitux original submission. That narrative didn't last though, and authorities pounced on this high-profile case.

Waksal received seven years in jail. James Comey, then a US Attorney in New York (who later gained fame in the 2016 US election before his subsequent dismissal by President Donald Trump) made the decision to prosecute Stewart. At the end of the day, Stewart and Bacanovic were each sentenced to five months in prison and five months home imprisonment and were each placed on probation for two years.

In the meantime, Erbitux went on to have real success. It was eventually approved by the FDA in 2004, who announced that during a trial of 329 patients, Erbitux had delayed tumor growth for about one and a half months in 10% of cases. While

QUALITY OF PEOPLE

Imclone was floated for sale in 2006 without success due to competing medicines, Eli Lilly and Co. eventually purchased ImClone in 2009 for about $6.8 billion.

Upon leaving prison, Waksal successfully launched another pharmaceutical company Kadmon Pharmaceuticals, though he was officially barred from serving as director due to SEC restrictions and appointed his brother Harlan—a man whose history included an arrest for allegedly carrying two pounds of cocaine through Fort Lauderdale Airport—as CEO.

As for Stewart, she managed to avoid too much negative PR and was reinstated to her position at Martha Stewart Living Omnimedia. In 2011, she was even inducted into the New Jersey Hall of Fame.

Key Takeaways

As with so many cases throughout this book, recklessness, deception and narcissism are not one-time events. They are sprinkled throughout the lives of people who display them. Sam Waksal couldn't walk straight if he were on a tightrope. Everything about him was crooked, from his labs to his finances.

What wasn't discovered until after the insider trading debacle was that Waksal was $75 million in debt. Of that, $44 million was lent by Bank of America, secured by a warrant (the right to buy ImClone shares in the future at a specified price) that was worth $19 million. Unbeknownst to Bank of America, Waksal had actually exercised the warrant a year or so earlier. In other words, the warrant no longer existed and the debt was fully uncollateralized. Needless to say, Waksal didn't just hide this fact from Bank of America, he even forged a document from his general counsel confirming that the warrant was still intact.

Waksal was a man whose life was mired by deception. While investors would not likely have been aware of his shenanigans with Bank of America or even the insider selling that drove down the stock, they could have been well aware of Waksal's checkered past before buying in.

* * *

If you forgive a fox for stealing your chickens, he will steal your sheep

—Georgian Proverb

JOHN MABRAY AND BEN MARKS'S TWO-FACED HOUSE IN TWO COUNTIES

When thinking of Wyoming, it's natural to picture its magnificent Yellowstone National Park and forget the rich history of its capital city, Cheyenne. Named after the Cheyenne group of Native Americans, Cheyenne was a village of 600 people when the Union Pacific Railroad arrived in 1867 and took off quickly thereafter. The new town soon sported a population of over 10,000, many of them desperate railroad jumpers traveling west for their fortunes, and it didn't take long for the new town to become a gambling hotbed. Into this fray stepped nineteen-year-old Ben Marks.

Tall and skinny, the Illinois-born Marks had been a liar from a young age. At thirteen, he convinced Army men that he was older than his actual age and joined the Union Army as a dispatch bearer during the American Civil War. He wandered around after the war, making money with various sleight-of-hand card games before finally moving to Cheyenne when the railroad arrived. At first, he tried doing what he did best: earning a living with card games on the streets. But with stiff competition on the crowded streets, he couldn't attract enough customers. Struck with a bold idea, he decided to move his card dealing into a store and put a loud sign on the front proclaiming that everything was being sold for less than a dollar. Of course,

Marks didn't actually sell anything; whenever customers would enter, they would be approached by a "salesman" who would hand them some whiskey and steer them toward card games.

Marks' operation took off and soon spawned copycats. Similar storefronts were set up throughout Cheyenne and Marks turned it into a national franchise, creating "Dollar Stores" in New York, Chicago and Council Bluffs, Iowa, right across the river from Omaha, Nebraska. They were so successful that even a legitimate Chicago department store owner turned his store into a card game arena because it was far more profitable. Marks himself settled in Council Bluffs and when a local official banned card games on the railroad trains, all the other card-game masters left the city for greener pastures, leaving Marks with a gaming monopoly in the city. He proceeded to buy the loyalty of the town's officials and built a good name among the locals, never drinking or smoking. Sporting a moustache that gave his tall figure a venerable look, he built a local casino in 1898 that featured trapdoors for drunks to cool off and was overall known as a "good guy."

But while Marks was making a good living, his ambition was insatiable. He built a mansion using logs from buildings of Omaha's 1898 Trans-Mississippi and International Exposition and located it precisely on the county line. The second and third floor served as a home for Marks and his wife Mary while the bottom floor was reserved for gambling. Being that it was precisely on the county line, the house's two halves were in two separate jurisdictions and when officers of one jurisdiction would raid one part of the house for illegal activities, Marks' cronies would simply move any evidence to the house's other half. Marks then built a horse race track near the mansion to expand the mansion's activities to sports betting and partnered with John Mabray, a con man who specialized in fixing and faking sporting events.

Mabray recruited a network of agents to act as "steerers." A steerer would approach its target, usually an affluent business-man traveling through the train station. The steerer, who we will call Joe, would take the target to a bar and after a few drinks, would claim to work for a certain wealthy railroad tycoon who we will call Mr. Richie. Aside from making millions off the rail-road and employing a host of servants, Mr. Richie also made a lot of money by promoting horse racing and would occasionally fix a match so that the underdog would win. Steerer Joe would proceed to claim that Mr. Richie would rake in all the money and abuse his hard-working Joe, and Joe now wanted revenge. Joe claimed that Mr. Richie was fixing an upcoming match but that he knew the owner of the underdog horse that Mr. Richie would be betting on and together, they agreed to have the underdog fall on the track. Joe could not bet against Mr. Richie, as that would look fishy, but if the target would, they would split the proceeds between Joe, the underdog's owner, and the target. In almost every case, upon hearing this story, the target would buy in.

On the day of the race, Joe would take the target to the rac-ing track. He would introduce him to "Mr. Richie," who would oftentimes be Ben Marks himself, and they would enjoy a raucous crowd track that included all the elites of town. They would deposit the target's money in a safe and watch the race. They would cheer together as the underdog would take the lead, and the target would send in more money. But then in a matter of complete and unexpected surprise, the leading horse would suddenly collapse amid an explosion of blood. A panic would ensue as a doctor came and Joe would whisk the target away and tell him to get out of town (such cheat-betting was definitely illegal and betting at all was illegal in places like Chicago), promising to retrieve the money from the safe and send it on. The target, who had then completely bought in to every word of Joe's, would listen and run.

Of course, the money was never sent. In fact, it was even removed from the safe before the race, in case the target had second thoughts. A pad of blood had been inserted into the horse's mouth, meant to explode at the right moment, and the "doctor" who examined the horse was an accomplice in the scam. The victim wouldn't tell police when he would realize the money would never be sent, as he would have to admit to joining in a cheating scam.

Mabray's horse-betting scam was extremely lucrative and it was soon featured at all of Marks' Dollar Stores. Mabray's agents became a national network and at one point, he had over 300 people working for him. But Mabray was careless. He accidentally sent a letter intended for one of his agents to a private detective, and then postal inspector J.S. Swenson got involved. Swenson figured out what was happening pretty quickly but since the targets didn't want to testify, he had a hard time finding evidence. Raids on headquarters didn't work either. Due to his wide-ranging network, Mabray was able to move his headquarters from place to place when he suspected something was amiss. Additionally, when Swenson tried raiding the headquarters in Council Bluffs, the police refused to cooperate, likely because Marks had them handsomely bought off.

But Swenson finally succeeded in 1909 when he conducted a raid in Little Rock, Arkansas, where Mabray had a stockpile of incriminating documents waiting for him. However, nothing they had was able to incriminate Marks, even after they convinced four targets and Mabray himself to testify. Mabray claimed that he gave eight or nine percent to Marks for police protection, but with no evidence to support this claim, Marks was let off. Mabray received a federal sentence of two years and a $10,000 fine, and more than eighty of his associates were rounded up and put in jail.

Marks returned to his house outside Council Bluffs and his wife Mary. He died at the age of seventy-one and his house still stands to this very day.

Key Takeaways

Mabray and Marks' horse-betting scam is an interesting case of fraud in that the victims thought they were defrauding others when, in fact, they were the fraud targets.

The lesson here lies in words uttered by Johnny Depp in his Oscar-nominated *Pirates of the Caribbean* role: "You can always trust a dishonest person to be dishonest." When you are included in a potentially lucrative opportunity from a known liar who is contravening some moral principles or the rule of law, no matter how profitable the opportunity, you may just be the mark in the con. Personal morality aside, every now and then you'll miss a golden opportunity, but often you'll avoid losing everything in the process.

* * *

AREN'T I TOO SMART TO FALL FOR THIS?

Psychologists have referred to it as the Lake Wobegun Effect. It is the illusory superiority bias driving our conviction that we are better than average in a whole host of domains. Whether this refers to our looks, our sense of humor or our ability to be deceived, we like to believe that we are uniquely special in society.

It is often our delusions that will get us in trouble. Whenever we think we're too smart to be defrauded, that will be the beginning of the end.

As we have already seen, contrary to conventional belief, investment fraud victims score higher on financial literacy measures than non-victims. Investment fraud victims had also attained a higher level of education and were more experienced with investments than the sample non-victim population.

And yet . . .

THE MAN WHO COULDN'T FACE THE MUSIC

During the Great Depression, F. Donald Coster was a highly respected man. Coster served as the president of McKesson & Robbins, a venerable drug company that was founded in the 1820s and continues as one of America's largest companies. Owning a twenty-eight room mansion in Fairfield, Connecticut and a castle in Monroe, Connecticut, he had all the outward trappings of a successful Wall Street executive. He was so well regarded that he was even asked to run on the Republican ticket to challenge incumbent president Franklin D. Roosevelt. But, Coster was intensely private, and there was a very good reason for him declining the presidential nomination. For starters, F. Donald Coster didn't actually exist. He was a con man named Philip Musica.

Musica was born in Naples, Italy in 1877. From there, his family moved to New York's Little Italy when he was seven. His father Antonio ran a small grocery store, importing products directly from abroad in an effort to beat out local retailers. Despite being a good student, Philip dropped out of school to join the business. While his father's approach was innovative, Philip thought there was far more money to be made and decided to take advantage of New York's corrupt waterfront by bribing officials to understate the amount he was importing, thereby lowering the tariffs on his goods. He was caught in 1909 and sentenced to a year in prison. In the end, he served only five months thanks to friends in high places, including the

Italian ambassador to the US, who convinced President Taft to pardon him.

Upon leaving prison, he founded United Hair Co., which on its surface imported high-quality human hair from Europe, which sold for as much as $80 a piece (roughly $2,500 today). In fact, he was selling hair collected from the floor of barber shops. That minor inconvenient detail didn't prevent him from taking the company public and becoming a millionaire within just a few years. However, the scale of his fraud became too ambitious. And when he tried selling $250 worth of hair for $350,000, he was eventually caught and then sentenced to another three years.

Once released, Musica wanted to restart his life and career. Thus emerged F. Donald Coster. Like his previous frauds, his alias was bold and creative. Musica claimed that he (F. Donald Coster) was born in Washington, D.C. and had managed to obtain a medical degree in far-off Germany. Shortly after creating his new alias, he founded Adelphi Pharmaceutical Manufacturing Company, specializing in hair content. That quickly fell apart, but within two years, he started a new venture, Girard and Co., which quickly struck gold. Like Adelphi, Girard and Co. specialized in hair products, but now Musica could reap the benefits of Prohibition. Due to his hair products, Musica was allowed access to government alcohol and he would buy massive amounts, not for his hair products, but rather to then sell the extra alcohol to bootleggers. The authorities suspected that Girard was doing something along those lines but with no evidence—and also with no knowledge that Musica/Coster was a convicted fraudster—Girard was allowed to continue unimpeded.

By 1925, he had amassed enough bootlegging profits to build something legitimate. That's when he bought McKesson & Robbins, a company that was quite established but still limited in scope, selling a selection of medications, but it was hardly a national powerhouse. Musica rolled up his sleeves and got to work. He rapidly expanded the company's operations, acquiring sixty-six other wholesale drug companies to help grow McKesson in the next twelve years. McKesson became a national chain so powerful it even withstood the Great Depression, employing workers in thirty-five states while claiming annual sales of $174 million. At the same time, he desperately avoided the public eye, not wanting to be connected with the young Italian fraudster he once was. He did not participate in board meetings nor did he allow himself to be photographed.

What no one realized was that Musica's past was as sham-saturated as his present. Firstly, he used McKesson & Robbins to launder his bootlegging profits while also embarking on a scheme to inflate earnings. He created a bogus sales agency named WW Smith and put his brother in charge of it. In reality, it was a printing station where they would type the names of various imaginary companies which supposedly ordered from McKesson & Robbins. Musica installed another one of his brothers at the shipping department, where documents were forged to show that they shipped inventory to the bogus customers and a third brother was put into the position of assistant treasurer, where he produced documents to create cash flows to match the fictitious sales.

To avoid connections with Musica's past, the brothers were all given the fake surname Dietrich. McKesson would pay commissions to the fictitious WW Smith and the brothers split the profits, with the mastermind Philip getting the most. Additionally, the brother concocted large amounts of phony inventory and with Philip being a 10% shareholder, the increased assets on the balance sheet and the subsequent rise in the stock price offered another benefit.

But it all ended in the hands of the company's actual treasurer, Julian Thompson. Suspicious of the many payments to WW Smith, he approached Dun and Bradstreet, which had supposedly given the credit reports for WW Smith that were then given to the company auditors. Turns out that D&B had never heard of any WW Smith. The SEC was notified and their investigation led to the quick halting of McKesson securities trading on the exchange.

Musica was arrested and then released on bail, but not before his fingerprints were taken. By the next day, his prints had been matched to Philip Musica and the police immediately went to his house. When they knocked on the door, they heard a loud bang. Musica had elected to shoot himself instead of facing more jail time, but not before he penned a multi-page suicide note where he declared his innocence and proclaimed himself "a victim of Wall Street plunder and blackmail in a struggle for honest existence." In a corny take on the situation, *Time* magazine proceeded to call him the man who "couldn't face the Musica."

Key Takeaways

Thanks to the Musica debacle, after this fraud was uncovered and 3,000 hours of testimony completed, the SEC proceeded to make serious regulatory changes. These included the requirement to have non-officer board members nominate the auditors and having the shareholders actually elect and receive the reporting by the auditors. Additionally, by the following year, the American Association of Certified Public Accountants made their first proclamation where they noted the auditors should have procedures to confirm accounts receivables and inventory, two of the main aspects of the McKesson fraud.

For today's investors, this case reminds us to pursue a simple method of due diligence that would have helped anyone stay out of Musica's way. When entering a deal with any prospective partner, employee and even vendor, trace their path to their earliest years. Even without dramatic aliases and fake identities, the discipline of tracing "back to kindergarten" allows you to avoid surprises in the future. If any of McKesson's shareholders had merely connected with a neighbor, a distant relative, a former classmate or a childhood friend, the eternal stain on McKesson's history could have been avoided.

* * *

IS DECEPTION A FUNCTION OF NATURE OR NURTURE?

Robert Feldman, the psychologist who spent several decades studying deception, says that upon meeting someone, on average, we lie approximately three times in first ten minutes of casual conversation. Some lie up to twelve times during that time span. In his book, The Liar in Your Life: The Way to Truthful Relationships, he claims that virtually no one refrains from lying altogether.

Most of the lies are not malicious nor terribly dramatic. They are generally "white lies" intended to keep the conversation going or to put on a positive impression. Whether it involves giving someone a compliment they do not deserve or exaggerating one's own value, it is generally quite harmless and not intended to harm.

Friedman's research suggests that there is something deeply human about deception, and that we must employ a great deal of effort and vigilance to limit or eliminate deception from our lives.

The three surprising elements of his findings are: how often we do it, how naturally we do it and (most surprising) that it still works. Recognizing how many lies are exchanged, one would think that we would become exceptional at spotting them. The reality is quite different. We generally have a truth bias and want to believe what others are telling us—in part, because that is what we want to hear.

FERDINAND WARD: HOW TO FOOL A PRESIDENT AND BECOME THE BEST-HATED MAN IN AMERICA

Ulysses S. Grant was known for many things. Hailed as a brilliant general during the American Civil War, he was popular enough to become president for two terms and later have his name stamped on the US fifty-dollar bill. But political savvy aside, he was a surprisingly gullible investor, paving the way for one of the biggest frauds of the nineteenth century.

It all started when Grant finished his second term as president and wanted both a vacation and a possible path to another Republican nomination in the 1880 election. Deciding to embark on a worldwide tour with his family, he started from Liverpool, England and traversed through Europe, ending in Asia, where he helped settle a longstanding Chinese-Japanese dispute and avoid war.

When Grant arrived in San Francisco's port after this two-year journey, he was greeted by cheering crowds and internal hopes to secure the 1880 nomination. Despite being the front runner for some time, his leading 304 first-ballot votes fell short of the 370-vote requirement and he eventually lost the nod to the surprise candidate from Ohio, James Garfield. Accepting his defeat and supporting Garfield, he began looking for a way to support himself in the private sector. In 1881, he moved to New York where his son, Ulysses Grant, Jr., seemed to be making a decent living.

Ulysses Jr., nicknamed Buck, had been educated in law and served as an assistant to his father during some of his presidential years. He then served as an Assistant Attorney General in New York before venturing out on his own and meeting a handsome, charismatic gentleman named Ferdinand Ward. A man with a gift for gab, Ward seemed to be born with a knack for trading. His trading profits in the aftermath of the Civil War had given him a massive estate in Connecticut and a townhouse in Manhattan by his twenties, where he was known as "the Napoleon of Wall Street."

Seeing an opportunity, Buck formed an investment firm, Grant & Ward, with the fast-talking trader. Hoping to provide for his family and believing in Ward's investment savvy, Grant Sr. joined the firm as a limited partner. He invested his entire savings of $200,000 (the equivalent of approximately $4.8 million in today's dollars) with Ward.

Back in the offices of Grant & Ward, the "Napoleon of Wall Street" was delighted. Ward surely knew that he was no investment guru, but also realized that with Grant on board he did not need to be. He reasoned that people would invest in his firm simply because the former president and war hero was involved. How right he was! Trusting Ward implicitly, Grant had convinced many of his army friends to invest in the firm. Many others followed suit, thinking Ward's "in" with Washington would bring the firm massive benefits, particularly in the realm of government contracts and insider information.

Using the same reasoning, the Marine National Bank lent out massive amounts to Ward. While Grant refused to lobby for government contracts due to what he thought was a breach in honesty, Ward still told everyone that a boatload of government contracts were coming. Even without that, investors piled in simply because of the perceived credibility created by Grant.

At first, all seemed well. The early investors in G&W received their payments and Grant now had a way to provide for his family. But what Grant did not know was that Ward was running what would later become known as a Ponzi scheme. He was paying earlier investors using money from subsequent investors and engaging in painfully poor trading in between. While Grant and his son were beaming to the public about their investment wunderkind, that wunderkind was busy siphoning off much of the money to finance his opulent lifestyle.

By 1884, Ward saw his end coming. His trading was terrible and with the massive loans outstanding from Marine National Bank, he knew that he would be personally responsible for its failure. Instead of owning up to the truth, the man of words spun an opposite tale. He told the elder Grant that while Grant & Ward was doing fine, Marine National was failing, and their fall might bring down their own firm. The complete opposite of the truth!

"I need $150,000[7] to save Marine National," said Ward to Grant. The man who paved his way through military mind games and American politics couldn't see past the face of his trusted partner and Grant immediately obliged.

He approached railroad boss and noted philanthropist William H. Vanderbilt and asked for a $150,000 loan. But Vanderbilt refused to lend Grant & Ward any money, saying

---

[7] The equivalent of approximately $3.7 million in today's dollars.

that "what I've heard about that firm would not justify me in lending it a dime." But in another game of misplaced trust, Vanderbilt agreed to lend Grant personally $150,000 and wrote out the check. For all of his honesty in not lobbying for government contracts, Grant pulled off a serious white lie and transferred the money immediately to Ward.

The next day, Ward was nowhere to be seen. He was long gone with his $150,000. When President Grant showed up at the offices the next day, he was greeted with this news by a very grave and solemn Buck. He locked himself in the office for a while and when he emerged, he spoke not a word. The crowd that gathered around Grant & Ward removed their hats in respect for their president and war hero and when it was revealed that June that Grant had a total of $200 to his name, he received a slew of checks in the mail from sympathetic well-wishers. Ward was caught and jailed shortly thereafter, but Grant & Ward had assets of $67,174 and liabilities of $16,792,640— almost a half-billion in today's dollars. With no money to pay back his $150,000 loan from Vanderbilt, Vanderbilt decided to be lenient on the former president and took some of Grant's war memorabilia as payment. Though the memorabilia was not worth nearly as much as the debt, Vanderbilt forgave the rest.

Grant was known as a man without a hint of a temper. However, he would dig his fingernails into the chair when Ward was mentioned and according to *The New York Times*, he said he would kill him "as I would a snake. I believe I should do it . . . but I do not wish to be hanged for such a wretch."

With his personal finances now far worse than when he started off on Wall Street, Grant accepted an offer from Mark

Twain's publishing company to write his memoirs. Doubting his own writing abilities, he had adamantly refused penning them for twenty years; but with nothing to lose, he began writing. He learned that he contracted throat cancer shortly after beginning his writing and hurried to finish it, with his son Fred doing the proofing and referencing. He finished just a few days before his death on July 23, 1885. With Grant's candid style, the memoir quickly became a national sensation, immediately selling over 300,000 copies, with the royalties providing an enduring income for his heirs. Later that year, William H. Vanderbilt also died, but not before returning Grant's memorabilia to his widow Julia and forgiving the large debt.

Locked in jail, Ward wallowed in self-pity and called himself "the best-hated man in the United States."

Key Takeaways

Former SEC enforcer-turned author Pat Huddleston notes how, of the many people who invested in Grant & Ward, few of them ever met Ward. While Ward did do some of his own promoting, even claiming to have government contracts coming when none in fact existed, his firm's attractiveness stemmed from Grant's involvement. In other words, Ward let Grant promote the company while he sat back in a lounge chair and siphoned off the money. A similar thing happened in the Bre-X mining fraud, where company executives promoted the company for their own personal gain without fully knowing that their gold samples were tainted.

The lesson for investors when any investment is promoted, whether it is a penny-stock, a boring magnet business or a promising fund manager, is the importance of distinguishing between the quality of the investment and quality of the promoter. Even the most qualified promoter might be less than fully informed, and your due diligence cannot be limited to, and/or reliant on their conscientiousness.

* * *

He that accomplishes his ends by deceit shall render up his soul in anguish

—Turkish Expression

WHITAKER WRIGHT: A BALLROOM UNDER A LAKE IS OF LITTLE CONSOL-ATION

In the same era when the Wright brothers of North Carolina gained fame for inventing the airplane, another Wright took a different path. J. Whitaker Wright was born in 1846 in England to James Wright, a Methodist minister, and Mathilda Whitaker. After quitting school at fifteen, the younger Wright first worked as a printer before becoming a Methodist preacher like his father, though he was soon forced to stop for health reasons. His younger brother, John Joseph, followed a similar course to the American Wrights, supposedly inventing the trolley pole but never patenting it. After the death of James Wright, Sr., the Wright family immigrated to Canada in 1867, coincidentally the same year that Canada was founded as an independent country.

With preaching no longer an option, Wright eventually made his way to Philadelphia, where he met seventeen-year-old Anna Edith Weightman and married her in 1878. He began his American career by trading in grain and petroleum but was determined to find something bigger. He decided to temporarily leave his wife and embark upon a journey west, traveling to Leadville, Colorado. There he rented a cabin with a few friends and somehow managed to acquire a mining claim for $325,000. Incorporated as the Denver City Consolidated Mining Company, Wright and Co. began selling shares to New York and Philadelphia investors with the claim that they had found plentiful ore. In truth, his ore was very low grade and Wright began a series of transactions to stall and keep up his pretense. Instead of selling the ore from his first mineshaft, he started constructing another mineshaft just 800 meters away. Even before he began shipping ore, he separated a part of his company as the Lee Basin Company and began selling its shares as well. It was soon obvious that neither of Wright's companies would accomplish much and both collapsed in 1882 without paying any dividends. Despite this, Wright somehow managed to emerge with money of his own, buying a lovely four-story house in Philadelphia and returning to his wife and family on an extremely high note.

But even as he returned to the City of Brotherly Love, his scams didn't stop. He led a group of investors in purchasing mining claims in New Mexico and floating them on the Philadelphia Mining Exchange. Unlike his previous investment, this time there actually was a limited quantity of rich ore and Wright and his partner George Roberts made sure potential investors would see its dazzling metal. The most successful of Wright's companies, the Sierra Grande Company, paid dividends to its investors. As the prices of Wright's companies soared, he sold them all off. By the very next year, the ore was depleted and the companies began their downturn, but with all of his shares sold, Wright had already become a millionaire. Being elected president of the Philadelphia Mining Exchange, Wright abandoned his first house to move to more fashionable neighborhoods and began announcing his wealth by buying yachts. One enraged investor attempted to have him arrested for the misuse of investor money in 1888, but the case was dropped.

In 1889, Wright returned to England with his wife and three children. Some say he planned to retire, while others counter that he had always longed to become part of Victorian society. Whatever the cause, Wright lost much of his money during the financial panic of 1893 and was fixed on reacquiring his old wealth. When discoveries of gold in Western Australia hit London investors with "gold fever," Wright turned back to his old tactics to rebuild his wealth.

Wright incorporated a new company in September 1894, the West Australia Exploring and Finance Corporation. And even with his questionable past, investors bought in. Wright's company began promoting many new mining companies and like his original Colorado one, none of them had much substance (and none ended up paying dividends). But Wright's tall figure, curvy moustache and small circular spectacles all helped him shine with sophistication and lure more investors into his mining exploits. The *Daily Mail* reported that in the year 1896 alone, he raised over £250,000 to dig for metals in Western Australia, the equivalent of nearly $35 million in today's dollars.

It wasn't Wright's presentations alone that endeared him to investors. He also pulled cunning tricks to get them to come. He named one of his companies Lake View Consols and another Paddington Consols, with the term "consol" being key. A consol was the nomenclature of the time for secure government-issued securities and many people thought that by investing with Wright, they were in fact investing securely with the government. Of course, Wright was in no way associated with the government. His mining company was in no way secure or reliable, but he gladly raked in the proceeds from his ignorant investors.

As more investors piled in, Wright became wealthy beyond his imagination, and, with a Victorian society to impress, he started spending with abandon. He bought a townhouse in a prestigious area of London and purchased a new yacht, Sybarita, which he used to race against world dignitaries; in one instance besting a boat belonging to Kaiser Wilhelm II at an international racing competition. But all the yachts and townhouses were mere crickets compared to Wright's favorite extravagance: his enormous mansion in the village of Witley.

After spending £250,000 to acquire the Lea Park estate from the Earl of Derby in 1896, "coincidentally" the same amount of money that he raised from investors that year, he proceeded to build a mansion that redefined the very nature of gaudiness. He hired 600 workers to construct a thirty-two-room house, digging out four lakes and removing hills that got in the way. Renovations cost an estimated £1.25 million. The finished mansion (costing as much as $210 million in today's dollars) featured an array of unique statues, a velodrome, stables for fifty horses, a theater, an observatory, and a massive ballroom constructed *under* a lake, allowing guests to look into the lake through the glass ceiling above.

In 1897, Wright set up another company, London and Globe Finance Corporation, targeting aristocratic investors. To give the company instant credibility, Wright appointed respected diplomat and politician, the Marquess of Dufferin and Ava, Frederick Blackwood, as chairman. To further boost his company, Wright acquired the already successful US mines of the Le Roi Mining and Smelting Company and renamed it the British America Corporation, floating it to British investors through London and Globe Finance with great success.

Investors were warned by financial experts that it was better to invest directly with the American mines than through the blind pool of London and Globe but Wright countered by hiring Bernard Macdonald, an accused but acquitted murderer, to put on an optimistic face to the public. Wright's sales were so successful that he started floating even more mines under the name Le Roi No. 2, with his London and Globe siphoning away £550,000 out of the £600,000 received from the public offering.

As time passed, problems began creeping up on Wright that he continually evaded. When investors became less excited about Le Roi 2, especially since it had yet to yield a dividend, Wright had London and Globe float a new mine for much more than its true worth and ordered British America Corporation to buy it up. Wright then faced a new challenge when the Western Australian gold fever he was milking began drying up. In response, he cunningly repackaged thirteen of his previously floated Australian companies as the new "Standard Exploration Company" in 1898 and investors fell for it again.

This trick, however, only bought him a short window of time. It didn't take long for Standard Exploration to join the rest of the industry in the red. At first, Wright hid the losses by shuffling money between his various companies, but he soon realized that to generate real profits he would have to enter a new industry. He did so by building the London-based Baker and Waterloo Railroad, not realizing that while Baker might eventually bring in profits, it would drain the present cash reserves that he desperately needed for his failing mining companies. With the shares of London and Globe falling, he moved £1 million of its liabilities into the British America Corporation with the help of his accountants (whose arms he twisted and protests he squelched), but that only caused both companies to go under. When this maneuver was discovered, along with his falsified balance sheets and systematic embezzlement from the British America Corporation for London and Globe's use, Wright was ousted from his position of control and the courts began debating whether Wright could be criminally prosecuted.

Always the wily fox, Wright took advantage of the courts' debates. Before they could reach a decision, he boarded the La Loraine to the United States under an assumed name and was suddenly nowhere to be found. Undeterred, Scotland Yard pursued him aggressively and New York detectives were waiting for Wright when he docked in the United States, He was immediately sent back to England to face trial. Charged with falsifying London and Globe's balance sheets in 1899 and 1900, Wright was sentenced to seven and a half years in prison. Unable to handle the shame, Wright took a cyanide pill after the verdict was issued. He died in January 1904, about a month after his American Wright namesakes successfully tested their first airplane.

As for his over-the-top Witley mansion, a 1952 fire destroyed most of the house, with the only remnants being a few stables and the ballroom under the lake, which can still be visited to the present day, a ghostly remnant of Wright's ill-gotten gains.

Key Takeaways

There are lessons here aplenty. Wright's history of enriching himself and living a highly ostentatious lifestyle without ever paying a dividend should have dissuaded any thoughtful investor.

The fact that he was able to pressure his accountants to transfer money between affiliates speaks volumes about their independence. As we've seen in other cases, if an accounting firm is so deeply dependent on any singular client, they cannot reject demands that would violate accounting best practices.

Additionally, the fact that Wright was able to repackage thirteen of his insolvent companies and sell them as one violated the blatantly obvious rule of 0+0=0. Then there's the fact that past performances in highly speculative industries like mining are far less indicative of future success than in other domains.

Furthermore, when investing directly is feasible, there is no need for an intermediary; i.e. for investors to give their money to Wright's London and Globe, which was merely a blind pool and promotion company. Including an intermediary tends to just increase the risk and cost for all involved.

All of these takeaways are meaningful and valid, but it is Wright's cunning manipulation of semantics that may be most salient. To earn the unwarranted trust every fraudster craves, they may employ a variety of tricks. One of Wright's approaches was to name two of his companies "consol," and appointing a government official as the chairman, giving the impression that they were safe and secure government bonds. The problem is that they weren't consols and Wright was not associated with the government in any way.

Semantics are important. When the employed terminology suggests an obvious misrepresentation, beware.

* * *

DO MEN AND WOMEN RESPOND SIMILARLY TO FRAUD?

Previous cases offered examples of specific sexes being targeted for specific frauds. For example, Ponzi targeted men while Howe exclusively targeted women, and there is evidence that each sex responds to different scams differently.

According to an AARP study, the victims of investment fraud are more likely to be male, while the victims of lottery fraud were overwhelmingly more likely to be female than the control group or the general population.

RAPE, PLUNDER AND LOOT: THE STORY OF THE FUGITIVE FINANCIER

Robert Lee Vesco was determined that his humble beginnings would not define him. Born to a Detroit autoworker in 1935, he lied about his age to begin working at an auto repair shop at age fifteen and then enrolled in night school to become an engineer. From there, he moved to New Jersey to work at a machine tool plant, eventually taking it over when it went bankrupt and dropping out of school to focus on promoting his business. In 1966, Vesco merged his defunct company with another equally unsuccessful enterprise to form a shell company named Cryogenics, which he referred to as a "fabulous moneymaking machine." He began borrowing oodles of money and specialized in finding weak companies on which to perform hostile takeovers.

Within a few years, the now-renamed International Controls Corp. (ICC) had sales of over $100 million, profits of $4.7 million and was a publicly traded company with over $40 million in shareholder equity. Most of the earnings came from a California manufacturing company, which he acquired through significant legal trouble, that gave him a bad reputation and prevented ICC from truly taking off. While he had backing from Bank of America and Prudential Insurance Company, Vesco wanted more. He found "more" in the ruins of Bernie Cornfeld.

Cornfeld was a celebrated playboy financier who, like Vesco, came from humble beginnings. Born in Turkey, he immigrated to the US with his parents at age three. He began his career as a socialist-leaning taxi driver before realizing that he enjoyed the conspicuous consumption of a flamboyant capitalist. Moving to France, he set up Investors Overseas Services (IOS), selling investment funds to US soldiers stationed abroad via door-to-door salesmen who offered soldiers $25-50 investments to help their families. His big attraction was his "Fund of Funds," a mutual fund investment in other mutual funds. With mutual funds being extremely popular in the 1950s and '60s, the idea of a "Fund of Funds" was very attractive to small investors and IOS soared.

Cornfeld's operations expanded to target the general European public that was eager to get "in" on the American boom of the '60s. By 1965, IOS trades made up five percent of all New York Stock Exchange trades. By 1969, Cornfeld had 13,000 salesmen and 750,000 customers in 110 countries. At the same time, he ran into serious trouble. The stock market had stagnated; sales were down, and over 20% of profits were needed to pay off long-term debt. Moreover, his operation was technically illegal, as the SEC required mutual funds to invest no more than three percent in other mutual funds.

Adding insult to injury, Cornfeld was being scammed himself. He had expected an upcoming downturn in the market and had invested $120 million in natural gas resources with a company led by former Republican congressman turned oil magnate John McCandish King. What Cornfeld didn't know was that King was sending him resources at twice the price he sent to other customers, at times jacking up prices as much as ten times their actual value.

The combination of these three factors hit IOS hard. With their stock price down fifty percent and their headquarters in complete disarray, the board fired Cornfeld and began looking for a "white knight." That prompted the thirty-four-year-old Vesco to take a June 1970 flight to Geneva to make his pitch.

Vesco presented well, with slicked back hair, long side-burns and a thick moustache that made him look like a reliably aggressive businessman. He mentioned to the board that he was backed by Bank of America and Prudential as prime lenders. However, when the board asked him if he had $5 million in cash on hand to lend, Vesco found himself in a bind. His Bank of America account only allowed him to withdraw $3 million.

He contacted Butlers Bank, a small Bahamas-based bank with solvency issues due to a recent $9 million construction of an office building. Its chairman, Allan Butler, was as risky and ambitious as Vesco. Butler, a former ski captain who was managing a multitude of simultaneous businesses and by then already on his fourth wife, Shirley, was eager to make a buck. So he gladly lent Vesco the $5 million to present to IOS as his own. By August, they had an agreement and Vesco proceeded to take charge of the company while also buying out Cornfeld's fifteen-percent share in IOS. Cornfeld had raised alarm bells about Vesco's integrity and did everything he could to avoid selling to Vesco, but through a series of shells and subsidiaries, Cornfeld ended up selling it to Vesco anyway without realizing.

With his hands firmly on the steering wheel of a completely dysfunctional company, Vesco put his mark on IOS fast. He began transferring IOS assets to companies that he owned without anyone catcing on due to IOS' continued dysfunctionality. To demonstrate his brash chutzpah, Vesco even considered setting up a company named RPL, an acronym for "Rape, Plunder and Loot" (he didn't due to some investigations beginning by US authorities). Before anybody could say anything, IOS was suddenly short $224 million. The SEC turned to Vesco, but he was long gone. He fled to the Caribbean on a commercial flight, only leaving behind $200,000 to donate to President Richard Nixon's 1972 re-election campaign in exchange for hopefully canceling the SEC investigation.

For a time, nobody quite knew where Vesco was. He resurfaced in Costa Rica, openly gallivanting around on his custom-made Boeing jet. Vesco's bribe was unsuccessful and caused him to be subsequently indicted by the US Attorney General. He managed to obtain immunity in Costa Rica from then-leader Jose Maria Figueres in exchange for investing $13 million into the local economy and promises to invest $42 million more. Despite some half-hearted requests by the US for extradition, Vesco lived comfortably for a while, even arranging to have his yacht that was confiscated by US authorities stolen back from a Fort Lauderdale port. When Figueres was accused of harboring criminals, he merely shrugged it off and said, "I wish we had more Vescos."

By 1978, however, he had worn out his welcome. A new leader had taken over Costa Rica and Vesco had founded a factory manufacturing weaponry that didn't sit well with the locals. Jumping from Nicaragua to Bahamas and narrowly avoiding an FBI trap at Bahamas' Nassau airport, Vesco was subject to an international manhunt that was followed closely by US news outlets. *Fortune* jounalist Arthur Herzog wrote a long profile on him called "Stalking Robert Vesco" and eventually wrote his biography. Vesco even tried (unsuccessfully) establishing his own country in the Caribbean island of Antigua. Vesco forged a close relationship with the Libyan government, even attempting to bribe the Carter administration to sell them weapons. All the while, Vesco managed to retain much of his wealth, enough to appear on *Forbes'* wealthiest in the world list.

Eventually, a urinary infection caused Vesco to find a place where he could receive healthcare, so he settled in Cuba where Fidel Castro claimed to accept him for "humanitarian reasons." In truth, he was allowed there in exchange for lending his financial acumen to the Cuban government, which was then trying to stay afloat despite a heavy US embargo. Vesco was asked to help them turn Cuba's Cayo Largo Island into a premiere tourist site. Growing a beard and passing himself off as Canadian citizen Tom Adams, he lived lavishly, chain-smoked and partied hard, all the while surrounding himself with an entourage of bodyguards and allegedly running a drug trafficking scheme, leading him to be named as the co-defendant in the trial against Florida drug dealer Carlos Lehder Rivas.

But Vesco made the capital mistake of "biting the hand that fed him," as he claimed to produce a "wonder drug" to cure a variety of ailments from cancer to a regular cold, in the process defrauding Fidel Castro's nephew, Antonio Fraga Castro. He was arrested shortly thereafter in 1995 and sentenced to thirteen years in prison. [Talk about snake oil treatments backfiring!] He was, however, released in 2005. According to friends, he lived quietly upon his release from prison, though he somehow managed to procure Italian citizenship in 2006 despite still being wanted by the US. Vesco died in November 2007, with his death only being discovered by the US five months later.

As for his IOS money, none of it was ever recovered, though Bernie Cornfeld and John McCandish King both served short jail stints for their roles in the company's demise. Allan Butler, head of the bank that gave Vesco the $5 million to scam the IOS board with, was named as a co-defendant in the SEC lawsuit against Vesco.

Key Takeaways

The one dynamic that has been consistent throughout this book and most acutely demonstrated in the Vesco-Cornfeld case is that fraudsters look for vulnerability. Cornfeld targeted soldiers who were removed from their trusted networks, away from the protective eye of North American regulators, and mindful of their susceptibility to death or the fragility of their family's financial affairs back home.

Vesco was equally enthused about the prospect of desperate shareholders and highly unstable corporate environments, where his chicanery would go unnoticed and anxiously distressed investors would place their blind trust in the confidence he exuded.

Their pursuit of vulnerability and desperation should serve as a reminder for all of us that distress-ridden circumstances are rarely optimal for making significant decisions with long-term implications. Desperation leads us to hope for that proverbial "knight in shining armor," embracing those that seemingly fit the bill, and forgetting that such glamorous rescuers are the ingredients of fairy tales.

Lastly, there's an old expression that when you lie down with dogs you should expect to get up with fleas. This dynamic is so powerful that the SEC actually introduced a Bad Actor rule, limiting the rights of those connected with scams and scammers. Whether they are an affiliated issuer, director, officer, general partner, significant beneficial owner, related promoter, et al., they will be disqualified from several important exemptions on the basis of their affiliation alone. This offers an important lesson that may have protected investors and shareholders from the likes of Vesco and Cornfeld. Both men surpassed grey areas and acquainted themselves with the most questionable of characters. Whether they were the victims or accomplices of these characters mattered less than the fact that they were surrounded by them. Similarly, a great many frauds can be sidestepped by simply avoiding those that reek of suspicion and whose friends seem to carry similar fleas.

* * *

HOW DOES FRAUD COMPARE TO OTHER CRIMES?

In the UK, approximately one out of every ten people has fallen victim to fraud in the last five years.

In the US, approximately, eleven percent of US adults, or an estimated 25.6 million people, pay for fraudulent products and services.

While these products and services are not necessarily or exclusively limited to investments, what's clear is that fraud has become the most prevalent crime in the developed world, and we are ten times more likely to be defrauded than to experience more traditional theft.

VALIDITY OF OPPORTUNITY

CHARLES PONZI: THE MAN WHO PROMOTED PETER AND PAUL

How fruitful were the Roaring '20s? Not very, if you invested with Charles Ponzi. Ponzi was a perennially well-dressed man whose smooth composure more than compensated for his five-foot-two height. He was born in 1882 as Carlo Pietro Giovanni Guglielmo Tebaldo Ponzi in Parma, Italy. [No wonder he went by Charles!] After four years at the University of Rome La Sapienza, he departed for the United States in 1903, accompanied by $200, a well-stocked wardrobe and a bursting desire to make money.

For all of his high hopes, Ponzi got off to a rough start. He lost all of his money at sea via gambling and drinking, arriving at Boston's harbor penniless. Four years of little success forced him to move around the Northeast before settling in Montreal, where he joined a shady local bank as a teller and was eventually arrested for trying to forge checks to himself after the bank's owner fled to Mexico. After spending three years in prison, he moved to Atlanta to join a ring that smuggled Italian immigrants into the U.S, which landed him another two years. All the while, Ponzi still claimed success and even wrote to his mother in Italy—from prison—that he had found success in America as a prison warden. Ultimately, it was his smooth-talking ability to spin something out of nothing that built his fraudulent empire.

It began in August 1919, while Ponzi was performing the simple act of opening his mail. The letter, which had been sent by a Spanish businessman inquiring about one of his previous failed ventures, included an International Reply Coupon (IRC), prepaid postage for the return letter. Whether Ponzi replied to that letter didn't cause ripples in the annals of history, but the idea that came to him then did.

Ponzi realized that one could buy an IRC in Europe and exchange it for a regular American stamp worth five cents. While that offered no profit on a face value, as the prices of stamps and IRCs were universally fixed, Ponzi knew that the European currencies were on the decline and he estimated that with the difference in currencies, an exchange could produce a 10% profit. Of course, 10% of five cents wasn't a whole lot, but when done on a large scale there was potential for profit.

Ponzi set out to find investors for his grand idea. He formed a company named the Securities Exchange Company. [Yes, quite ironically the "SEC"]. Ponzi claimed that he was paying agents to buy IRCs in Europe and then send them to America, where he would redeem them for stamps and sell the stamps for a 10% profit. Recruiting very aggressively, Ponzi hired commissioned agents to lure investors, first promising returns of 50% in ninety days and subsequently claiming those same returns in just forty-five days. While many were skeptical at first, sure enough, when the allotted amount of days expired, Ponzi handed his investors their promised returns. The investors were naturally jubilant, and word spread that Ponzi was the latest financial genius in town.

By the summer of 1920, he was on the cover of all Boston newspapers and police had to be deployed near his offices, which were so flooded with enthusiastic investors that they were blocking traffic. It did not take long for word to spread throughout the country and soon enough, Ponzi had amassed $10 million from 10,000 investors, and was receiving approximately $250,000 in new investments each day.

The problem was that he didn't have a network of agents and he didn't even try to obtain one. A later audit discovered that he only had $61 worth of coupons. So what was Ponzi doing? Simple. He was making his money from his investors, using money from later investors to pay the previous ones. His promise of enormous returns brought hordes to his door and as long as he had new investors, he had money to pay all of his debts.

Then Clarence Barron got involved. Barron, owner of the *Wall Street Journal*, realized something was amiss. He launched a full-scale investigation into Ponzi and his findings were reported on the front page of *The Boston Post*, a paper that had been promoting Ponzi highly for quite some time. Unfortunately for Ponzi, this time was different.

Barron noted that Ponzi's claims for exorbitant returns were not only unlikely, they were simply impossible. Unlike the frenzied investors, Barron actually sat down, crunched the numbers and discovered that in order for Ponzi to be making his returns, he'd need to be trading 160 million IRCs around the globe. But here's the technical glitch: there were only 27,000 of them in the entire world.

So charismatic and convincing was Ponzi that many of his investors chose to ignore Barron's report. It wasn't until the government got involved that his scheme finally fell. A government raid found that he did not have a large supply of coupons and since he had used mail to tell his investors how well he was performing, he was also charged with mail fraud. In total, he was brought to court with eighty-six charges on two different indictments. After pleading guilty to one, he was sentenced to five years in prison. Serving three and a half, he was released and deported to Italy. He made his way to Rio de Janeiro and lived as a poor man, dying unceremoniously in 1949. His only life achievement was scamming investors out of an estimated $20 million and causing the "borrowing from Peter to pay Paul" ruse to be forever named the Ponzi scheme.

Key Takeaways

Ponzi was far from the first to use the "borrow from Peter to pay Paul" scam. In fact, there was a similar scam in Boston a mere decade before conducted by former fortune teller, Sarah Howe.

Howe founded the Ladies' Deposit, a charitable organization for women. Only accepting investments from fellow females, Howe promised astounding returns of 8% per month and maintained an aura of exclusivity by only allowing new members who were recruited by other members. The exclusivity didn't stop Howe from amassing 1,200 investors and $500,000 in invested capital, the equivalent of tens of millions today. Cleverly, she instituted that investors could only withdraw their interest and not their principal, claiming that she didn't want "frivolous spending." The real reason was simple. She was running the same scheme as Ponzi, using money from later investors to pay interest on prior investors' funds. As with Ponzi, pesky journalists got involved and the *Boston Daily Advertiser* soon discovered the fraud, landing Howe in jail for three years.

Almost comically, when she was released, she proceeded to conduct the same scheme and raise $50,000, this time disappearing with the money before anybody could catch on.

These are just two early examples of the now infamous Ponzi schemes, which were particularly publicized after the Bernie Madoff affair. Investors the world over began clamoring for information, looking for tips and red flags on how to avoid Ponzi schemes, the most obvious advice being the old adage that some things are just "too good to be true." Since a Ponzi scheme usually does not have a legitimate way of making money, it is fully reliant on new investors as the source of income. Hence, to tease in new investors, the operators need to offer unusually high returns, which Ponzi and Howe did to the tee.

Often, there is a comparable industry to help flush out what is considered to be true. For example, Howe claiming 8% monthly returns, which translates to 96% returns in a single year. Which institutional investor makes that much money? In a modern-day example, Nicholas Cosmo, whose $400 million Ponzi scheme earned him the title "mini Madoff," promised returns up to 80% in the bridge loan industry, where returns (in the best of circumstances) are in the 15-25% range.

And sometimes there is no clear comparison, as with Charles Ponzi's fictitious innovation in arbitraging the currency differences in the IRC industry. That said, in all cases, anyone claiming to repeatedly provide 50% returns in 45 or 90 days is selling a pipe dream. If they were based on any real business activity everyone and their uncle would quickly jump into the same business, but, remarkably, Ponzi had no competition.

Returns like this should be a red flag to any investor, no matter what the industry is. They signaled caution to Clarence Barron, and they should signal caution to you.

* * *

WHO ARE SOME OF THE SWINDLER'S FIRST TARGETS?

You may not want to hear this, but the most frequently targeted victims are those within the community in which the swindler resides—whether it is a physical community, spiritual, social or professional community. Fraudsters brazenly engage those that are nearest and dearest to them.

While most people take refuge and comfort investing with members of their own community, charlatans will take advantage of this preference and recognize that people lower their guards when investing with "one of our own".

Particularly with investment frauds, this is so common that the industry has given this phenomenon the official moniker of affinity fraud.

OPRAH'S CARPET CLEANING MOGUL STEALING GRANDMA'S JEWELRY: THE CRAZY LIFE OF BARRY MINKOW

Few American entrepreneurs were adored more in the late 1980s than Barry Minkow. Minkow founded ZZZZ Best Carpet Cleaning while still in high school and took the company public at the young age of twenty. He was a guest on the *Oprah Winfrey* show and was largely hailed as the prototypical American rags-to-riches story, the "Rocky of the carpet cleaning industry." The problem was that there might have been rags, but very few riches.

Founded in his parents' garage while he was still a high school sophomore, ZZZZ Best did not rocket to an all-star beginning. Minkow's company struggled mightily at first. Banks didn't allow him to open his own account because he was a minor. Faced with the challenge of meeting his payroll, he resorted to check kiting[8], charging customer credit cards for nonexistent services, and even stealing his own grandmother's jewelry. But even with all that, ZZZZ Best was floundering. Minkow knew that something needed to be done and for that he turned to his good friend Tom Padgett.

---

[8] Check kiting is a shell game, involving multiple accounts, where the fraudster utilizes checks to access funds from the bank, when in fact there are no funds in the checking account from which the check was written.

Padgett, a workout buff who could press more than 300 pounds, first met Minkow at a local gym when the latter was just fourteen. He was initially annoyed by the high school kid who professed an interest in training with him, but Minkow knew how to win friends. And boy, did he ever win Padgett over. Padgett, an insurance claims adjuster at Allstate who didn't see a growing future for himself, had turned to boxing, only to be knocked out so badly and so frequently that sunglasses became a staple accessory. While many at the gym poked fun at him, it was Minkow who lambasted them for not even mustering the guts to enter the ring. Soon after, Minkow and Padgett were good friends, with Padgett taking out a loan of $4,500 for Minkow when he started ZZZZ Best and referring him insurance jobs that he came across at Allstate. So, with ZZZZ Best still in trouble, Minkow turned to Padgett yet again.

He told Padgett that aside from carpet cleaning, he was also doing insurance restoration jobs, repairing damaged buildings. He asked Padgett, who had since been fired from Allstate but was now working as an auto appraiser at Travelers Insurance, to send him some stationery from Travelers to show bankers that he wasn't getting all of his insurance work from one place. While Padgett suspected something was amiss, he obliged. After his boss learned of this, he was summarily fired from Travelers as well.

But neither of them was deterred. With Padgett desperate to make money to impress his fiancée, Debbie, and Minkow being Minkow, they formed a fake insurance company, Interstate Appraisal Services, which supposedly sent ZZZZ Best a boatload of insurance restoration jobs. Minkow hired Mark

Morze, a former college linebacker turned tax accountant, to cook the books. Miraculously, the paperwork showed a carpet cleaning company garnering 50% returns on their insurance restoration projects. In a short while, 86% of ZZZZ Best's "revenues" were coming from their insurance restoration division. With the paperwork to prove it in hand, Minkow was able to borrow large sums of money from banks and expand ZZZZ Best's carpet cleaning division across Southern California.

While ZZZZ Best was functioning, and its carpet cleaning received high marks for quality, they were still not making much profit. That's when Minkow decided to take the company public, hoping that the money received from his Initial Public Offering (IPO) would be enough to turn his company legitimate before any securities laws would crack down on him. But as time went on, auditors began to insist on inspecting his insurance business and while Minkow managed to delay them at first, a $7 million-dollar contract was coming his way and the auditor wouldn't let up.

In a stroke of sheer brilliance, Minkow pulled off the illusion of the century. He would take the auditor to his "headquarters" . . . on a Saturday, when nobody was at work. He chose a brand-new Sacramento building to pose as his headquarters and then bribed the security guard to pretend that they knew each other. After decorating an entire floor with the trappings appropriate for his "business," he took the auditor on a lovely tour and got his $7 million contract. Minkow's company was listed on NASDAQ in January 1986, trading at a $280 million valuation, and he became the youngest American to lead a company through an IPO.

With an estimated net worth of $100 million, Minkow was riding high. He went on the hunt for acquisitions and in early 1987 struck a $25 million deal to merge with KeyServ, a nationwide carpet cleaning firm that cleaned carpets for Sears' customers and had $80 million in revenues the prior year. He also planned a hostile takeover of ServiceMaster, the leader of the carpet cleaning industry with over $1 billion in annual revenues. He even began discussions to purchase a major league baseball team, the Seattle Mariners.

But even as Minkow fooled auditors and sophisticated Wall Street investors, it was one of Minkow's early carpet cleaning clients that broke it all up; a woman who noticed when he began charging her credit card for nonexistent services. She spoke with other ZZZZ Best clients and found a total of at least $72,000 in fraudulent credit card charges in 1984 and 1985. She brought her discoveries to the *LA Times*, and then the dominoes started to fall. The stock's price fell from the bad publicity, and, when a reporter went back to the Sacramento office building and discovered that it was a phony, short-sellers smelled a rat and bet against the stock. Before you knew it, investors lost over $100 million.

Minkow, Padgett, Morze and eight others were eventually indicted while Minkow was ordered to pay $26 million in restitution to go along with a twenty-five-year prison sentence.

Key Takeaways

While the amount of fraud committed by Minkow varied in nature, it was his insurance restoration division that caused the most damage. Investors and banks were thrilled with the opportunity offering 50% returns, headed by the popular wunderkind, and they lost an estimated $100 million in ZZZZ Best's demise. However, for those who actually gave it a second thought, the viability of such an investment was dubious all along.

Mark Morze, who headed the division, recounted how surprised he was at how long the fraud continued. The division had many flaws. The fact that a multimillion dollar division only had one listed employee, or the fact that all those involved were inexperienced and had checkered pasts, or that ZZZZ Best wasn't licensed to be involved in insurance restoration should have all been red flags. But most glaring was how ZZZZ Best compared to its industry peers. The insurance restoration industry was not one that typically garnered 50% margins or returns. In fact, margins were slim and standard returns were in single digits. Yet, investors threw their money into a 50% return promise.

When investing in any enterprise, comparable industry participants are always a necessary and critical benchmark. If there is a large discrepancy between the enterprise and all of its peers, it warrants asking some difficult questions. And if there is no obvious difference in the strategy driving those returns, there is likely a problem with the accounting underpinning them. By ignoring this basic principle, investors lost millions and allowed the ZZZZ Best story to live on in infamy.

* * *

Nothing in this world is more dangerous than sincere ignorance and conscientious stupidity

—Dr. Martin Luther King Jr.

EVEN THE JARGON COULDN'T SAVE HIM: HOW KIRK WRIGHT GOT SACKED

Long-time Denver Broncos safety Steven Atwater, nick-named the "Smiling Assassin," was largely known as one of the fiercest hitters in NFL history. He signed many lucrative contracts, his last being an $8 million deal with the New York Jets. And when he finally signed a one-day contract to retire with the Broncos, he surely thought that his retirement was set. But he had made the unfortunate mistake of trusting Kirk Wright, a hedge fund manager at his self-founded International Management Associates (IMA).

Kirk Sean Wright was born in the Bronx in 1970 and received an undergraduate degree from Binghamton University. He then attended Harvard from 1993 to 1995, where he gathered $2,000 from his classmates to invest. He earned a Master's in public administration and worked at Kaiser Associates for a year before venturing off on his own to form IMA, using relatives and acquaintances as his first investors. Based out of his Manassas, Virginia home, Wright incorporated IMA in 1997 as a hedge fund. While just one year at Kaiser didn't give him the background to be a hedge fund manager, he told potential investors that he been investing since he was nineteen, after receiving a large insurance settlement from a car crash.

As an African American, Wright began to attract customers from Atlanta's black community at a time when a great cultural change was occurring in Atlanta's black community. According to the *Wall Street Journal*, Atlanta's community was somewhat insular in the 1970s. Most middle-class African Americans put their money into the one African American-owned bank but began expanding in the 1980s to the point where it became a hub for young black professionals. These professionals became the building block of Wright's non-familial client base.

In 1998, Wright met Nelson Bond and Fitz Harper, two African American doctors who invested with him, referred him to their friends and eventually became partners in IMA. He moved his office to Atlanta in 1999, when he had about $7 million under management; with the help of Bond and Harper's referrals and claims of high returns, IMA began taking off. By the end of 2003, the *Wall Street Journal* reported that he had $84 million under management and was claiming average annual returns of 27% when the S&P's average was 5%. Wright was listed as an approved financial adviser by the NFL Players Association (NFLPA) in 2004, which led to Steve Atwater recruiting six of his friends to invest a total of $20 million in IMA. He established offices in Las Vegas, Los Angeles, and New York, creating a total of seven hedge funds. By 2006, he was managing nearly $200 million.

As IMA found great success, Wright made sure to impress accordingly. He expanded his suburban house and purchased a fleet of cars that included a Bentley, a Jaguar, an Aston Martin, a BMW and a Lamborghini. He bought flashy jewelry and rented expensive suites at Falcons and Hawks games, entertaining potential clients there. When he divorced his high school sweetheart in 2003 and then married his second wife in 2005, his wedding was an over-the-top lavish affair costing an estimated $500,000.

Lost in all the charisma, spending and promises of high returns was the obvious question: What was Wright doing with the money? How did he get those 27% returns? His responses were always loaded with jargon vaguer than the murky waters of the Hudson. According to Pat Huddleston's *The Vigilant Investor,* Wright described one fund's strategy as capitalizing "volumetrically on a few select opportunities characterized by moderate to high valuations, compelling business fundamentals, and strong management teams." Then there's the *Wall Street Journal* report that his main fund, the Taurus fund, had marketing materials proclaiming that its "objectives are achieved through a top-down, bottom-up process that identifies disparities in the economy or security sectors creating +/- changes in market perception."

For the life of me, I could not decipher that nonsense, and neither did Wright's clients. They were merely impressed by his multi-syllable words and trusted his client testimonials, assuming that his sophisticated-sounding phrases were as impressive as his actions.

Reuben McDaniel III, the African American manager of Atlanta's Jackson Securities, did not invest with Wright when he couldn't articulate just how he achieved the returns he claimed. How right he was. According to Pat Huddleston, Wright's main strategy was short selling, where one borrows on securities in anticipation that their price will drop with the intention to buy them at a lower price to pay back the lender. Yet, Wright failed at it. Miserably. His trades suffered tremendous losses and he hid them by fabricating spreadsheets for his clients showing massive gains. All the while, he had been diverting most of the funds for his own use, funding his lavish lifestyle.

He kept the real brokerage statements from his trading hidden to all. Even his own partners, Drs. Bond and Harper, had no idea what Wright was really up to. They innocently hired an accountant named Kenneth Turchin for one of the newer funds and when he was finally able to access the statements, he noticed that they differed greatly from the returns that Wright claimed. He passed on the information to Dr. Harper.

Steve Atwater, who had earned a degree in business and finance and had since become an employee of Wright's, also heard the news and became suspicious when Wright's answers were evasive at best. He, the other former NFL players and some of Wright's other clients tried withdrawing their money, but Wright never delivered it. Atwater formed a group to sue Wright for fraud. The feds closed Wright's funds and froze his accounts. The SEC and FBI were both investigating, but by the time they had seen enough to make an arrest, Wright had already fled.

Wright was on the run for over two months, not returning calls from his investors after one called and threatened to kill him. Police eventually tracked Wright to a plush Miami Beach hotel, where he was lounging by the pool with a cocktail. He was found to have a number of aliases on hand, as well as $30,000 in cash, a Mercedes, and had already made a down payment on a condo.

Wright was brought to trial and convicted in May 2008 for forty-seven counts of fraud. He faced up to 710 years in prison, a fine of up to $16 million, and restitution payments for all of his clients' losses. Whether it was the shame or the upcoming loss of his once-grandiose image, the thirty-seven-year-old Wright couldn't take it. He was found hanging dead from a rope in his jail cell less than two weeks after his conviction.

Atwater and his fellow NFL players proceeded to sue the NFL for keeping Wright on their list of financial advisers. Ruben McDaniel, an African American himself, publicly blasted Wright for taking advantage of the trust of the black community: "In all candor, what he [Wright] did was say, 'I can wine and dine African Americans who are not sophisticated in the investment field and get their money.'" While most of his investors were not black, it was from his first African American investors that he gained the credibility to reach for a larger audience.

The total losses for investors were estimated to be over $185 million.

Key Takeaways

The first takeaway speaks to the pervasiveness of affinity fraud, as many schemers take advantage of the trust within their own community to build their client base, whether those communities are religious, racial or local. Gerald Payne took advantage of his Christian community. Tom Petters took advantage of the local Minnesota community. Bernie Madoff took advantage of the Jewish community. Oscar Hartzell took advantage of Midwestern and farming communities. And Wright took advantage of the African American community. While it is easier to trust someone within your own community, it is never prudent to trust someone to the point of neglecting proper due diligence.

While that is a valuable takeaway on its own, the more salient lesson is that investors who give their money to a money manager or a fiduciary owe it to themselves to at least understand what their money is doing. A fraudulent fiduciary or manager may take other people's money and pretend that he or she is deploying it for productive purposes, instead spending it on their own extravagances. If they were actually successful traders and investors, they would have a simple method of explaining what they do—much like any other professional who has practiced on thousands of people, simply articulating what they do. Conversely, those who have something to hide tend to introduce unnecessary complexity and jargon language, as the less their investors (and partners) know, the better.

When presented with an investment you can't understand, and the manager can't explain, remember Kirk Wright and his 185 million reasons to stay away.

* * *

Real knowledge is to know the extent of one's ignorance

—Confucius

THE CROCODILE TEARS OF LAWRENCE SALANDER

By all indications, Lawrence Salander was a massive success. A prominent New York art dealer and artist, Salander's clients included tennis legend John McEnroe, who was so close with him that McEnroe was named the godfather to Salander's child. His other close friendships included the likes of Liam Neeson, Robert De Niro, and Bruce Springsteen. Salander-O'Reilly Galleries, which was located in a large townhouse in the Upper West Side of Manhattan, was named by the glossy *Robb Report* as the world's best art gallery and housed paintings by De Niro's father, Robert De Niro, Sr. However, after a series of lawsuits beginning in 2007, it was soon revealed that Salander was a heartless con man, one who would endear himself to his clients and funnel away their works for himself.

Back in 1949, young Larry was born in Long Island to a middle-class family, with his father working as the proud owner of a small art gallery. When the elder Salander died in 1969, nineteen-year-old Larry became the primary breadwinner for his mother and sisters and promptly dropped out of his studies at University of Miami to run his father's operation.

After three years and gaining much expertise, he opened his own gallery in Connecticut. In 1976, he partnered to create a more upscale second location in Manhattan, the Salander-O'Reilly Galleries. He became the youngest member elected to the Appraiser's Association of America in 1977 and built himself and his gallery into known staples of the art world. According to friends interviewed by Anthony Amore for his *The Art of the Con*, Salander "didn't sleep at night." He "ate, drank and breathed art." Despite being balding, stocky, and embracing his middle-class upbringing, Salander soon attracted wealthy clientele, including Wall Street businessmen and a range of artsy celebrities. His own paintings were successful as well, garnering nine solo exhibitions and ten group shows.

Before long, the art dealer began living like his clients. He bought a $5 million house in the Upper East Side and a sixty-acre estate in Millbrook, New York, which included tennis courts and a baseball field for his children to play on. He began flying exclusively on private jets to the point where even De Niro was surprised: "I saw that I had a plane and Larry had a plane. It just didn't add up to me." He gave a half-million dollars in jewels to his second wife, Julie, and threw a $60,000 birthday party for her when she turned forty. His townhouse gallery cost $150,000 in monthly rent, as it included three floors of exhibitions and a lavish greenhouse roof.

But with increasing expenditures came increasing pressures. With Salander's habit of overdoing everything, merely covering his wife, six children and ex-wife's expenses became a tremendous burden. Additionally, as an art connoisseur, he had a personal drive to bring back Renaissance art but acquiring such paintings was very costly. Add that to the increased rent and the results were almost crippling. So, Salander had to get "creative" to keep his ambitions afloat.

First, there was Stuart Davis. Known as one of America's premier modernist painters, Davis died at a young age and left all of his works to his son Earl, who had become a good friend of Salander's. Earl entrusted his father's paintings to Salander and agreed to give up a 10-20% commission should anything be sold, but he explicitly requested that Salander not sell anything without permission. Unfortunately for Earl, his "friend" had been selling off his father's paintings since the mid-1990s and keeping all of the profits for himself, eventually selling over ninety works that were worth more than $30 million.

The same was true for Dr. Alexander Pearlman, who regularly visited the gallery and would hug Salander whenever they would see each other. Upon Pearlman's death, Salander came to the funeral and cried with Dr. Pearlman's children but all the while sold off the $2 million worth of paintings that Dr. Pearlman's children entrusted him with. Salander betrayed De Niro as well, selling $77,000 worth of his father's paintings without notice.

Over time, Salander's frauds grew more and more diverse. In 2004, he gave his child's godfather John McEnroe the opportunity to invest $2 million in a set of paintings he was buying. McEnroe would own one half and Salander would own the other half, until it was sold off at a profit. What McEnroe did not know was that Salander made the same deal with two other people and raised more than $2 million from each.

Salander even toyed with Wall Street investors at their own game. He asked investment banker Roy Lennox (whom he met at their children's shared posh nursery) to lend him $400,000 to help him buy a $800,000 painting which he planned on flipping for $1.25 million, guaranteeing Lennox a 56% gain on the loan. When payment time came, Salander simply came up with "another great deal" and asked Lennox to reinvest the money for further gains. Lennox dutifully obliged, eventually giving $3.6 million and never receiving a penny in return. He also forged documents for one of the financers of his Renaissance art expansion, the Renaissance Art Investors, claiming $42 million in art purchases when, in fact, they were worth far less.

But Salander's brazenness became a ticking time bomb. A number of clients soon discovered that Salander had sold off their paintings without permission, including Maurice Katz, whose $125,000 painting had been sold without his knowledge. Katz contacted major art publications and began telling other clients of Salander's behavior. Salander followed the fraudster playbook and threatened to sue Katz for libel but rumors were already flying; many clients began showing up to the gallery and personally removing their paintings. By 2007, lawsuits were being filed right and left. At that point, Donald Schupak, head of the Renaissance Art Investors consortium, contacted the New York Supreme Court and hired a private security team to surround Salander's gallery.

In 2009, Salander was arrested on 100 counts of scamming $88 million from twenty-six victims. His personal finances included a $15 million mortgage on his Manhattan house and a whopping $55 million in debt against his painting investments. Although his second wife left him, his children did appear at their father's hearing, only to see their father's head slumped over in defeat. At one arraignment, he even showed up in a moth-eaten sweatshirt and a lawyer begged for mercy, showing that Salander was in fact substance-addicted and had even suffered from a stroke. Even as he pleaded guilty to what was now a $120 million fraud, the judge showed no mercy for the man who had signed his friendly emails with "love" while using others' monies as his own, and sentenced him to six to eighteen years in prison with $115 million in restitution payments.

Salander is serving his sentence in New York's Riker Island prison while his "friends" are busy trying to recoup their missing money and lost sense of trust.

Key Takeaways

Salander basically committed two forms of fraud. First, selling other's paintings without their knowledge—i.e. pure theft. Second, committing investment fraud by overvaluing paintings and claiming he could arrange profitable sales as he did to Roy Lennox. The takeaway for both, however, is rather similar.

For the former, there is a clear need for independent oversight. This may be difficult in the context of an art gallery, where the simplest way for investors to know whether their paintings were still in the gallery was simply to go to the gallery and check up on them, which is both arduous and time consuming. The alternative is to hire some sort of third-party custodian to verify that the asset is still there and when a sale actually happens, the owner is both apprised and in agreement.

For the latter, there is a clear need for independent valuation. The arts are generally rife with subjectivity, which is especially murky for those not deeply familiar with the industry. Successful hedge fund manager Roy Lennox claimed that his main takeaway from this experience was "not [to] do business in markets you don't have a deep understanding of. You're tak-

ing someone's word for it. If it doesn't work out, it's your fault."
While Lennox focused on the fact that he wasn't educated in
the industry, it was the subjectivity of value that allowed him to
be fleeced. When assets have a clear and objective value, lying
about their value is hard, even if it's to a layman. For those
investing in subjectively-valued assets, there's a heightened risk
of speculation and abuse, with a need for trusted third-party
appraisals to get a better sense of valuations.

In the arts, Salander was able to claim things were worth
more than they were worth. He could claim that he purchased
a painting that he could resell for a 67% profit. With his clients
trusting Salander as they had, all they could later blame was his
blinding greed . . . and their own blinding trust.

* * *

WHERE DO SWINDLERS HAVE THE GREATEST EDGE?

In brief, unfamiliar markets. Investors in markets, industries or assets they don't understand are particularly ripe targets for fraud, as it creates an asymmetry of information where the seller has much more information than the buyer and takes advantage accordingly. This is no different than the original snake oil salesman and namesake of this book, Clark Stanley, who claimed that every ailment—from simple nausea to arthritis to skin disease—could be cured by his magical elixir, which was nothing more than mineral oil. Stanley knew that his buyers didn't know medicine and capitalized on their ignorance.

THE SALAD OIL KING
WHO TOPPLED AMEX AND
ELEVATED BUFFET

Anyone who spends time in a kitchen is aware that oil and water don't mix. In fact, if one pours oil and water into a cup simultaneously, the oil will rise to the top while the water will sink to the bottom. Oddly enough, this chemistry tidbit led to one of the most unusual corporate frauds in American history.

Anthony De Angelis was born in 1915 to Italian immigrants in the Bronx. Nicknamed Tino, he dropped out of school to become a meat packer and developed a specialty in his ability to cut meat quickly. Using his talents well, he was able to move up until he borrowed enough money to start his own meat plant during the Great Depression. As with many other industries, World War II helped him grow and he contracted with the American government to supply them with meat. When the war ended, he even began selling meat to foreign governments; in the process, he moved his meat plants to Bayonne, New Jersey and set up offices there.

From the outset, De Angelis seemed to care more about the quantity of his sales instead of the quality of his meat, and his clients made him pay for it. Foreign governments often sued him for selling them inferior meat. Two federal agencies began to levy charges against him when he supplied school lunch programs with two million pounds of uninspected meat and overcharged the government by $31,000. He was brought to bankruptcy court in the early 1950s. Though the process took a while, with Tino not actually going bankrupt until 1958, he began to see that real profits lay elsewhere. At that time, vegetable oil derivatives, both soybean oil and cottonseed oil, were hot tickets, with heavy demand in the US and abroad. So Tino entered the market by opening Allied Crude Vegetable Oil Refining Corporation in 1955. He established offices in New York, but set up the plant again in Bayonne, New Jersey, by buying petroleum tanks and having them cleaned for storing oil instead.

He then launched his business in the most unusual fashion. Since Tino owned farms and had no way to manufacture the oil himself, he bought the oils from Midwestern farmers for above market price and sold them to foreign buyers at market prices. It was basically buying high and selling low. Logically, there was no way it should have worked, let alone be profitable. But Tino kept on selling, at one point accounting for 75% of American vegetable oil exports and was nicknamed the "Salad Oil King." This was all despite having no apparent path to profitability.

The answer to that dilemma lay in his Bayonne oil plant. The plant was under the supervision of American Express Warehousing Corporation (AEWC), a subsidiary of the American Express company, which was involved in the business of financing inventory. AEWC would guarantee the existence of the inventory for a third party who would in turn use the inventory as collateral to borrow. Now, should the borrower default, the lender would have the right to the inventory. All the while, the inventory owner would be issued receipts for the value of the inventory and those receipts could be exchanged for cash. De Angelis had gone around to different banks throughout the '50s looking for someone to agree to this arrangement. Only American Express did, as they had recently entered the field of warehouse financing and wanted to get in on any big customer they could find.

Turns out, all the other banks were no fools. American Express was blindsided by De Angelis, who figured that with 138 huge tanks to manage and inspect, they would never actually complete the job. As such he didn't fill the tanks with oil, instead putting large portions of water to make it look like there was more oil than there actually was. Creating a system of pipes connecting all of the tanks, De Angelis arranged for oil to be pumped from one tank to another before American Express inspections would take place and each tank would only contain a small percentage of oil, with the rest being water. If inspectors would take off the tanks' tops, they would only see oil. If they would look in the pipes connecting the tanks, they would again only see oil. In short, American Express thought De Angelis had full tanks of oil when they were really diluted. Over the course of many years, American Express used De Angelis' oils to guarantee over $200 million on that assumption, not realizing that De Angelis' claims of inventory exceeded the total amount of all the salad oil produced in America.

At the same time, De Angelis was running a double-scheme, as he felt that he could increase his profits even further if he managed to bump up the prices of salad oil, and the increased value of his inventory as collateral value. He did so by buying up the futures market, in the hopes of driving up the prices.

And for the most part, he was successful. De Angelis took this to such a level of excess that at one point he held more than 90 percent of the cottonseed oil futures and 40 percent of the soybean oil futures on the New York Produce Exchange.

It was these ventures into the futures market that caused his downfall. While the salad oil industry was booming during De Angelis' reign as the Salad Oil King, nothing this good lasts forever. Salad oil prices began to fall (in part because authorities began investigating De Angelis' heavy involvement on the futures market, along with the fact that they were tipped off about various briberies) and De Angelis' futures began to plummet as well. At that time, De Angelis was so heavily invested in the soybean oils futures market that for every one percent drop in price he lost $13 million. By November 1963, he was short $19 million on his margin calls and Allied declared bankruptcy. When creditors and borrowers both rushed to check on their collateral, they were surprised to find more than half of the oil to be non-existent.

Over fifty companies who issued loans underpinned by Allied's collateral were left holding the empty bag, and the two brokerage firms that Allied used were temporarily banned by the NYSE, leaving all of their holdings in serious disarray. Then the world stopped, as President John F. Kennedy was shot dead on Friday, November 22. Once the terrible news began making its way to the trading floor, people began to start panic selling and the NYSE halted trading midway through the afternoon. It remained shut the next Monday and only opened on Tuesday, giving the NYSE time to address the De Angelis issue and restore securities to the holdings of the two banned brokerage firms.

Federal investigators soon discovered that while De Angelis declared bankruptcy, he actually had a half-million dollars stored in a Swiss bank account. With contempt of court added to his swindling charges, De Angelis was sentenced to seven years in prison. When he got out, he proceeded to embark on another Ponzi scheme that (thankfully) was not nearly as successful.

As a result of the De Angelis fiasco, American Express' stock fell drastically, and the company was almost bankrupt. As a result, some little-known textile entrepreneur from Omaha, named Warren Buffet, invested $20 million to buy a 5% share in American Express thinking that the company was experiencing a temporary blip and would rebound well. As they say, the rest is history.

Key Takeaways

There are several key takeaways here, which are recurring themes throughout the book. Firstly, as we have seen time and again, individuals with a checkered past tend to have a checkered future. De Angelis' past indiscretions with scamming the government should have led American Express to be more cautious.

Even if American Express was not privy to who De Angelis was, or conducted zero due diligence on him, the lack of a sustainable business model underpinning any financial activity (i.e., clarity on how money is made) should have kept them at bay. In De Angelis' case, he was buying oil high and selling it low. Any seven-year-old knows that this is not a durable business strategy, and it should have raised red flags for anyone that put their trust in him.

Lastly, and perhaps the most unique takeaway in this case, was the inappropriate conflation of risks. Entrepreneurs do not, typically, make money in the futures markets. Futures markets are the most volatile and levered of all asset classes[9], thereby the only prudent use of commodities is as a hedge against the rapid rise or fall of the specific commodity the business is exposed to. De Angelis went far beyond hedging his risk; he entered the world of extreme speculation.

There are few traders that have successfully survived the vicious volatility of commodities. Even fewer–if any–entrepreneurs have created consistent profits through such speculative gambles alongside their business. And anyone that claims to do so is either ultra-greedy, ultra-foolish or ultra-dishonest. More likely, as with De Angelis, it is a combination of all three. His lenders should have known better.

* * *

---

[9] Given that a $100 futures contract can be purchased with as little as $5 cash, even a 5 percent loss in the price of the contract can wipe out 100 percent of the capital invested.

WHO (OR WHAT) IS A FRAUDSTER'S PRIMARY ACCOMPLICE?

When behavioral economists Jeff Langenderfer and Terence Shimp, studied what factors make someone most susceptible to fraud, they concluded that victims serve as cooperating accomplices by succumbing to either greed or fear.

While greed is self-evident, people forget that fear is among the most utilized methods employed by con artists. If they can unearth your anxieties or bring disconcerting issues to focus, and immediately provide the remedy, there is a good chance you will bite.

Clark Stanley, the previously referenced snake oil salesman with a useless mineral oil concoction, would remind people of the ailments they were susceptible to and then dramatically demonstrated how his elixir could cure virtually every illness under the sun. Others in the 20th century, like John Brinkley, adopted Stanley's fearmongering ways to offer solutions for male impotence, via a goat testicles transplant, and sold countless vulnerable men on a promise they could not deliver.

BOILER ROOMS AND SUPERLOADERS: HOW WALTER TELLIER RULED THE '50S

One of the most prominent poster boys for how to deceitfully promote stocks was Walter Tellier. His New Jersey-based brokerage firm, Tellier & Co., was the largest over-the-counter security selling organization in the US. He was the Jordan Belfort of the 1950s. Same dashing three-piece suits, same lies and consequent profits. Belfort's only edge on Tellier was youth and a fuller head of hair. Otherwise, Belfort may have been the Wolf of Wall Street, but Tellier was its monarch. And to this day he is remembered as the Penny Stock King.

Penny stocks are distinct not just for their bargain basement prices[10], but also their extreme volatility and their often-speculative nature. They are not generally traded on major exchanges, such as the NYSE or NASDAQ, instead trading on over-the-counter forums such as Pink Sheets and Over-the-Counter Bulletin Board (OTCBB).

Tellier, a former cosmetics salesman from Hartford, Connecticut, began successfully trading securities in the Roaring '20s and kept doing so even into the Great Depression. While working for various Wall Street brokerage houses in 1931, his bosses suggested that he move from Hartford to New York. He

---

[10] In the US, the SEC defines penny stocks as securities that trade for under $5 per share.

did so, and soon after his arrival he was hit with what would be the first of multiple mail fraud and conspiracy charges.

Though the charges were eventually dismissed, Tellier kept a low profile for a while, trading securities legitimately until the 1950s rolled around. In the aftermath of World War II, where a raging bull market resulted in the Dow Jones quickly tripling in value, Tellier roared into the public eye.

He began selling "miracle" penny stocks to inexperienced investors, with promises that these stocks would rise to extraordinary levels while costing investors fifty cents or less. And in a market where all the prices were rising, every penny stock Tellier touched seemed like a winner. Of course, in any bull market, when everybody is making money nobody bothers to ask questions.

But Tellier didn't only target inexperienced investors that happened to come his way. He made a conscious effort to grow his operation using "boiler rooms." In the penny stock world, boiler rooms were makeshift offices crammed into abandoned or remote commercial or residential buildings where nobody would bother looking. After setting up shop, the boiler room creator would recruit "salesmen," often other con men, to call unsuspecting people under the guise of being experienced Wall Street brokers. The salesmen would convince those on the other end to invest in the stock that's destined for its stratospheric rise. And in the early days of investor ignorance these brokers were frequently successful. After all, when a sophisticated Wall Street guru calls and tells you a stock is about to jump through the roof, you don't want to miss out on the fun.

Boiler rooms wreaked havoc in the '50s, with $150 million of investor money being lost in 1956 alone (the equivalent of $1.35 billion today), and Tellier was leading the pack. As recounted in Ken Fisher's *100 Minds that Made the Market*, Tellier's callers would refer their victims to more experienced thieves called "loaders," who would find out more about their victims and see if they had any other assets they could take advantage of. His loaders would even convince their victims to trade in their safe blue-chip stocks for Tellier's securities, as his shares could skyrocket, unlike Wall Street's typically boring names. "Superloaders," the con men a step above the ordinary "loaders," would even convince their prey to steal and rob in order to buy Tellier shares. Tellier would advertise continuously on the radio and in the *New York Times*, and his name recognition only helped his boiler room salesmen sell their penny stocks faster. Their ads also included send-in coupons, which Tellier's salespeople used to squeeze additional information from their targets and take them in for even more. As Tellier and Co. quickly grew into the largest over-the-counter security seller in North America, Tellier's reputation as the undisputed "Penny Stock King" swelled as well.

But Tellier and Co. didn't simply sell penny stocks, they also manipulated their prices. With all of their claims of XYZ penny stock being the next "miracle" stock, Tellier was then able to jack up their prices. And if that was not enough, should the customer, who we will call Customer A, wish to sell that stock, he would encounter an entirely new set of problems. Because penny stocks weren't traded on the regular exchange, Tellier and Co. was the only brokerage firm who would buy the shares back from Customer A. Being that they were the only buyer, they were able to demand even a lower price than they originally received for the security.

And the fraud didn't stop there. They would then flip the switch and sell Customer A's rebought shares in other geographic locations (for prices that were commonly higher than the original price, with which they had already ripped-off Customer A). For example, Tellier and Co. might sell a stock for $1.25 to someone in southern New Jersey. Being the only brokerage who could buy back the stock, they would then buy the same stock back for 30 cents and make a new glorified boiler room pitch to someone in New York, re-selling it to them for $2.50. This geographically enhanced "pump and dump" strategy gave Tellier millions, allowing him to live luxuriously in Englewood, in New Jersey's most exclusive neighborhood. And his boiler room staff were equally flush with their absurdly high and unjustly earned salaries.

Tellier's biggest hit was Consolidated Uranium Inc., a one-cent stock that he claimed had 85,000 acres of land loaded with uranium, with $1,000,000 worth of uranium being discovered in just one of those 85,000 acres. His salesmen pitched to this tune, and hordes of people bought jacked-up shares in what they thought would become an $85 million company. This was despite Consolidated's own president saying, in an interview with *Time* magazine, that Tellier was exaggerating their resources. In reality, Consolidated's net worth was a mere $1 million. Tellier was eventually called in for a Congressional hearing and the SEC began investigating him.

Just weeks after his hearing, Tellier was charged in another case completely unrelated to Consolidated. Apparently, he also sold $1,000,000 worth of unsecured bonds of the nearly bankrupt Alaska Telephone Company, swindling 1,400 investors in the process. Six months later the SEC brought the Consolidated charges against him, charging that he had defrauded investors of $15 million ($135 million in today's dollars) through stock manipulation. Tellier proceeded to publicly berate both the SEC and Congress, claiming that they weren't willing to let the American uranium industry grow.

In 1958, after an unsuccessful attempt to bribe a government witness to get off his case, Tellier was sentenced to four and a half years in prison and an $18,000 fine. And so, the "Penny Stock King" was dethroned.

Key Takeaways

Much can be gleaned from the mess created by Walter Tellier. Besides avoiding individuals with previous indictments and recognizing that no penny stocks are "sure things," as Tellier claimed, the main takeaway is avoiding opportunities that are rife with conflicts of interests. The vulnerability of penny stocks is the fact that these markets have limited price discovery or liquidity and are easily susceptible to manipulation.

In traditional public markets, there is some element of fair competition. If one broker wants to pump up the price, an investor can simply go to another broker to buy the stock. In penny stock scams like Tellier's, competitive forces are limited. If Tellier is the only one who can buy or sell the securities, this creates a number of highly-toxic conflicts of interest. Boiler room salesmen could willingly raise prices for their promoted stocks, and simultaneously add insult to injury by buying the same stocks back for a much lower price. This dynamic can be avoided with markets that have other legitimate buyers.

To this day, many still copy Tellier's methods to produce their own penny stock scams, the only difference being that the modern-day boiler rooms consist of better-equipped offices and the use of various internet-based tactics.

Should you choose to pursue investments in penny stocks, beware that the industry is rife with manipulation, overcharging, limited liquidity and various "pump and dump" strategies. Investing in this space requires intimate knowledge of the company, its management and the sector in which it operates - rather than relying on an enticing pitch from a snake oil salesman.

* * *

Tricks and treachery are the practice of fools, that don't have enough brains to be honest

—Benjamin Franklin

NAMI YEN: CAME DOWN FROM HEAVEN AND WENT UP IN SMOKE

Japan is a country of paradox. On the one hand, it has one of the lowest crime rates; truly miniscule when compared to other countries. When 2011's 9.0 earthquake and tsunami hit the east coast of Japan, the world marveled at how starving citizens patiently waited in lines by the supermarket. The looting we witnessed following the New Orleans and Haiti disasters did not make its way to the East Asian islands.

At the same time, a 2009 *Forbes* article relays the stark contrast when it comes to white-collar scamming. In 2008 alone, over 20,000 scams were reported in Japan. Japanese fraudsters have no problem targeting the elderly. One of those scammers was Kazutsugi Nami, whose scheming exploits have caused him to be dubbed the Japanese Madoff.

Nami's early years were spent conducting fraud. In the 1970s, he served as vice president of a car parts company where he was involved in a pyramid scheme selling car exhausts that drew in 250,000 investors. When that failed, he founded a new company that sold stones which he claimed could convert tap water into mineral water, a scam that briefly sent him to jail.

By 1987, it seemed that jail had worked and Nami finally founded a legitimate business named the Ladies and Gentlemen Company, which sold bedding supplies and health products. Things at L&G seemed to go smoothly enough for almost a decade and a half. In 2001, one would have thought that the sixty-six-year-old Nami would be on the brink of retirement. Yet the still-youthful-looking Nami did no such thing. Instead, he started a new venture that made his magical stone scam look like crickets. Claiming that a recession was coming that would force the world into a new digital currency, L&G began pitching a new product to investors, the "enten" ("yenten" in Japanese), meaning "yen from heaven." Nami claimed that his new digital currency would double in value and become the main international currency, all while erasing world hunger and being unlimited in supply.

While that claim alone sounds far too dubious to be true, Nami knew how to pitch to investors. He would throw lavish parties at hotels and convention centers where he would convince investors to buy in with promises of 36% annual gains. Investors who gave 100,000 yen or more would benefit from an added bonus by receiving an equivalent amount in enten to go along with their cash returns. Nami asked his investors to recruit their friends and families into the fold and posted lengthy daily blogs to his investors. Going out of his way to attract media attention, Nami became very well known throughout Japan and his L&G investor group became a quasi-cult.

In total, L&G amassed 126 billion yen from 37,000 investors between 2001 and 2007 (with the US dollar-to-yen exchange rate ranging between 100 and 160 during those years, according to statista.com), with some reports saying that it was 226 billion from 50,000 investors. Of course, it was merely an elaborate Ponzi scheme, using new investors' money to pay up the old investors, with Nami and his associates pocketing much of the difference.

But like every Ponzi scheme, its time was limited. In February 2007, L&G was running short on cash and began paying its investors in enten. L&G filed for bankruptcy later that year and police raided their offices in October. Even as an investigation ensued, Nami loudly proclaimed his innocence on his blog and any other platform he could get. Comparing himself to sixteenth-century Japanese warlord Oda Nobunaga, Nami claimed he was a visionary whose enten would surely become world famous.[11] Media interviewers began following him closely due to police hints at upcoming arrests and apparently predicting an upcoming arrest himself. Nami even showed a journalist a checklist of things he wanted to do in jail.

Seventy-five-year-old Nami was arrested in February 2009, while eating breakfast at a local café with an entourage of reporters surrounding him. When asked if he had any remorse, he loudly said "No; why do I have to apologize? I'm the poorest victim. Nobody lost more than I did. You should be aware that high returns come with a high risk."

Of his associates, twenty-one were arrested in what proved to be the largest Japanese scam since Toyota Shoji (not associated with the car company) stole 202 billion yen from investors, selling gold bars in the 1980s. In 2010, Nami was sentenced to eighteen years in prison, with his scheduled release coming at the ripe old age of ninety-three.

The losses from this scam translated to nearly $1.5 billion USD.

---

[11] Notwithstanding his deceitful intentions, to Nami's credit, he was actually ahead of his time, predicting that cryptocurrencies would evolve into the force we're witnessing today.

Key Takeaways

The most obvious red flag, which we've already highlighted in a wide variety of scams, were the high returns of 36%. This return target is absurd in both its quantity and in its specificity. Currency cannot offer a specific rate of return. Currency is simply a medium of exchange, offering a unitized basis for trade. Yes, as currency achieves greater adoption, its value can rise. However, the magnitude of that rise is both unpredictable and unreliable.

Another glaring red flag was that currency, by definition, cannot be unlimited, and its value is driven by its scarcity. It is the simplest rule of economics that when supply increases, demand decreases. When the money supply increases, inflation takes over. By suggesting that the currency will be unlimited, Nami was also suggesting that it will be worthless, which was certainly accurate.

Even if there was a shred of merit and legitimacy to the investment, the fact that Nami asked his investors to recruit their friends and family should have also served as a red flag. Investments that offer above-market returns are aggressively chased after by investors, not aggressively marketed by promoters. However, given the need to repay old investors with new money, a deep reliance on an ever-expanding investor base was critical for Nami's operation.

Perhaps the most obvious takeaway, which is a running theme throughout the book, was the pedigree of the individual involved. Nami had already conducted a pyramid scheme and falsely claimed to have water purifying stones in a fraud that landed him in jail. Why would investors then trust him again when he claimed to have "yen from heaven," a claim that was just as dubious and fantastical as his magical stones?

Of course, there are many fraudsters that turn straight and build legitimate businesses (just look at the story of Frank Abagnale, Jr., recounted in Steven Spielberg's Academy Award-nominated *Catch Me if You Can*), and even L&G started as a legitimate business. When confronting any proven liar and hearing his dubious claims about currency from heaven and unusually high returns, the only appropriate response is running the other way.

* * *

CAN'T TRULY SAVVY AND INTELLIGENT INDIVIDUALS SPOT FRAUDS?

Intelligence and savviness alone does not preclude one from falling victim to fraud. In one comical example, decades apart, both Napoleon Bonaparte and Benjamin Franklin—two of the savviest men in history—found themselves investing in a Mechanical Turk, which was purported to be the world's first chess-playing machine. What impressed both men was the fact that they believed they were beaten by the Mechanical Turk they had seen. In reality, a chess grand master was concealed in a cabinet beneath the board, manipulating the pieces into what looked like automated moves.

AN ECCENTRIC VIGILANTE'S WAR ON THE WORLD'S BIGGEST PIGEON FRAUD

I f you live in an urban area like New York City, you likely know all about pigeons, those pesky birds that peck at garbage bags on street corners, frolic in puddles, and interfere with your leisurely strolls. In case you thought that's all the damage they're capable of, you'll be surprised to learn that pigeons were front and center in one of the most creative Ponzi schemes in recent memory.

Pigeon King International was a company founded by Canadian pigeon breeder Arlan Galbraith. According to Galbraith's own accounts, his fascination with pigeons began when he was six years old, when some of his neighbors in Stouffville, Ontario, introduced him to the sport of pigeon racing. Despite the sport's long history, it wasn't terribly popular when Galbraith was growing up in the 1950s. Though, that didn't prevent Galbraith from getting into it.

As life went on, Arlan dropped out of high school and founded a pig and cattle farm with his family, all the while remaining active in the pigeon racing and breeding communities. His farm eventually went bankrupt in the 1980s and he resorted to various forms of farm work as well as animal breeding to sustain his family, which then included his wife Elizabeth and their two children. In 1989, Elizabeth was hit in a snowstorm-induced car crash, leaving her a quadriplegic. In a touching move that could hardly be associated with a soon-to-be fraudster, Galbraith remained at his wife's side for many years and cared for her and the children. The family told *New York Times* reporter Jon Mooallem that even when the couple did separate, it was done so on Elizabeth's request, and that Arlan did not want to leave because he felt a "strong sense of duty."

Despite this touching story that would surely interest Hollywood directors, Galbraith used his still-active pigeon hobby to branch into an area which would bring him infamy. In 2001, he decided upon a move—later employed by star basketball player LeBron James—and crowned himself "king," more specifically, the "Pigeon King."

Claiming that he had developed his own genetic line of pigeons, he started advertising for Pigeon King International. He presented a new program where he would sell breeding pigeons to farmers with a promise that he would buy back the baby chicks at fixed prices that would give the original buyer an attractive return with payouts in either five or ten years, giving separate contracts for either option.

Why would Galbraith want to do this? "Racing," he told investors.

The pigeon racing industry had grown since Galbraith was a child and become much more professionalized. He claimed that he had buyers waiting for his special line of pigeons in the Middle East and that famed boxer Mike Tyson, who was a well-known pigeon racer, also bought pigeons from him. He targeted rural farmers, promising them that their returns would allow them to work less and spend more time with their children.

Despite being low pressure and not having the aggressive salesman attitude that generally gets things sold, Pigeon King International began seeing success. Investors paid money to receive their pigeons and Galbraith began his expansion by hiring salesmen in Ontario, Pennsylvania, and other American rural Midwest communities. He even founded a *Pigeon Post* newsletter for his investors and created a pseudo-community of followers. By 2007, he was paying back his early investors in the five-year program with their expected returns.

In short, business was booming and it might have remained booming were it not for one man: an elderly Amish vigilante named David J. Thornton.

Eccentric by nature, Thornton had a burning passion to catch fraudsters. This led him to launch a website called CrimeBustersNow while living off a pension and residing in a friend's basement in Quebec. When he was informed of the Pigeon King, he decided to do his usual research and immediately decided that there was no way Galbraith was running anything but a Ponzi scheme.

The eccentric Thornton began blindly calling people in farming areas as well as their banks, warning them of the Pigeon King's true operation and asking them to spread the word. He even traveled to the police station near Galbraith's headquarters. When they kicked him out, he stood outside and announced his perceived doomsday on a bullhorn. While many saw Thornton as a lunatic, some began to think twice about investing with Galbraith. With banks referring potential borrowers to CrimeBustersNow, the tide of new investors began to slow.

Others joined on the Galbraith-bashing bandwagon and in December 2007, a tremendous journalistic effort by *Better Farming* magazine rose to the top. *Better Farming*, a small operation that was headquartered in Robert Irwin's (its editor) Ontario farm, published a special on Pigeon King International. *Better Farming* reported that based on gathered agricultural data, it was impossible for there to be a market that allowed Galbraith to sell the number of pigeons he claimed to have sold. The sixteen-page report, the longest ever done by Irwin and his staff, was entirely damning.

Galbraith's response was fierce. He blasted Thornton and Irwin as fearmongers in his *Pigeon Post*. He announced that he was expanding even more with the construction of a new plant in Northern Ontario, one that would produce edible squab. Contrary to his earlier claims that his pigeons were for racing, he now claimed that he was selling his pigeons as meat, better known as squab, which require superior breeding. Galbraith claimed that the demand for his pigeons was virtually unlimited, so Pigeon King International would be ever-more successful.

But this was just a front for Galbraith's growing problems. Not only was he losing new investors, he also faced a growing logistical challenge. His scheme had a problem that other Ponzi charlatans like Bernie Madoff, Allan Stanford and Gerald Payne didn't confront. Galbraith actually did buy and sell pigeons, and unlike other commodities such as cash or securities, pigeons have actual needs. They need to be stored, fed and cared for in order to be properly resold to subsequent investors. Hence, Galbraith wasn't simply failing to re-sell his birds to the Middle East, he was also bleeding due to the cost of their upkeep. This had been manageable when he began his operation, but as hordes of investors began selling him back their pigeons after their first five years, it left him as the pigeon caretaker. Just in the province of Ontario, he had fourteen barns that he needed to care for, with the largest holding approximately 40,000 pigeons. Galbraith knew that unless he could sell them off at a miraculous pace, he was done for. In June 2008, Galbraith admitted in the *Pigeon Post* that Pigeon King International had collapsed, although he blamed it primarily on Thornton and his gang of "jealous fearmongers."

Investors were left with thousands of pigeons and nobody to whom they could be sold. Ken Wagler, one of Galbraith's salesmen who had invested in the company and had no idea that the company was a Ponzi scheme, called a meeting of a large group of investors in Stratford, Ontario. They decided to sell the pigeons for meat and collaborated with a food industry entrepeneur to come up with a range of pigeon-based products. While at first it appeared that they might receive a return on their money, they were shocked to discover that each pigeon only produced enough meat to feed two people, hardly a viable return for their $30 cost. Moreover, when they then tried selling them for racing, they were equally surprised to learn that their pigeons were too large to race. Pigeon experts began examining the Pigeon King's birds and found them, in the words of one expert, to be hopeless "junk and crossbreeds."

In total, nearly one thousand American and Canadian breeders choked up $42 million for useless birds and were left with pigeons that Galbraith promised to buy back for a total of $356 million, sales that would never materialize.

In Ontario alone, some 400,000 pigeons lay uselessly in the hands of owners and Ontario's agricultural officials were terrified that should they be released into the wild, Toronto would be flooded with a pigeon apocalypse. Farmers were told to kill their pigeons and the government sent out teams to help dispose of them.

Galbraith went bankrupt along with his company and was subjected to an increasingly wild trial. Prosecution uncovered witnesses to tear off Galbraith's nice-guy veneer. Some witnesses who had worked for Galbraith attested that he had threatened any employees who might expose the Ponzi scheme. Galbraith refused to hire a lawyer and represented himself, bizarrely cross-examining the witnesses with strange and overburdening questions and getting into shouting-filled confrontations with witnesses to whom he had once sold pigeons.

In the end, Galbraith was sentenced to seven years and three months in prison. With no money to pay any sort of restitution, he left hundreds of farmers scrambling in his wake.

Key Takeaways

There are many important lessons that can be learned from Galbraith but perhaps the most striking is that when investing in a company that is built off selling a certain product, the investor needs to verify the existence of a market for that product and to check whether the sales match the stated demand.

Galbraith told his investors that his pigeons were needed for pigeon racing in the Middle East. But how large was their pigeon racing market? Was the demand sizeable enough to need thousands upon thousands of pigeons to keep it going? The *Better Farming* editorial staff asked this question; the investors did not.

The second question was equally ignored: Were his birds fit for racing? Did the product match the professed "market?" It would have been very easy to ask pigeon experts and find the answer. Nobody did.

The lesson from the self-proclaimed Pigeon King: when investing in a market, do your homework to make sure the supply-demand fundamentals are actually there, and that the products truly address the needs of that market.

* * *

HOW DO FRAUDSTERS FABRICATE TRUST?

Soren Kierkegaard once said, "There are two ways to be fooled. One is to believe what isn't true; the other is to refuse to believe what is true." This underlying principle has been coined the approach-avoidance model by social psychologists Eric Knowles and Jay Linn, who claimed that the most persuasive tactics simultaneously entice you to approach something and give you no reason to avoid it. They call these two groups of tactics alpha and omega.

Alpha tactics, which are easier to employ and most frequently utilized, are meant to increase the attractiveness of a proposition. Whereas, omega tactics are intended to lower one's guard and reduce their resistance to a proposition.

By creating a scenario that appears to be a win-win, or no lose proposition, the fraudster has artificially manufactured trust.

WILLIAM MILLER: THE 520% MAN

People associate Ponzi schemes with Boston's Charles Ponzi, but some historians claim that Ponzi took his cues from the playbook of Brooklyn's William Miller. Thin, scrawny and not as presentable as the finely manicured and dapper Charles Ponzi, Miller did not have the glamour but his story was essentially the same.

In February of 1899, a wheezy William Miller was then twenty-one and facing increasing financial pressure. He was married with a sick wife and a child and his meager bookkeeping training could not provide enough to cover his costs because he had a habit of venturing into speculations. It was then that he was struck with an idea.

He started a simple operation with his friends at a Bible study group, promising that he knew of high-potential investments coming from inside information. The returns, he said, would be 10% weekly. At first, he based himself out of a candy store and went around hand delivering the returns and soliciting more investors, but the operation began to grow quickly. He quickly hired four delivery boys to help and began calling himself the Franklin Syndicate, renting an upper-story room of a house at 144 Floyd Street in Brooklyn. Solicitations by mail to far-off places then followed, with Miller receiving inquiries from Louisiana to Manitoba.

With Miller becoming known as "the 520% man" due to his ridiculous annual returns, it didn't take long for his Brooklyn home to become flooded with a combination of mail and eager investors. He rented the entire house and hired fifty clerks to handle the onslaught of investors. Fridays were the worst, as people wanted to deposit their money before the weekend to get a chance at next week's 10% returns. Money was shoved into cabinets and pantries and when those were full, it was simply dumped on the floor, where Miller and his assistants waded through it while handing green and pink receipts to the investors clamoring for their proof. By that very October, just nine months after he began the operation, Miller had to make the unfortunate rule that he could no longer accept investments of less than fifty dollars, but the money kept pouring in. The advertisements were still being sent out en masse and, deciding he couldn't handle it alone, Miller hired an agent, Rudolph Guenther, to manage the advertising full-time and brought in a partner, Edward Schlesinger, to help manage the Boston office.

But the Franklin Syndicate had plenty of skeptics, notably the media and perhaps most formidably, *The Boston Post,* who referred to the entire operation as a swindle. Things got worse when an editor of a financial paper, E.L Blake, warned all his subscribers to avoid Miller. One disturbed investor asked Miller why Blake would doubt him. Miller proceeded to call Blake a "blackmailer", and Blake responded by threatening Miller with a libel suit. Suddenly, the audacious twenty-one-year-old felt out of his league and he enlisted the help of Robert Adam "Colonel" Ammon, a lawyer specializing in helping shady bucket shops all but break the law.

Ammon told Miller to incorporate and exchange his outstanding liabilities for shares in the Franklin Syndicate. Ammon even managed to get Wells Fargo on board with a certificate of deposit of $100,000. Since Ammon was a broad and imposing figure who (unlike the scrawny Miller) exerted extreme confidence, he drove to Boston to help stop the flow of nervous investors influenced by *The Post*. And he successfully managed to keep $28,000 of potential redemptions in the Franklin fold. Lastly, he told Miller to avoid any further public statements.

For Miller, the last piece of advice came a bit too late. While Ammon was trying to rejig the Franklin Syndicate, Blake was still hurting from his fight with Miller and decided to move ahead by filing a $50,000 libel suit. As there is no honor among thieves, the suit scared Schlesinger, prompting him to take $150,000 from the Boston offices and leave for Europe, settling in the Riviera. Police began looking into the situation and Ammon began to hear from behind closed doors that warrants were in the process of being issued. Miller fled to Canada, taking hordes of money along with him, and also gave Ammon $180,000 to be allocated toward the care of his wife and child. Ammon, who had skirted the law on plenty of occasions, remained behind to manage the Franklin Syndicate.

Remarkably, hundreds of investors couldn't bring themselves to believe the negative reports and were still pouring money in, even after Miller had fled or "disappeared." But authorities had seen enough and approached Ammon asking for Miller. Initially, Ammon pretended he didn't know him, but being hardly interested in Miller's long-term interests, he eventually caved to police pressure. In another display of deception, he sent Miller a message instructing him to return, claiming that he would get him a reduced sentence. When the naïve Miller returned, he was sentenced to ten years in prison. Police asked him to testify against Ammon. He refused. That is, until he discovered that Ammon, who had promised to fully support his family while he was gone, had given the ill wife and child only five dollars a week. Infuriated, Miller, who had become sick in prison and was now a shriveled version of his skinny self, appeared in court to testify against Ammon. In exchange, his sentence was reduced to five years. In the end, about one million dollars was unaccounted for, an amount that would be equal to $25 million in current-day currency.

Unfortunately, the romantic side of the story didn't end well, as Miller divorced his wife in 1914. However, unlike some other notable fraudsters, he decided to keep clean when he eventually left prison. He ran a grocery store in Long Island, staying far away from finance and going by the ironic nickname of "Honest Bill."

As for the Miller's old partner, the now-runaway Edward Schlesinger, he lived lavishly in Europe until he died of gastro-enterological complications due to excessive overeating.

Key Takeaways

Besides the fact that no one really knew or asked what Miller did to create wealth, shockingly the entire fiasco played out in less than two years. And the gush of interest that chased after Miller in such a short period of time is as astonishing as it is recurring.

There is a common refrain within the financial world that the most naïve and unsophisticated investors chase performance. On the face of it, what could be wrong with chasing performance? Isn't that what every investor is seeking?

In reality, chasing short-term performance is a quick path towards oblivion. When it comes to legitimate money managers, even average performers have large positive aberrations. And almost immediately after those upswings arrive, investors that chase performance pile in, only to be met by a sharp reversion to the mean, leaving performance chasers badly burned.

Thoughtful investing requires patient observation and time as it allows most schemers and charlatans to burn themselves in the process of burning the money of others. The combination of seedy (and unreliable) characters that surround them, the unsustainable need for increasing inflows and the external suspicions that will inevitably surface, lead virtually all frauds to unravel in time. As such, perhaps the easiest way for investors to deal with suspicious sounding opportunities is simply to wait and see.

* * *

The worst of all deceptions is self-deception

—Plato

Nothing is easier than to deceive ourselves, as our affections are subtle persuaders

—Demosthenes

FROM COWSHEDS TO LAUNDROMATS: THE RASTOGI'S IMAGINARY EMPIRE

The only thing worse than a debt deal gone wrong is a debt deal that never existed!

At the turn of the century, two brothers managed to convince banks around the world to lend billions for factoring deals that did not exist. Factoring is simply the sale of one's accounts receivables for a discount, usually in order to shore up some liquidity. The only factoring that Narendra and Virendra Rastogi did was factoring in the misplaced trust of their victims, who were as large and prominent as JP Morgan Chase and General Motors.

The brothers convinced institutions worldwide that they needed capital for fictitious metal-trading deals. The premise was simple. By virtue of the metal deals they claimed to broker, they would be entitled to fees. The challenge was that these fees would not be paid until the metal reached its ultimate buyer, which—especially when most of the metal traveled by ship—could take many months. In order to smooth out their cash flow and match revenues to liabilities, they convinced banks to loan them money against the fees that would inevitably be received.

The con operation the Rastogi brothers engineered was likely more sophisticated and intricate than what a legitimate business would have required. While Narendra oversaw Allied Deals in the US, Virendra supposedly supervised RBG Resources (which they claimed to be a metal and mineral producer) in London.

To secure the loans, they employed 324 nonexistent shell companies, countless counterfeit documents—invoices, purchase orders, etc.—of 200 sham multi-million-dollar corporations in twenty different countries, and fake bills of lading[12] that served as collateral for the banks. Each of these companies had phony bank accounts, formal letterhead, receptionists (in case the auditors called), and even hired over a dozen actors pretending to be metal traders in key markets around the world, such as Hong Kong, Singapore and Dubai. And if that wasn't enough, they even concocted a rating agency that issued bogus credit reports on the bogus companies they claimed to have on their client list.

When authorities would eventually launch a formal investigation, attempting to visit the customers the Rastogis claimed to have had, they instead found themselves standing in front of random locales. They were brought everywhere from a cowshed in India to a laundromat in New Jersey to the home of an elderly woman selling scrapbooks, a far cry from any creditworthy "metal buyers" they claimed to work with. In short, authorities discovered one of the most convoluted and meticulously planned transaction frauds in history.

The brothers could have carried on hiving off funds into their British Virgin Island trusts for longer if it wasn't for a mindless mistake of a Hong Kong-based employee. In what could only be described as fateful, the employee accidentally sent eight fake letters from "customers" to the Rastogis' audi-

---

[12] Bills of lading are documents issued by shippers to attest the kinds and quantity of goods that the carrier has on board. Naturally, since they weren't real to begin with, the Rastogis used the same bill of lading for multiple loans and with multiple banks.

tor, PricewaterhouseCoopers, rather than Virendra Rastogi, for whom they were intended.

Once the accounting firm claimed that they doubted the veracity of these transactions, the gig was up. Authorities raided Virendra's London office, where they found him frantically shredding documents which offered evidence of their entire duplicitous operation. Simultaneously, the US authorities raided their New Jersey office, arresting Narendra and his staff.

As we said earlier, there's no loyalty among thieves. And it seems the truism stands even among thieving brothers, as Narendra gave evidence against his own brother and named him as a co-conspirator as part of his plea bargain. Narendra pled guilty and was ultimately sentenced to seven years in prison, in addition to his obligation to repay the $683.6 million he milked from investors. Virendra, whose admission wasn't nearly as quick, was sentenced to nine-and-a-half years in prison. And while several of their top deputies also received prison sentences, other members of the family avoided prosecution. Their niece, Sheetal Rastogi, who was intimately involved in the fraud, escaped to India a month before the raid on the London office.

Key Takaways

The Rastogis could have written the playbook on the infrastructure for fraud. However, they did trigger several red flags that can provide meaningful lessons for investors.

For starters, the terms they had with customers were simply inexplicable. Most vendors give their customers anywhere from ten to thirty days (in extreme cases sixty to ninety days) to pay their bills. To have a 180-day credit window, as RBG Resources had, is virtually unprecedented. What would be the benefit of having such unusually long periods for accounts receivable? If the customers themselves would not have expected it, why would the Rastogis offer it, especially given the long delays in receiving the metals to begin with? Only a company that didn't actually earn those accounts receivable would be comfortable giving such long payment dates. Any time someone offers unusually generous terms, which no one would need or expect, it should raise a fair number of questions.

Furthermore, the extent of their borrowing and how much they were willing to pay for servicing the debt also seemed to be far beyond that of anyone in the industry. Records indicate that they borrowed half of their annual revenues. The number of credit lines they had with numerous institutions was another significant red flag (not to mention credit risk), as it made no economic sense. A much cleaner, more common and efficient arrangement would involve working with an agent bank that farmed out pieces of the loan to other financial institutions.

Lastly, and most importantly for investors, was the utter absence of "skin in the game." As alleged brokers of these trans-actions, the one thing the Rastogi brothers were actually trans-parent about from day one was the fact that they put no capital at risk. While it is not a sign of fraud per se, any prudent lender or investor that's involved in complex, overseas transactions should expect and demand greater alignment of interest before putting any significant capital at risk. A $683 million loss may not put the future of financial institutions at risk, but for pri-vate investors the results can be catastrophic.

* * *

WHY CAN'T INVESTORS SIMPLY RELY ON THE AUDITORS?

Surprisingly, you cannot. The fundamental problem with relying on auditors is that their incentives are structurally misaligned. Auditors are paid by their clients (i.e. the corporations) to do work for the benefit of non-clients (i.e. investors). And since any service provider is incentivized to do whatever it takes to retain their client base—especially those clients that pay hefty fees—their loyalty is to the companies, not the investors thereof. If this misaligned dynamic is not enough, historically, auditors could not even be held accountable for their negligence, as they have no duty of care to investors.

In a landmark 1997 case involving Hercules Management Ltd., auditors should have clearly discerned impropriety, but didn't. In this case, the court shockingly ruled that individuals who base their investment decisions on the audited financials do so at their own peril. Corporations or officers and directors can be sued, but the auditors walk away scot-free. This decision was challenged in 2016, when a court ruled that Deloitte & Touche was, in fact, liable in the Livent fraud and that, specifically with public companies, there must be a higher standard of care. While this was a promising improvement, we are still woefully far from being able to rely on the auditing establishment to protect us.

RUDY GIULIANI'S BIG, GREEDY FISH: THE STORY OF IVAN BOESKY

The tall and silver-haired Gordon Gekko is one of Hollywood's most famous characters. Played by Michael Douglas in Oliver Stone's 1987 film *Wall Street,* Gekko is listed as No. 24 on the America Film Institute's current list of cinema's most iconic villains, garnering Douglas his only acting Oscar.[13] In perhaps one of Gekko's most famous lines, he gave an impassioned speech about how "greed is good," words that were inspired in real-life by Ivan Boesky.

Boesky was born in Detroit to a restaurant chain-owning family in 1937 and from his early childhood, Boesky was all about work ethic. Though his family was well off, he still sold ice cream from a truck in high school and violated his license numerous times by selling ice cream after 7 p.m. He claimed to be a high school dropout, but he did actually complete high school before moving on to law school and graduating in 1964. In that time, he married Seema Silberstein, the daughter of a wealthy local family whose assets included the Beverly Hills Hotel in Los Angeles. Boesky worked in the family business until his father-in-law gave his son-in-law and daughter their dream gift: an apartment on New York's Park Avenue. Boesky had always wanted to live in NYC and hoped to make money off arbitrage on Wall Street, a process of buying and selling

---

[13] He received another Oscar for producing *One Flew Over Cuckoo's Nest.*

items in different places with the goal of producing profits due to price differentials.

While Boesky did not lack in excitement or work ethic, his body of work was very poor. He got fired from his first job when he lost $20,000 on a single trade and he singlehandedly bankrupted the second firm he worked for, a small outfit with only $1 million in capital. He was even slapped with a $10,000 fine from the SEC for selling securities that the firm had yet to acquire. With a trading resume that would hardly get him hired, his in-laws came to the rescue, gifting him $700,000 to start his own firm, Ivan F. Boesky and Co.

Having his own company didn't improve Boesky's trading, nor his desire to make profits at any cost. He began looking for insider information to help his trading and found his perfect insider: his tennis partner, a well-respected investment banker and mergers guru, Martin Siegel. He paid Siegel for information about upcoming mergers and Siegel thought that even though insider trading was illegal, no harm would come of it. After all, reasoned Siegel, it'll only affect a few trades of the many Boesky was making. Nobody would catch on.

Siegel told Boesky about the upcoming acquisitions of Getty Oil by Texaco and other oil industry deals. Very quickly, the once-floundering Boesky and Co. was off like a rocket, with Boesky raking in $65 million in 1984 alone. He got another $50 million the next year through Philip Morris' acquisition of General Foods. In addition to Siegel, Boesky had spread his wings to gather information from junk bond dealers such as Drexel Burnham's bond-trading head Michael Milken—known as the Junk Bond King for earning more than $1 billion in junk bond revenues in the 1980s—and its manager Dennis Levine. Boesky was in on just about every major deal of the 1980s, oftentimes buying stocks only a short time before a major merger happened. In one blatant example, just three days before Maxaam Group paid $80 million to acquire Pacific Lumber, Boesky acquired 10,000 Pacific Lumber shares.

In a charmingly perceived rags-to-riches story, the once-terrible trader now found himself as Wall Street's top arbitrageur. The well-dressed Boesky became the symbol of Wall Street success; suddenly, arbitrage trading was sexy and everyone wanted to know how to predict the markets like Boesky. Hordes of people rushed to give their money to Ivan F. Boesky and Co. and he was put in charge of numerous funds located in the far reaches of the world. Riding his wave of publicity, Boesky went on a campaign detailing the wonders of arbitrage. Boesky penned a book on arbitrage and how to predict mergers entitled *Merger Mania*. He was even featured on the cover of *Time* magazine in 1986. According to one top arbitrageur later interviewed by the *New York Times*, Boesky "put arbitrage on the map" when it had largely gone out of style.

Even with his huge success, he kept on working hard. He was at the office every morning at 7 a.m., where he had 160 telephone lines on which he "kept tabs" on the market while predicting the next mergers. Of course, those lines were simply used to collect tips from his insiders, something that much of Wall Street suspected but nobody in the SEC apparently cared about. According to *New York* magazine writer-turned-TV personality James Cramer: "It was pretty much an open secret that he trafficked in inside information. My boss at Goldman Sachs,

Bob Rubin, had told me repeatedly to be careful of Boesky. Funny thing, it mattered to ethical people like Rubin, but it didn't appear to matter to the Feds. As long as it didn't seem to matter to the Feds that he bought stocks ahead of takeovers, why should it matter to anyone else?"

To the public, Boesky kept an impressive face. Making over $200 million from his trades, he purchased a 260-acre estate in suburban New York with dog patrols and visited his daughter's boarding school via private helicopter. He was invited to speak at the commencement of University of California where he famously spoke about how he thought "greed is good" and "greed is healthy," the inspiration for Gekko.

But while the SEC had no idea about the widespread corruption happening on Wall Street, they were eventually informed about Boesky's accomplice, Dennis Levine. Levine had moved his assets to a Swiss bank, Bank Leu, where he thought he would be safe from regulators. The bank soon realized that Levine was engaged in insider trading. However, instead of turning him in, they wanted a piece of the pie. They began following his trades and covered their own tracks by splitting Levine's trades among several brokers, one of them being from Merrill Lynch. Merrill Lynch tipped off the SEC, who brought Levine in on charges of securities fraud, tax evasion and perjury.

Soon-to-be New York mayor Rudy Giuliani, fresh off indicting eleven members of a mafia ring, enthusiastically prosecuted the case. Levine pleaded guilty and agreed to cooperate with authorities for a reduced two-year sentence. He was banned from securities trading for life and coughed up the largest sum of money ever in an insider trading case at the time: $11.5 million. He also agreed to turn in his network of insiders, which included Boesky and Siegel. Boesky was the big fish though, and as Giuliani brought him to court, Boesky followed Levine's suit and cooperated with authorities. He allowed authorities to tap him while he went about his daily business of contacting insiders and the SEC uncovered an entire chain of insiders in Wall Street, headed by Boesky himself and Michael Milken.

Boesky gave up $100 million and his allowance of authority wiretapping turned in Michael Milken, who was eventually slapped with a $600 million dollar fine and ten years in prison with Giuliani acting as the prosecuting attorney. Boesky was sentenced to three-and-a-half years in a California federal prison, a sentence that Giuliani was reportedly "very happy" with, though he was released after two for good behavior. Even so, the man whose face was once plastered on *Time* had his reputation eviscerated. He divorced his wife, the mother of his four children in 1991 and the institutions that he supported took his name off their walls. According to a later interview with his cousin, Boesky retreated to a quiet life near San Diego, far from the hubbub of Wall Street that had made him famous.

The arrests of Levine, Boesky, Siegel, Milken and others ended the 1980s era of a Wall Street where insider trading and corruption ruled. The US Attorney's office mentioned in its sentencing memorandum that "not since the legislative hearings leading to the passage of the 1933 and 1934 Securities Acts has the Government learned so much at one time about securities law violations." The SEC adopted numerous methods to stop insider trading in Wall Street and end the corruption there. Unfortunately, the subprime mortgage crisis of the late 2000s revealed an entirely new angle of corruption and insider fraud, which the SEC would regrettably discover too late.

Key Takeaways

Many on Wall Street had suspected that Boesky was involved in insider trading. They merely swept that fact aside since the authorities didn't care. But while that may have been obvious to the kingpins of Wall Street, the average layman likely thought Boesky could predict the markets just by keeping incredibly up to date. The premise of that belief is simply false. Nobody can fully predict mergers and acquisitions solely based "on the market."

As an analogy, consider the world of sports. At every sports trading deadline, there are rumors swirling around about potential trades. Team X may need this player while Team Y needs that player, but there are a multitude of bidders and external factors to weigh in before major events happen. The only people who seem to have a feel about what will happen are the reporters who remain in constant contact with the general managers and are, hence, insiders. Wall Street is a lot more complicated than the average baseball team. If anybody claims that they can perfectly predict what will happen and somehow be correct on nearly every major deal, insider trading (rather than market analysis) is likely involved.

The bottom line is that any form of trading is risky, and those that do it well may be right only 55% of the time. You can make educated guesses and take calculated risks, but ultimately no one can know what the future holds. That is one of the lessons learned from the insider trading scandals of the 1980s; along with the fact that, contrary to the claims of Gordon Gekko, greed is not necessarily good.

* * *

HOW DID "INSIDER TRADING" EVOLVE INTO A CRIME?

Until the 1930s, insider trading was merely considered good business sense. Sentiment on insider trading changed during the Crash of 1929 when Albert H. Wiggin, then the Chairman of Chase National Bank had made a fortune by shorting—betting AGAINST—his own company. To put it in perspective, Wiggin was one of the most distinguished financiers of the era. He sat on the board of directors of over fifty major American companies and made Chase the fourth-largest bank in America. And for him to net $4 million (the equivalent of over $56,400,000 today) in 1929, by betting against the institution that he was encouraging others to invest in, seemed criminal. In 1934, they revised the Securities Act to include insider trading as an explicit violation—a change that has been comically referred to as the "Wiggin Act."

The SEC did not take any meaningful action against violators until 1959. At that time, Texas Gulf Sulfur, a public exploration company, hit a bonanza mineral find of copper, silver, etc. in northern Ontario. The executives, however, downplayed the find to stealthily buy as many shares as possible at low market prices. Of course, when the extraordinary find was announced, the stock price exploded, making every executive extremely wealthy. The case proved to be so egregious that Texas Gulf was charged with insider trading, a message sent to Wall Street that this illicit benefit bestowed on insiders would no longer be tolerated.

THE TAPED INSIDER: A GLIMPSE INTO THE RISE AND FALL OF RAJ RAJARATNAM

In the early 2000s, there was perhaps no better symbol of the American dream than Raj Rajaratnam. Born in Sri Lanka to a sewing factory manager, Raj attended college in the United Kingdom, and his intellectual prowess got him accepted into Pennsylvania's prestigious Wharton School of Business in 1981. Everything went uphill from there.

After earning his business degree in 1983, Rajaratnam joined Chase's technology group as a lending officer. Seeming to create a niche for himself in the technology industry, he then joined Needham and Co., a small investment bank that has since ballooned to a larger firm with offices in five cities and over $200 billion in transactions, including the underwriting of Google's initial public offering. With his tech industry expertise, Raj rose to the top of Needham's technology group and founded a Needham-affiliated hedge fund, Needham Emerging Growth Partners, in 1992. He remained at Needham for five more years, all the while developing a sterling reputation in technology, which coincided nicely with the dotcom bubble.

When Raj left Needham in 1997 to found his own hedge fund specializing in the technology sector, everybody wanted to be a part of it. Naming his fund Galleon Group after the sixteenth-century war ships, he attracted conservative investors like the Swiss bank giant UBS and New Jersey's state pension plan.

Using a "mosaic" strategy, through which Galleon aggressively collected information about a company to paint a broader picture of it before investing, Galleon Group grew into one of the world's largest hedge funds. At its height, it managed over $7 billion, paying $300 million in annual trading commissions to respected investment banks such as Morgan Stanley and Goldman Sachs. All the while, Raj benefited handsomely. At his peak, Forbes listed his net worth at $2.6 billion, with annual earnings of $300 million in 2006, according to *Traders Monthly*.

But what made Raj even more endearing was the fact that he never forgot his Sri Lankan roots. He and his wife, Asha, lived on Sutton Place on Manhattan's East Side with their three children and housed Raj's parents. They donated heavily to help AIDS and HIV victims in India and Sri Lanka and added more to landmine clearing initiatives in Sri Lanka, all while helping the local Harlem Children's Zone. Raj pledged a million dollars to support the recovery of Sri Lankan's "LTTE" rebels (itself a debatable move, as LTTE was classified as a terrorist organization in 32 countries) and founded a charity to help the nation recover after a devastating tsunami struck in 2004. Through their involvement in various charitable initiatives, the family was well known in political and celebrity circles, donating over $100,000 to various Democratic Party campaigns, including those of Barack Obama and Hillary Clinton.

Even when the 2007 recession hit, Raj remained confident. A fiercely competitive person and an equally fierce sports fan, Raj compared his trading during the recession to Mohammad Ali in the boxing ring in a *New York Times* quote: "I'm feeling the pain, but they can't kill me. I'm a warrior."

But little did Raj know that thanks to Andrew Michaelson, he was then under heavy investigation. Michaelson, who had graduated Harvard Law in 2003 and joined the SEC in 2006, had quickly found something that his older colleagues were completely unaware of. While looking at emails between Raj and his brother Rengan, who worked at Galleon before founding his own firm that Michaelson was then investigating, he saw indicators of insider trading. At first the investigation was slow, but it sped up when authorities discovered a text message sent to Rajaratnam from an IBM employee long suspected of tipping, which advised not to buy Polycom stock until "I can get guidance; want to make sure guidance OK."

The FBI secretly wiretapped Galleon's phones and their findings made jaws drop. Apparently, Raj had taken his "mosaic" strategy much too far, brazenly acquiring insider tips from corporate insiders and other traders, including a few of his old classmates at Wharton. He even got tips from Robert Moffat, senior vice president of IBM and widely considered to be the company's CEO-in-waiting. All in all, a wide network of insiders was discovered, all recorded on tape over a nine-month period in 2008.

On an early October morning in 2009, Rajaratnam was arrested. Charges were also brought against twenty-four other executives, with twenty-one of them pleading guilty. Raj kept on fighting, claiming that he had done nothing wrong. Even as he had to shut down his hedge fund, he and his lawyers claimed that all he had done was access legal information that was available to all as part of his "mosaic" strategy. His defense also collected over 200 letters of support to be presented at the trial.

The prosecution, which included Andrew Michaelson, countered in a surprise move by agreeing that most of his trading was legal, but that at least $63 million were obtained through illegal tips and forty-five RBI-recorded taped recordings of Rajaratnam were produced at the trial. Being right in the middle of a large government crackdown on insider trading, with forty-seven charges brought in a span of eighteen months, the use of tapes prompted the *Wall Street Journal* to call it "the first insider trading prosecution to use methods mainly reserved for organized crime, drug and terrorism related cases." The vast list of tips included ones about Google and another about a $5 billion investment by Warren Buffett in Goldman Sachs during the economic crisis of 2007.

The twelve-member jury deliberated for twelve days before concluding that Rajaratnam was guilty of all fourteen charges; Rajaratnam remained silent as the verdict was proclaimed. He was sentenced to eleven years in prison, the longest ever for an insider trading case, and he's scheduled to be released on July 4, 2021—and on Independence Day, he'll commemorate with the lessons of his crashed American dream.

Key Takeaways

Many people became collateral damage in the wake of the Galleon insider trading scandal. Some of these individuals had merely wanted to share in the collaborative spirit that permeates Silicon Valley. It is important to recognize that when this transparency relates to public securities, it can come at great personal cost and caution is warranted.

Another significant takeaway speaks to the difficulty of avoiding victimization by insider trading frauds, or even finding oneself guilty thereof. On the one hand, standard due diligence involves talking to many other people, gathering as much information as possible about the inner dynamics of the company and finding an analytical edge against other investors. That is a basic best practice of any astute investor. On the other hand, making investment decisions based on non-public information that is known only by insiders is a violation of securities laws. This is a difficult tightrope to walk, with lots of grey areas and insider trading laws which are materially different from country to country. It is equally difficult for investors to ascertain whether an opportunity to make money with a certain manager is real or whether that manager is simply benefiting from tips.

To limit the possibility that you are invested with a money manager who is guilty of insider trading, simply ensure that you understand how value and conviction is established. Is their analysis based on the deep understanding of a company or industry or simply a function of what they learned from others "on the street?" Raj's vague "mosaic" description did not explain what he had expertise in identifying or what fundamental analysis he performed. As a consequence, his investors paid the price of guilt by association.

* * *

CONSISTENCY & ALIGNMENT

THE DEFRAUDED FRAUDSTER: THE UNBELIEVEABLE BAYOU STORY

Born in Louisiana to a family of successful traders, Samuel Israel III was determined to follow the family tradition. So upon graduating from Hackley High School in New York, he skipped college to embark on a trading career.

After working at several menial jobs in the New York Stock Exchange and other brokerages in the 1980s, he founded the Bayou hedge fund in 1996 with his friends Jimmy Marquez and Dan Marino.[14] Similar to Bernie Madoff before him, Israel developed an electronic program which he believed would separate him from his competition. He called it the "Forward Propagation" program, a system that would predict the market with 86% accuracy.

Israel began small, attracting capital from his family and friends for the hedge fund, and trading through Israel's own brokerage firm, Bayou Securities, which ran as a parallel business to the fund.

As the face of the hedge fund, Israel presented himself impressively, touting his rich family history and the prominent firms he had worked for (conspicuously failing to mention the insignificance of his roles at those institutions) while Marquez was the main trader and Marino worked the books.

---

[14] Not to be confused with legendary quarterback Dan Marino.

Early trading activity gave Bayou 20% gains, but then the tide quickly turned against them. Marquez had predicted a dramatic rise in gold and piled heavily into Barrick Gold, which had just made a pact with the Indonesian government to buy an extraordinarily large gold deposit. But Barrick was confronted with an expensive lawsuit and its Indonesian deal was slowed, followed by the temporary fall of the entire gold market. Suddenly, Bayou was facing a 14% loss for its first year.

Terrified that their investors would leave, the three partners began searching for answers and it was Marino who came up with one. Bayou's loss for the year was about $161,000 but it had paid $400,000 in commissions to Israel's brokerage, Bayou Securities. Why not rebate the commissions for the year? While that would the give the brokerage a loss, the fund would still come out with a remarkable 40% gain if the money was rebated in full. Marino reasoned that this would temporarily prop up the fund until successful trading would dig them out of their hole. Marino convinced the hedge fund's auditors, Grant Thornton, to reluctantly accept this scheme. Investors were informed of the year's 40% gain and Bayou lived on another day, hiding its losses from everyone, including Israel's responsibly minded wife Janice. This especially pained Israel, as he knew that Janice, herself an accountant, would immediately demand that he should demonstrate honesty by admitting to Bayou's failure.

Marino's imaginative "save" proved to be fleeting. By 1998, Bayou still wasn't trading well, suffering an 18% loss while the market went up 30%. No amount of of rebates could make up for that loss. To make matters worse, at Marquez's insistence, Bayou had also moved its headquarters from Israel's basement to an area in Connecticut known as "Hedge Fund's Row," an added expense of $18,000 a month. Despite Israel's cool and confident demeanor, the firm was failing, as was Israel himself. Feeling estranged from Janice for hiding the fund's losses, he resorted to crack and alcohol. And if that wasn't enough, Marino revealed that Bayou would fail its audit and that Grant Thornton's $50,000 fee was too much for Bayou to handle.

With a sense of impending despair, the three partners met in their new office, where Marino again concocted a solution. They would fake an audit by creating their own accounting firm. Despite the reluctance of the partners, they were not willing to face the honest alternative, so they proceeded with the plan. Using their previous Grant Thornton statements as reference, Marino created faked audited financial statements under the name of the "Richmond Fairfield" accounting firm. The statements included completely fictional numbers to make Bayou look good. Marquez and Israel concocted fake trading returns to match the financial statements and by the year's end, the public was informed that Bayou had a 22% gain. The firm was still small on paper, with its year's gross income hovering around $520,000, but it was "on the rise."

Money began pouring in but even so, Marquez's trading abilities had not improved. He deliberately avoided rising internet stocks and stubbornly stuck to collapsing commodities.

In 1999, personal problems wrecked the team. Marino contracted cancer; Marquez felt like he was ruining both his and Israel's futures, and Israel's crack and alcohol addictions worsened as he tried to keep up with the Joneses on Wall Street. Marquez and Israel got into a fight and Israel decided that he would do his own investing in tech and internet stocks. He did OK, but nowhere near enough to climb out of the hole Bayou was in. By 2001, the team had raised $70 million of investors' money but still had $12 million in losses. By then, Marquez agreed to leave the firm, saddling Israel with the burden of getting them out of their rut.

On September 10, 2001, Israel's Forward Propagation system told him to go all-in on long-term stocks. Confident that this would be his final savior, he went all in. Of course, when planes penetrated the World Trade Center the following morning and trading stopped, Israel knew he would be in for a massive loss. Marino wanted to shut down the fund, arguing that they now had the ability to hide their fraud and just claim they lost money with the small market crash following 9/11. But going bankrupt would put Israel into $2 million of personal debt and ruin his trading career, so he refused.

To keep Bayou going, even though they continued trading, they needed a Ponzi scheme. Through it all, Marino forged the audits and continued issuing rebates from Bayou Securities to Bayou Hedge Fund and Israel gave descriptive letters to his investors about the global markets. By the year's end, he had almost $80 million under management. Looking on enviously, Marquez regretted his decision to leave and demanded his share of compensation or else he would turn Israel in. With no other options, Israel gave him 20% of the gains.

Slowly, Israel's humorous and entertaining personality, as well as his impressive numbers, began to attract more capital. To the world, Israel was brilliant. But on the inside he was crushed. He was making money but not enough. His marriage with Janice was failing. In January 2003, he needed a series of dangerous surgeries and even when he recovered, he traded terribly that year, losing almost $30 million. His marriage finally folded when he got drunk at a reconciliatory Thanksgiving dinner. Israel decided to aim for a new life and moved into a mansion owned by Donald Trump from whom he rented.

By the end of 2003, Israel was managing $150 million with growing losses. The thrill of investing was entirely gone. All he wanted was a get-rich-quick scheme to get out of his troubles, so he sent Marino to find venture capital opportunities.[15] In the process, Marino met and introduced Israel to former actor Jack O'Halleron. Israel developed an instant bond with O'Halleron and shared with him his need for a quick money option. O'Halleron referred him to Robert Booth Nichols, a man he described as Jason Bourne-like "black-ops CIA" who "really knows the goings on of the world."

After investigating Nichols online, Israel was not disappointed. He came across a manuscript linking Nichols with "PROMIS," a supposed high-tech CIA database with the ability to monitor all financial transactions. Beset by personal troubles, Israel's now-deluded mind convinced him that this was his way out of debt. If he had access to PROMIS and knew whenever financial transactions took place, he would consistently be one step ahead of the entire market.

---

[15] Venture capital generally refers to investing in new or start-up companies that have yet to establish themselves. While venture capital investments have the potential for extraordinary gains, they are also highly speculative with greater potential for losses than virtually any other asset class.

O'Halloran arranged a meeting where Israel mentioned PROMIS, prompting Booth to gesture for Israel to meet him later. After arranging a secret meeting, Nichols and Israel had some "deep, meaningful conversation" in which he explained how the world was run by a group of thirteen families, with all of the world governments and intelligence agencies serving as covers. In the background of this all was a shadow market where one could make astronomical returns; enough returns to pay off Bayou's old debts and much more. Israel was so taken by Nichols and flew Marino in to meet him as well.

Convinced that he would become the next George Soros and use his newfound wealth to cure AIDS, Israel transferred Bayou's $150 million into an account at the Barclays bank in London intended to be immediately wired out to one of Nichols' cronies. Luckily, Israel needed to make a withdrawal himself and undid the wire before it could reach Nichols' co-conspirators. While Israel still didn't suspect Nichols, the wires triggered intense FBI interest.

In a true twist of irony, when $150 million almost left Israel's account, the FBI merely thought Israel was a victim of Nichols' fraud, without suspecting that Bayou was an actual Ponzi scheme! It took the FBI one interview to realize that something was wrong in Israel's head. Although they began investigating Nichols, they still didn't bother looking into Bayou itself. And so, the fund continued until Cameron Holmes, who worked in the Arizona Attorney General's office, figured something was up when Israel moved $100 million that was originally meant for Nichols' investments. Holmes did some digging and, confident that Israel was about to get scammed, froze the funds. Without that $100 million, Bayou had no money to pay its investors, because the rest of their money had been invested by Marino into risky venture capital propositions that didn't yield good results. In July 2005, Bayou closed, leaving Israel and Marino in much personal debt, which they began paying off with bounced checks.

The fraud was discovered when a creditor of Marino's uncovered a Marino-composed suicide note detailing the fraud. Police were alerted and arrested Marino before he could commit suicide. With a warrant on the way for Israel, Israel faked his own suicide by parking an SUV by a bridge and leaving a note saying "suicide is painless." The police weren't fooled. A two-month manhunt ensued for Israel and his girlfriend, Debra Ryan, who aided and abetted his escape. After the pair was featured on *America's Most Wanted*, Israel surrendered to federal authorities.

In the end, Bayou investors lost $450 million, making it the largest hedge fund Ponzi scheme until Bernie Madoff later surpassed him.

In April 2008, Israel and Marino were sentenced to twenty years in federal prison. When Israel failed to report for his prison appointment, authorities pressured his girlfriend to admit his attempt to escape. He was eventually tracked down and, on July 2, 2008, Israel surrendered. As a consequence, he was further sentenced to an additional two years in. Not to be forgotten, Jimmy Marquez joined his merry band of thieves behind bars for four years and three months.

Key Takeaways

One of the most obvious takeaways from the Bayou case is the need for a hedge fund to have an independent broker, since there is an inherent conflict of interest with being both the broker as well as the hedge fund manager. The more Israel traded, the more his brokerage, Bayou Securities, gained, even if the hedge fund lost money in those trades. While that is true, lacking an independent broker was not the *cause* of Israel's fraud.

Israel traded heavily because he wanted to get his fund out of the black hole they had dug. Being that the hedge fund was his main business, he even rebated money from the broker to the fund to keep the fund afloat (at least on paper). He would have probably traded heavily regardless of who their broker was. Being their own broker did enable the fraud to begin through Marino's rebates of the commission fees. That should have been the responsibility for the auditor to figure out, not the investor, and here the auditor happened to be Richmond Fairfield, a product of Marino's imagination.

The main takeaway for investors, therefore, relates to Bayou's change of auditors. Whenever a company changes auditors you should begin probing why. This is especially true when a manager shifts from a respected blue-chip firm to an unknown entity. The trajectory of most funds is typically the opposite; i.e., work with someone local and unknown when you are small, and progress to a blue-chip name when the fund and the assets it manages grow. Why did Bayou suddenly stop using Grant Thornton as their auditor in 1999 when their financial statements showed profits of 40% and 22% in the previous years? If those returns were valid, they should have been able to easily afford the $50,000 fee and not need to switch to the little-known (and nonexistent) "Richmond Fairfield" firm.

Additional takeaways for investors relate to basic due diligence. Notwithstanding Israel's employment at various recognized organizations, all anyone needed to do was to call any former employer to verify that Israel hadn't the slightest bit of investment capability, pedigree or experience. The fact was, Israel's "Forward Propagation" program was an attempt to sell investors on a shinier crystal ball, which even the best in the business don't seem to have. And how an amateur can develop such a solution is, in hindsight, an obvious question to ask.

* * *

DESPERATION AND FRAUD: A CHICKEN AND THE EGG CONUNDRUM?

Desperation can lead individuals to commit fraud and to serve as a firebrand for becoming victimized by it. Sam Israel proved to be the classic example. While he was running his own Ponzi scheme, his desperate need for a quick and sizeable return on his capital made him a ripe target for scam artist Robert Booth Nichols.

Frequently, desperation will make even the greatest skeptics abandon their good judgment. It is perhaps the very reason that retirees, who are 15% of the population, account for 30% of fraud victims (Huddleston). Individuals who have no prospect for recreating their savings or those that desperately need something to survive often have the largest targets on their backs.

Of those that historically preyed on others' desperation, among the worst offenders was the father of perhaps the greatest philanthropist in American history: William "Bill" Rockefeller, the father of industrialist John D. Rockefeller. Bill concocted a snake oil of his own, calling it Rock Oil, claiming it that it had the ability to cure all cancers and charging the desperate victims the equivalent two months' salary for the "cure." Bill showed no greater concern for his family. After philandering Bill left his wife and children penniless, young John D. committed early on that he'd have a life that was opposite his father's.

WOOD RIVER'S SUNSET
IN SUN VALLEY

The name Whittier carried significant weight in the computer industry of the 1980s. Ronald Whittier, after all, was an early employee at IBM who went on to become senior vice president of Intel. He was entirely self made, spending time in the army, attending both UC Berkeley and then Stanford for his doctorate before joining IBM, where he was eventually granted stock options to the tune of almost $80 million. His son John, though, had a far less glamorous life.

Growing up in Silicon Valley as one of three siblings, he followed the family tradition of attending UC Berkeley in 1984 where he took an interest in politics. Majoring in political economics, he joined the Young Republicans club and spent a summer interning in the San Francisco office for California's Republican Senator Pete Wilson. At the same time, he took an interest in investing, interning one summer for Bear Stearns. When he eventually graduated in 1989, he stuck to politics and went on to work for Wilson's gubernatorial campaign. Wilson managed to win the governorship due to a large domestic deficit that he went on to fix. His victory left Whittier wondering whether he should continue in politics or move to the greener, more lucrative pastures of Wall Street. He followed the money.

He moved to New York and began working for investment bank Donaldson, Lufkin and Jenrette (DLJ), a respected firm which had trading revenues as high as $3 billion, until it was eventually bought by Credit Suisse for over $10 billion.

Working as an analyst, his time at DLJ was unremarkable, with recommendations that were usually positive (like everybody's in the '90s). One friend recalls that his only claim to fame was that he was Ronald Whittier's son.

In 1997, Whittier left DLJ to form his own private investing group named Wood River Capital Fund, LLC and he amassed $30 million from family and friends. At the beginning, all seemed peachy. Whittier invested heavily in tech stocks, which went well with the dotcom bubble of the late '90s. In 1997, the year the NASDAQ went up 87%, Wood River's memorandum proudly claimed that it had more than doubled in value. Thirty-three and tiring of New York, Whittier left with his wife and kids for the greener scenery of Sun Valley, Idaho, home to the actual Wood River after which his hedge fund was named. He settled in the Sun Valley area of Ketchum, a mountain town with a population of under 3,000, notable as the home of actor Tom Hanks, writer Ernest Hemingway and many other celebrities. It also happened to be home to many former Wall Street money managers. Whittier established a Wood River office out of his temporary home in downtown Ketchum while beginning construction on a massive house nearby.

After settling in to Ketchum, Whittier's second year wasn't bad either. While the NASDAQ fell almost 40% in 2000 as the dotcom bubble burst, Wood River was able to boast to its investors that it had gained two percent, which while not great, was far better than the index. Whittier took this as a sign of success and began his ostentatious expansion, returning to his Silicon Valley roots. He signed a five-year lease on a sizeable office in San Francisco with annual rent over $375,000.

The trouble was Whittier's grandiosity did not match his performance. While he was able to maintain slight gains for 2000 despite the fall of the market, the next two years brought significant losses. Unlike the first two years, he relayed no specifics in his memorandum to his investors, merely claiming that the portfolio "declined in value (although still outperforming the benchmark)." And Whittier's performance was not his only source of trouble. He neglected to pay $45,000 worth of taxes that year in California, and, at the same time, Credit Suisse filed suit against Whittier's New York-based operations, claiming that Whittier had not provided them with over $1.6 million worth of securities that they were owed in trades.

With all of this over his head, Whittier charged forward and decided to move on from managing family and friends' money, and to open a more formalized hedge fund. Just three weeks after the Credit Suisse suit, he formed Wood River Partners LP, and began to raise capital. But that August more bad news kept coming, including an $80,000 tax lien from the state of Idaho and his San Francisco office filing suit over him not paying rent. He managed to settle the suit by paying most of the first month's rent.

Despite all of these personal issues, Whittier was able to raise enough money for his hedge fund to get started by promising high returns, usually over twenty percent, without ever outlining any specific strategies. In fact, in one meeting with potential investors, he causally described his strategies as both qualitative and quantitative, investing long term while also looking for short-term opportunities. He often met with potential clients casually in his home office while wearing a baseball cap. To many of these potential investors, it seemed like his strategies were equally haphazard. The lack of clarity steered some investors away but others bought in, even sophisticated investors like BNP Paribas and PNM Resources.

By the end of 2003, he claimed thirty-four percent net returns. A new tax lien came up, this one again from California for a sum of $54,088. Whittier plowed on and at the end of 2004, he was claiming twenty-two-percent returns while also promising good things for the future, including the hiring of four more employees. He also noted that Wood River had significant opportunity in "smaller investment companies" with "disproportionally favorable risk/reward characteristics."

On that note, Whittier wasn't completely lying. He promptly invested a fortune in a small Silicon Valley telecommunications company, Endwave, putting in a position that counted for over sixty-five percent of the fund's $265 million in assets. He even set up a special offshore account in the Cayman Islands where 98% of its content was Endwave stock. Despite being legally required to disclose any purchase of more than ten percent of a company's shares to the SEC, Whittier made no such disclosure. Nor did he tell his own investors, who were promised in the memorandum that Wood River would not invest more than ten percent in any long position.

What Whittier saw in Endwave was highly dubious, as Endwave suffered losses in each of the preceding years (despite reaching its highest stock price of $54) and sure enough, Endwave proceeded to have a most miserable summer. Between July and September, its stock price fell from $53 to $31. By the end of September, it was less than $15. Perhaps trying to find a

"Hail Mary," Whittier also invested in the penny stock Mbay, a hotly advertised internet stock at the time. However, once again, he did not disclose it. Clients began to call demanding their money back. To the first batch, Whittier replied that he couldn't. Soon thereafter, Whittier simply stopped answering the phone.

When all was said and done, investors suffered losses of $88 million. Wood River's demise was discovered shortly after the massive fall of Samuel Israel's Bayou hedge fund, then the largest Ponzi scheme in history, and calls began to come out for more regulation in the hedge fund industry. Whittier at first faced between fifteen-and-a-half and nineteen-and-a-half years in prison, but he eventually received a compassion sentence of only three years because he was needed at home to help raise his autistic son. Whittier forfeited $5.5 million personally while the court-appointed receiver sold many of the Endwave shares back to the company.

After Whittier was released from jail, he returned home to Sun Valley where his LinkedIn profile now says he works in business development. Notably, his profile has a large gap between the Berkeley years in 1989 and his business development beginnings in 2009.

Key Takeaways

One of the telltale signs of integrity is how someone shares bad news. Even those with questionable integrity will often take issue with outright lies, usually preferring to tell a white lie or simply masking the truth. These are not insignificant red flags.

Knowing that nothing truly qualified him to run a hedge fund, his investment strategies were as vaporous as a London fog, and that his only claim to fame was his father, Whittier had nothing but immediate results to fall back on. And he couldn't bear to share bad news.

Whittier would trumpet to his investors the exact percentage of returns when he performed well but failed to do so when his performance faltered. Instead of being transparent or providing any meaningful details, his only comment was that investors did better than "the benchmark."

This may seem insignificant. Some may even sympathize with Whittier's predicament, but truly thoughtful fiduciaries and managers make a habit of sharing bad news fast and are slow to bask in self-adulation.

The more salient message is, how someone does anything tends to be how they do everything. In Whittier's case, his inability to honor his commitments was glaring. He didn't pay tax liens and other obligations, had standing suits against him, had switched prime brokers three times in seven months, and had no audited financials for the last four years he was in business.

While it may have been hard for investors to keep track of these moving parts, especially since some of the claims stemmed from New York, others from Idaho and others from California, proper due diligence should have unearthed one or two commitments unmet.

* * *

HOW STRICTLY DO THE AUTHORITIES RESPOND TO FRAUD?

Due to the variability of the judicial system, many convicted scam artists receive mitigated sentences for reasons that have nothing to do with the case or the crime committed. In the case of John Whittier, he received a lighter sentence than expected because of his claim that he needed to be home to care for an autistic child. Even for those that claim that Whittier was a not a truly bad guy and did not originally set out to defraud, when con men serve mitigated sentences, justice appears to go unserved.

SUBPRIME-RICH AND CASH-POOR: THE STORY OF RALPH CIOFFI AND THE DOWNFALL OF BEAR STEARNS

s the old adage goes, "pride comes before down-fall." That's what happened to Bear Stearns, which from 2005 to 2007 consistently topped *Fortune*'s "America's Most Admired Companies" and in 2006 boasted capital of approximately $67 billion. It was hard to imagine that anything could go wrong for the financial giant. But then the mortgage crisis hit, and Bear Stearns had a front row seat in the chair of Ralph Cioffi.

According to an extensive *Bloomberg* report (Goldstein, 2007) , Cioffi was once considered a rising star at the illustrious securities firm. After his 1978 graduation from Saint Michael's College in Vermont, Cioffi eventually moved to the Big Apple and became a bond salesman for Bear Stearns. Four years later, he was promoted to head of Bear Stearns' group selling fixed-income securities. Cioffi was so successful that by 2002, he strongly considered leaving Bear Stearns to create his own hedge fund, but Bear Stearns bribed him into staying by allowing him to run his hedge fund out of their offices.

At first, it seemed that Bear Stearns had hit a home run by keeping Cioffi. Not only had Cioffi successfully founded his flagship hedge fund, but by 2006, he added another fund to the mix, the "Enhanced Fund," which used more leverage to generate better returns. In short, both funds were doing quite well. Amazingly, for the five years until 2007, neither fund reported a single losing month!

His method wasn't a breakthrough genius. He would take investor money, couple it with other loans, and buy Collateralized Debt Obligations (CDOs), which were securities created by repackaging assets into a financial structure that was backed by mortgages. Of course, the neglected detail was that many of these were subprime mortgages, where the borrower would have difficulty paying back the debt. Cioffi became one of the pioneers of the CDO strategy and since it was working so well, everyone simply adopted the old adage of "if it aint broke, don't fix it."

Cioffi continued his torrid pace of buying securities to create CDOs, purchasing so many of them that their yields dropped, prompting the vicious cycle of needing to buy even more. But that didn't pose a problem, as banks were delighted to lend money to one of Bear Stearns' most prominent hedge fund managers and a leader in the CDO world. Cioffi's operation continued until he had over $30 billion worth of securities in 2006. Less than 1% of their assets were in cash, a far cry from the 10% that most hedge funds kept in their reserves, causing Cioffi's auditor Deloitte to issue a warning to his investors. Deloitte issued another warning as they discovered that Cioffi's own team was aggressively valuing their securities more than their actual worth, a problem that was then rampant across many hedge funds. Naturally, both of these warnings were ignored as Cioffi continued producing returns and investors gladly accepted them.

When the mortgage crisis of 2007 hit, Cioffi was entirely unprepared. Not only were the funds heavily invested in subprime mortgages and other allegedly overvalued securities whose values dropped precipitously, but they also had virtually no cash on hand. Had Cioffi heeded Deloitte's warnings, he may have weathered the storm, but he compounded his problems by borrowing oodles of money without saving for a rainy day. With security prices collapsing and debts looming large, the two funds were facing their first downturn in an extremely dramatic fashion.

To make matters worse, Cioffi's "Enhanced Fund" was having a problem of its own. The fund had been set up with the help of the British bank, Barclays, who had seeded the fund with an astounding $275 million to become its sole equity investor. With the markets flailing in 2007, Barclays wanted out, as Cioffi had always given his investors the ability to redeem their money whenever they wished. However, Barclay's pullout would collapse the fund.

As all of his investors began panicking, Cioffi tried to remain calm. He assured investors that despite the current mortgage downturn, things would eventually level out. It was just a temporary dislocation that would soon be corrected. But on the inside, he was a nervous wreck. Email exchanges between him and fellow manager Matthew Tannin revealed that they were keenly aware that their firm might go under, even as the two of them publicly claimed that the fund would get out of it.

However, their public optimism didn't do much. In mid-2007, the two funds collapsed, causing investors to lose over $1.6 billion. Cioffi's two collapsed funds led to a domino effect that eventually caused all of Bear Stearns to go under, with America's favorite securities firm eventually being sold to J.P. Morgan one year later.

Cioffi and Tannin both faced criminal charges for lying to their investors, with the prosecution's cases bolstered when the authorities uncovered email exchanges between the two of them where they had clearly expressed worry. Both of them proclaimed their innocence loudly and were eventually acquitted. In 2012, a civil SEC suit forced Cioffi to pay $800,000 along with a three-year ban from the securities industry and Tannin had to pay $250,000 along with a two-year ban. According to the *Observer*, Cioffi sold off his New Jersey home to go live with his family near his parents in Florida. Understandably, he can't find work and instead quietly manages his own money while following the New York Yankees.

Key Takeaways

Unlike many of the other people in this book, it is probable that Cioffi never meant to defraud anybody. That said, many things were troubling about his investing practices. Pouring all of one's assets into securities without any cash buffer is dangerous in the best of times, but virtually insane when one is applying further leverage on top.

The fact that Cioffi's securities were (over-)valued by his own team was also disconcerting. While these two attributes may have been sufficient to keep investors away, I would like to focus on another consideration, which could have caused the collapse even had the market not gone extremely sour; that being Cioffi's unusual arrangement with Barclays.

Cioffi's second fund was literally at the mercy of Barclays. Should they decide to withdraw their capital, the fund would be done, and being that Cioffi allowed redemptions at any time, there was nothing he could do to stop them. True, Cioffi cannot be blamed for failing to predict the timing of the subprime mortgage crisis, but even a smaller crisis or any internal disaster at Barclays could have prompted them to demand their money back, leaving Cioffi and other shareholders at risk.

There was also the pesky issue of insufficient disclosure. Investors in Cioffi's first fund weren't told that the Enhanced Fund was reliant on Barclays. And even investors in Enhanced Fund were only privy to a vague disclosure in one line on the fiftieth page of the fund's memorandum, stating that Barclays' "interest in terminating the Leverage instrument might conflict with the interest of the shareholders."

In addition, Cioffi allegedly withdrew $2 million of his own money from the hedge fund in March 2007 without disclosing it to other investors. According to the SEC, "Cioffi's clandestine redemption caused the Enhanced Leverage Fund to pay out $2 million at a time when the markets were weak, and the fund was facing another month of losses, as well as escalating margin calls and forced sales." In other words, his sale adversely affected those that didn't sell a thing and created misalignment with his investors.

Aside from demanding complete disclosure, this is a reminder to ensure our investments are independent from the potentially reckless actions of any other investors, to our detriment.

* * *

Rather fail with honor than succeed with fraud

—Sophocles

THE UNSAFE HARBOR OF
PORTUS ASSET MANAGEMENT

John Pearson, the Canadian Crown prosecutor in the case of Portus Asset Management, pointed out the irony that while Portus means "safe harbor," the assets it held were "anything but . . ."

Portus was co-founded by two individuals that didn't really fit together. First was the tall Boaz Manor, with blonde spiky hair, who was known as the brains behind Portus' investments. He was born in Israel to entrepreneur Daniel Manor, who had moved the family to Toronto and found great success developing technology for traffic cameras. When his young Boaz graduated from University of Toronto with a bachelor's in applied science in 1996, it was first expected that he would enter the family business. Boaz did so for a little while, but quickly grew tired of it and soon met entrepreneur Michael Mendelson.

The round-faced Mendelson, who hailed from Texas and somehow ended up in Toronto, teamed up with Manor and they began investing in venture capital firms. As hedge funds became more popular, the two were drawn into the hedge fund party. Manor even went to New York's Paradigm Global Advisors hedge fund to study under its head, James Park. They first co-founded Paradigm Asset Management back in Toronto, with Manor as the investor and Mendelson as the CEO, but soon changed it to Portus Asset Management when Park found out and asked that they not use his fund's name.

Despite being founded by two people with limited hedge fund experience, Portus took off. Promising high returns of 12% and guaranteeing the principle was certainly attractive to many. The main attraction, however, was the referrals. Portus promised high referral fees to anybody who would bring them clients, and even convinced Canadian insurance giant Manulife to be a referral source. Manor and Mendelson were also very aggressive salesmen, and one professor from the University of Toronto remembered Manor as a perfect salesman, "young, brash and tenacious." They also offered something rarely found in hedge funds: the ability to liquidate your investments in any given week. This was virtually unheard of, as most hedge funds only allow redemption on an annual or quarterly basis, often with thirty to ninety days' notice. Within two years, Portus amassed 26,000 investors, with $750 million coming from Canadians and another $50 million from across the American border. Already the fastest-growing hedge fund in Canada, Portus soon became the largest. Manor was proclaimed the newest financial wunderkind.

However, Portus' internal story was entirely different. Instead of sending all the funds where they were supposed to be sent, it was all commingled together into one large pool. Of that, close to $110 million was used to pay sales commissions, salaries, rent utilities and the unusually high referral fees. Another $185 million was used to purchase notes from the French bank Societe General (Soc Gen); yet another $93 million simply wasn't invested at all and another $50 million gathered from 700 investors specifically into an offshore account for the sake of investing also lay there unused. Even when they did do trading, most of it was done with entities that were connected to Portus. Unlike many other frauds, none of the money was siphoned away for personal uses; it was instead used differently than it was expected to be and sometimes it wasn't used at all.

In 2005, the Ontario Securities Commission stepped in. They had been conducting an investigation of Portus since January 2005 and found numerous problems among the bookkeeping and Know Your Client (KYC) procedures.[16] The OSC put Portus into receivership, ordering both Mendelson and Manor to cooperate with the appointed receiver, KPMG. Quickly, Mendelson withdrew $320,000 for his own use, but Manor did something a lot flashier.

He fled to his home country, Israel, and on the way, he misappropriated $8.8 million in Portus money that was being held in Hong Kong to buy diamonds. Even when Manor eventually consented to go to court, he claimed to have no idea where the diamonds were and court-appointed receivers couldn't find them. To this day, they remain missing.

In the meantime, Mendelson had a change of heart (or a smart lawyer) and decided to cooperate with authorities. He pleaded guilty to one count of fraud and was sentenced to two years in prison and a permanent ban from securities trading. He eventually got out on parole after six months but still had to repay the $320,000. He now works as an independent business consultant specializing in, of all things, business ethics.

---

[16] Money managers are obliged to give their investors a variety of forms to fill out outlining their financial needs, their risk tolerance, their financial knowledge and extent of personal wealth. These are stringent regulatory requirements, which all registrants must comply with.

To his credit, Mendelson's website makes full mention of his Portus dealings, detailing how the humiliation and jail time prompted self-examination that turned him from being "ego driven and self-grasping to practicing living a life of service, using his skills and talents to help others achieve their goals." With the number of fraudsters who claimed to become clean only to be the same old selves on the inside, only time will tell if that is indeed the case. For now, Mendelson is a professor at Toronto's Schulich School of Business.

Manor did not get off as easy. The RCMP said they would press criminal charges if he wouldn't return to Canada, so Manor came back to face the justice. Without trial, he pleaded guilty to one count of fraud and another count for disobeying a court order when fleeing the country. He was sentenced to four years in prison along with a permanent securities ban and was ordered to pay the $8.8 million that he had used to buy diamonds. Already bankrupt, Manor had no way to pay back the cost of the diamonds and claimed that they must have been stolen by a middleman. Manor filed action against the middleman who he thinks has the diamonds and the results are ongoing.

More than 97% of Portus' investor money has been recovered by KPMG. Much of it came from the French Bank's SocGen notes, which guaranteed Portus' investments, and also from firms who referred their clients to Portus, who gave up their referral fees in exchange for not being held accountable for their lack of due diligence. That, along with the fact that Manor and Mendelson did not regularly siphon off money for themselves (Manor's diamonds and Mendelson's $320,000 notwithstanding), got the two of them smaller sentences than other white-collar criminals.

Key Takeaways

Thankfully, the OSC stepped in before anything terrible happened. Unlike other fraudsters who treated others' monies like their own bank accounts, the case of Portus almost defies logic. The only stealing happened at the end, when Portus was already in receivership, but the fraud was shut down for simply not following its own procedures and using money in the way it wasn't intended for, which is a red flag in and of itself.

The term "strategy drift," referring to a change in the specific way money has been invested or how the fund was promoted, has long been the fear and focus of intelligent capital allocators. However, it could and should be a warning sign for anyone. If money is not being invested according the mandate that has been outlined by the manager, irrespective of the performance, the investment needs to be reconsidered.

The main red flag in the case was the terms of liquidity. Unless one is dealing in treasuries or high-grade corporate bonds, offering weekly liquidity is either asking for trouble or making a promise you may not be able to keep. That is why most hedge funds that invest in a variety of opportunities with varying degrees of liquidity, there is usually a period during which investors can't withdraw their money or at least where several months' notice is required. For example, some small- or micro-cap stocks, which may offer the most lucrative opportunities, do not have much trading volume. In other words, someone that tries to unload a fair bit of stock will quickly drive down the share price and adversely affect every investor, not just the one redeeming. So, while investors may not like restricting access to their money, a hedge fund needs the flexibility to liquidate assets in an orderly fashion over time. The question that begs to be asked is: Why didn't Portus recognize that you can't own illiquid assets within a highly liquid structure? If they were actually trading as they claimed to be, how could they offer such liquidity? This simple answer is: they weren't.

Always ensure the liquidity of the vehicle matches the liquidity of the underlying assets. Even if that limits your own access to the capital, it will avoid some serious disappointment down the road.

* * *

WHY DO PONZI SCHEMES (SEEM TO) ENDURE?

It is shocking when Ponzi schemes have a durability to them, often lasting 10, 15 or even 20 years. Some infamous examples include: James Lewis Jr., Gerald Payne, Bernie Madoff, and Lou Pearlman—whose talent agency managed the BackStreet Boys and 'NSync bands. Both Madoff and Pearlman ran their Ponzi schemes for over 20 years. The question is why? How did they get away with it for so long?

Professor Tamar Frankel, from Boston University, claims that the answer is reinvestment. Ponzi schemes last longer than expected because people reinvest their paper profits, rather than taking capital out and thoughtfully rebalancing over time.

Any disciplined investor who somehow found themselves in an enduring Ponzi scheme would have withdrawn their capital through the disciplined practice rebalancing, leaving a relatively small residual position with the manager, long before everyone felt the pain of total loss.

THE ONLY HITTER WITH A .966 BATTING AVERAGE: BERNARD L. MADOFF

If one would have said the name "Bernie" in New York in the early 2000s, it would have inspired nostalgia and pride. Bernie, of course, was Bernie Williams, one of the most beloved New York Yankees of all time, a winner of an MVP award, four Gold Gloves, and member of four World Series Championship teams. By the late 2000s, however, "Bernie" became associated with a different New Yorker, who inspired frowns, grimaces and disgrace: Bernie Madoff.

In writing this book, I had hoped to avoid profiling Madoff, due to the barrels of ink already spilled on his case and exhaustive coverage he has received. Upon reflection, however, it dawned on me that he introduced so many innovations in his fraud that not highlighting them would be a public disservice. So, let's begin with his story.

Bernard Madoff was born in Queens, New York to Ralph Madoff, a plumber/stockbroker, and Sylvia Munter. After graduating from Hofstra University in 1960 and briefly starting law school, Madoff dropped out to follow in his father's footsteps, using the $5,000 he earned as a lifeguard and sprinkler installer to begin trading penny stocks. And after receiving a $50,000 loan from his father-in-law, Saul Alpern, he set up Bernard L. Madoff Investment Securities LLC (BLM). BLM was a "market maker," buying securities and keeping them in inventory for the sake of profitably reselling them to prospective investors. With his father-in-law continually referring Madoff to his friends, the firm began to grow. Like all market makers, Madoff initially used the National Quotation Bureau's "Pink Sheets," a system that informs potential buyers about the prices and liquidity of the various securities in which they are interested. However, in order to compete with other trading firms on the New York Stock Exchange (NYSE), Madoff's firm developed a computerized system to inform buyers of quotes, a system which later became the NASDAQ. Madoff became so successful that he grew into one of the largest market makers on Wall Street, the largest at the NASDAQ, and also its first chairman.

Aside from this legitimate and influential enterprise, Bernie had a sideline investment management business that was largely unadvertised. In this side business, Madoff claimed to invest in "blue-chip stocks" and reputable companies like Walmart, Microsoft, or Walt Disney, employing various "collar" or "split-strike conversion" strategies. These strategies involved purchasing *options*, offering Madoff the right, but not the obligation to buy or sell the securities at a future date for a specified price.[17] He claimed these were effectively hedging strategies limiting the portfolio's risk and providing a steady return.

What most people didn't realize is that taking advantage of these options also requires near-perfect market timing, and if his timing was so perfect, why employ a hedging strategy at all?

Unlike's Madoff's predecessors (e.g. Ponzi, Miller, et al.), his innovation was that his scheme did not offer unusually high returns

---

[17] The right to *purchase* a security at a later date and a pre-agreed upon price is often referred to as a *call option*; the right to *sell* a security at a later date at a pre-agreed upon price is often referred to as a *put option*.

to his investors. Instead, he offered unusually steady returns, hovering around 10% per year. He did not reveal how he knew which securities to target for his split-strike conversion, but that did not prevent investors from running to him in droves. And his well-maintained aura of exclusivity only further enhanced his reputation as one of the most successful and reliable hedge fund specialists in the world.

Enter Harry Markopolos. Markopolos, a Pennsylvanian financial analyst and portfolio manager who worked at Rampart Investment Management in Boston, was asked by his boss to look into Madoff, as one of Rampart's trading partners was heavily invested with him. Markopolos spent mere minutes looking at Madoff's revenue stream and began shaking his head at one massive red flag. How was it possible that Madoff, who was trading constantly in a market that by its very nature was volatile, provided such impeccably consistent positive returns? In a 1992 interview with the *Wall Street Journal*, Madoff claimed that his 10% returns were not out of the ordinary because the S&P returned over 16% during the same period. That being true, those S&P returns came with significant volatility along the way.

Picking up on this, Markopolos compared Madoff's returns from the previous seven years to that of the S&P 500 and found something astonishing. The S&P reported twenty-eight losing months while Madoff only reported three. Markopolos would later complain in Congress that Madoff was like a baseball player who batted .966 the entire season, a feat that even Bernie Williams in his prime couldn't accomplish.

A math whiz by nature, Markopolos spent countless hours working the numbers, trying to see how investing in the split-strike conversion strategy allegedly used by Madoff would give such constant returns. Every possible attempt or permutation he attempted proved unsuccessful. In short, he concluded that Madoff, who was then assumed to manage approximately $6 billion and the largest hedge fund in the world, was either a front-runner (one who buys stocks in advance of their clients, knowing what the clients will buy) or a massive Ponzi scheme, and Markopolos suspected that it was most likely the latter.

Markopolos wrote a seventeen-page memo detailing what he thought were a total of thirty red flags in Madoff's operation, headlined by the fact that Madoff's perfectly consistent returns were impossible. Markopolos feared that going to the FBI without the backing of the Security Exchange Committe (SEC) would cause him to be ignored. As early as 2000, Markopolos sent multiple reports to Boston's SEC office, who did nothing.

In 2005, Markopolos brought his findings to John Wilke, a *Wall Street Journal* investigative reporter. Wilke elected not to pursue the story at the time. And when Markopolos finally managed to convince Mike Garrity, the chair at the Boston SEC office, that Madoff was at least breaking the law, Garrity replied that he couldn't take action because Madoff was not based in New England. Markopolos sent it in to the New York SEC office, but they dismissed him because Rampart Investment Management, where Markopolos worked, was a competitor of Madoff. He sent an anonymous package to Eliot Spitzer, then the Attorney General of New York who had successfully prosecuted many for numerous white-collar crimes, and nothing happened. All along, Markopolos was afraid to send in his findings to the National Association of Securities Dealers, which at the time was the body that self-regulated the industry, as Peter Madoff, Bernie's brother and the Chief Compliance Officer in the Madoff Fund, was the former vice chairman there and wielded significant influence in the organization. Markopolos also feared that Madoff had organized crime connections that would endanger him and his family.

And so, the Madoff fraud went on uninterrupted until the market collapse of 2008. The global financial crisis forced investors in need of liquidity to withdraw approximately $7 billion from Madoff. By then, Madoff had long stopped his trading entirely and his only profits came from his investors, causing him to go scrambling for new investors to meet the $7 billion-worth of redemptions. But as the market was failing, people were hesitant to invest their capital and Madoff had to face the fact that his Ponzi scheme was about to collapse. He ordered his sons Mark and Andrew, who worked at the firm but had no knowledge of its true nature, to dole out $170 million in bonuses from the $200 million the firm had in assets. When they asked how he could do that when they hadn't paid their investors, Madoff admitted that the asset management division was a Ponzi scheme, "one big lie" in his own words. Mark and Andrew subsequently turned their father in to the authorities.

When all was said and done, Madoff's $826 million in assets were frozen and he was sentenced to a maximum 150 years in prison and ordered to pay $170 billion in restitution. Prosecutors estimated the scope of the fraud to be approximately $65 billion, the largest Ponzi scheme ever.

Key Takeaways

Besides triggering almost every "red flag," such as the absence of independent custodians, administrators, auditors and an inexplicable investment strategy, the Madoff fiasco was remarkably unique in its size and scope. It became the largest Ponzi scheme precisely because the promised returns were not exorbitant. The value proposition Madoff offered was the consistency of returns, not their magnitude.

Furthermore, Madoff's ability to leverage external credibility was unprecedented. He piggybacked on the legitimacy of his market-making business and his long-term relationships with the business, political and entertainment Who's Who. These associations and his chairmanships of NASDAQ and the National Association of Securities Dealers gave him undue authority, bringing in a gush of new capital and shrouding him with the cloak of exclusivity.

For investors, this is yet another reminder that authority in investing must be established, not merely presumed by association. There is always the possibility that a fox (i.e. Madoff) finds itself as the guardian of the henhouse. Much of the blame for Madoff's ability to perpetuate his scheme falls on the SEC, which failed to acknowledge Markopolos' many warnings. Investors should have recognized the most blatant red flag: the realities of capital markets. Anyone investing in securities and options, such as those in which Madoff invested, will have ups and downs, good days and bad days.

Any one who claims some securities can *definitely* deliver you a specific rate of return is a false prophet. It took Markopolos five minutes to figure this out. For investors, it took $65 billion.[18]

* * *

---

[18] Putting aside all the red flags, it is astonishing how many people had most or ALL of their money with Madoff, failing to adhere to the most basic elements of diversification and the common sense policy of not having all your assets with one investment manager.

WHAT WERE THE UNTOLD CONSEQUENCES OF THE MADOFF AFFAIR?

Besides the unprecedented financial loss, the Madoff affair resulted in at least four suicides directly linked to their second-degree involvement. They included René-Thierry Magon de la Villehuchet (co-founder of Access International Advisors LLC) who slit his wrists after discovering that all his family's wealth and 75% of the $3 billion he managed for others was lost with Madoff. William Foxton, a decorated British soldier, shot himself after having lost all his family's savings in Madoff feeder funds. Mark Madoff, Bernie's elder son, hanged himself inside his New York apartment after experiencing unsuccessful attempts to secure a Wall Street trading job, federal prosecutors' tax-fraud probes, and potential lawsuits by the court-appointed trustee. Charles Murphy, a hedge fund executive who invested more than $7 billion with Madoff, including nearly $50 million of personal wealth, leaped from the 24th floor of the Sofitel New York Hotel.

A study by University of Texas in Dallas looked at the assets managed by nearly 4,000 investment advisors at 97,000 bank branches in more than 20,000 ZIP codes. The study found that after the fraud was discovered, investors with connections to, or living near, Madoff's victims lost trust in the financial system and withdrew $363 billion from their advisors, migrating to cash. In the years that followed, as the S&P almost doubled in value, those who removed their assets from the market missed out on those returns. Simultaneously, many well-meaning advisors in the affected areas went out of business. Firms with clients in affected regions were more than forty percent more likely to close in the aftermath of the Madoff affair.

BEING TOO EARLY DOESN'T COUNT: MICHAEL BERGER'S DOOMSDAY BET

There's an old joke about the financial analyst that predicted nine of the last two recessions. Well, in the late 1990s, that analyst was Michael Berger. Berger would rant about bubbles and financial collapses, raging about the corporate world being rife with fraud and that even the world's largest companies were overvalued by as much as 40% due to various shenanigans.

Strangely enough, he was somewhat correct, as corporate frauds such as WorldCom, Tyco and Enron were exposed, revealing the very same shenanigans that Berger had predicted. In fact, Berger predicted a 70 to 90% fall for WorldCom and accused Tyco of shady accounting practices. Having said that, he also predicted similar results for almost every major American company, especially those involved in tech, and he proved to be partly correct there as well. But the most ironic of all was Berger being the pot calling the kettle black, as he was soon discovered to be fleecing investors of $400 million through a hedge fund fraud of his own.

Born in Austria, Berger left college to enroll in a teller training program for a savings and loan bank where he worked in their money management arm. He moved to New York in 1993 and launched his Manhattan Hedge Fund in August 1995. Thinking that the market was overvalued and that stock prices were going to plummet, Berger began short selling, a strategy where one borrows securities and sells them, only to buy them back at a lower price when the stock goes down.

Short selling is always a risky strategy (as stock losses cannot exceed 100% but gains on stocks could be much greater, meaning a short-seller's liability could be much greater than the size of their investment) and it was especially risky for Berger, who began using shorts to bet against the conventional market at a time when the market was on a meteoric rise. The current bull market didn't concern Berger, as he was convinced that even the most successful companies were grossly overvalued and a correction was due.

Berger's losses began right away. In April 1996, he received his first investment of $2 million and proceeded to lose 30% of it by June. He did well in the summer months though, was able to recruit new investors, and did nearly well enough to make up for his initial loss. But then September rolled around and with it came poor short-selling and losses of almost 40%. Manhattan Fund's administrator, a Bermuda-based outfit associated with Ernst and Young, noticed the losses and got ready to send a report to Berger's investors, who would surely withdraw from the start-up fund. Berger's nervousness began to mount. It seemed like a four-cornered certainty that his fund wouldn't make it out of its first year.

Quite a shame, Berger thought. After all, his trading had been successful in the summer. Clearly, his strategy would eventually work. All he needed to do was push the right buttons to sway his administrator, and ultimately the investors.

The solution was simple. His administrator had been getting information from Berger's prime broker, the well-respected firm Bear Stearns. He needed to come up with a counteracting source of information and for that, he turned to another one of his brokers, Financial Asset Management (FAM). FAM was a small Ohio firm that served as Berger's introducing broker, the go-between between Berger and the prime broker, Bear Stearns. He proceeded to cook the books, typing up a spreadsheet showing 14% gains instead of his true losses and sent it to FAM. He claimed that Bear Stearns' numbers were incorrect, as they could only service some of his trades due to his varied portfolio, and that these new numbers were the real ones, including the many trades he made using other brokers. The small Ohio-based company, which received large commissions on Berger's trades, was more than happy to accept his explanation. So Berger proudly faxed his FAM-certified spreadsheets to the administrator, who bought the story as well.

Sighing an elongated sigh of relief, Berger was able to go back to trading, where he would surely fare better in the upcoming year. But as the markets continued to rise and Berger's short-selling continued to fail, Berger found himself constantly cooking the books. He soon had to sell the same "Bear Stearns has limited access" story to his auditor, another Bermuda-based outfit, this one being an affiliate of Deloitte and Touche. All the while, Bear Stearns notified FAM, the administrator, the auditor and even the investors that according to their records, Berger's trades were in fact failing, but Berger was able to sell his fudged numbers to FAM and everyone else chose to believe the FAM statements instead of Bear Stearns.

Talk about naïve optimism and not reading fine print. If investors would have taken a look at Manhattan Hedge Fund's prospectus, they would have seen clearly that Bear Stearns was Berger's *only* broker for his trades, despite Berger's current assertions.

The same story carried on for a few years. With the bull market of the late 1990s, short-sellers across America lost money in four of the five years between 1995 and 1999, but Manhattan Hedge Fund somehow managed to turn in profits, as much as 30% in 1997. Through those years, Berger kept on proclaiming boldly doomsday for America's largest corporations and kept on being wrong. He did have to alter his external proclamations and give all sorts of excuses why it hadn't fallen yet, but inwardly, he still thought it was only a matter of time before he was right.

With every passing year, Berger became more audacious and his statements more fabricated. In December 1996, Bear Stearns claimed that he had $5.6 million in assets while his FAM statements claimed he had $15.6 million. By 1997, Bear Stearns claimed he only had $39 million while the FAM statements said he had $81 million. The discrepancy between the two more than quadrupled in one year. In 1998, the differences were at an astounding $260 million and by 1999, it was $400 million. Bear Stearns kept warning everyone they could get their hands on about the discrepancies in the numbers, but it was only in late 1999 that they really suspected fraud and contacted the SEC. The SEC shut down the fund in January 2000, Berger was arrested, and the SEC brought criminal charges against him. By then, the losses were estimated to be $400 million from 300 investors.

Berger first pleaded not guilty but did waive an indictment to show he would cooperate with authorities. He later pleaded guilty to falsifying documents going back to 1996 and after being released on bail, was scheduled to be sentenced in a New York court on March 1, 2002. But when the day of judgment came, Berger did not show up in court. He had fled the country.

For a while, nobody knew where the missing fund manager was. In 2007, authorities both in the US and abroad intensified their search and narrowed down their search to Berger's hometown in Austria. Berger was wanted in Austria as well, as at least four of his victims were Austrian institutions that lost around $50 million, and fifteen Austrian policemen were sent to find him. He was accosted while driving a red car on a rural highway and was taken into custody. Being an Austrian citizen, he wasn't extradited to the US, where he would have faced more than ten years in prison when combining his frauds with leaving the country while on bail. Instead, he was imprisoned in Austria for only two years.

Manhattan was one of the earliest hedge funds to collapse in the early 2000s, causing many on Wall Street to get nervous. Investors tried suing Bear Stearns for their losses, but the suit was quickly dismissed. With Bear Stearns giving them constant warnings in advance, investors had nobody to blame but themselves.

Key Takeaways

In this otherwise classic cooking-the-books fraud, the greatest red flag was the simple fact Berger was making profits in what was then an unprofitable strategy and all of the companies on his "to-fall" list just kept on climbing. Investors should have taken notice.

The easiest way to spot a fraud is when someone's investment theses or predictions are contradicted by reality, and yet they still manage to generate a healthy return. It makes no sense!

Even more shockingly, investors ignored Bear Stearns' repeated warnings that the numbers didn't match up. They ignored (or didn't read) Berger's own prospectus, which indicated that Bear Stearns was his only prime broker.

Any time a credible institution raises a red flag, a prompt and thorough investigation is warranted. Perhaps they trusted Berger due to the other credible institutions involved. Bear Stearns was his prime broker and custodian, but he also had an independent administrator and an independent auditor from Big Four accounting firms that may have given investors false comfort.

Either way, investors placed too much trust in the manager, ignored the warning signs and were left with a reminder that regardless of what the financials say, nothing substitutes for common sense.

* * *

IN WHAT MARKETS DO FRAUDS TEND TO THRIVE?

Frauds are most likely to proliferate during periods of transformation, revolution and change. Whether those changes are technological (e.g. the dot-com era), geopolitical (e.g. Industrial Revolution), opportunistic (e.g. the gold rush), legal (e.g. cannabis), or cultural (e.g. social media), swindlers will take advantage of the increased uncertainty.

This proliferation of frauds goes into further overdrive if the change is coupled with rising markets. It is in this environment that people optimistically adjust their expectations upwards and become ill-prepared for drawdowns. Studies during the late 1990s, when markets were booming, showed investors believed that returns from the stock market would be in the high teens for the decade ahead, notwithstanding that the historic returns on equities was under ten percent (Konnikova, 206).

This was supported by economists Hyman Minsky and Charles Kindleberger, who claimed that if you apply a macroeconomic view to frauds, you'll discover that the most intense clustering of frauds occurs in the midst of (or immediately following) bull markets, when returns come easy and people ask far fewer questions than they should. Similarly, the majority of frauds are discovered in a bear market, when investors get skittish, start pulling capital or begin asking the questions they needed to ask all along.

In summary, the combination of dramatic changes and heated markets create the optimal environment for fraud, where investors don't realize that something is truly too good to be true.

COMPUTER ASSOCIATES: CREATING THE 35-DAY MONTH

There was a time when IBM had a virtual monopoly on the hardware industry, but regulatory pressure clamped down, forcing them to start selling a wide range of products. It was then that an unlikely partnership formed between bombastic Chinese immigrant Charles Wang and a quiet programmer Russell Artzt.

At first, they began selling and developing IBM products with moderate success. Then they aimed higher. They formed a partnership with Swiss company Computer Associates to begin selling a data management product, CA-Sort, which had sold well in Europe but never quite made it in the US. Combining aggressive sales techniques with a "steal" of a product, Wang had great success and realized that for his company to thrive, all he needed to do was sell products, not develop them.

Wang proceeded to go on an acquisition binge that lasted decades. In the early 1980s alone, he spent over $60 million acquiring other companies and gaining the rights to sell their products, including dishing out $22 million for a Phoenix-based software company and $27 million for an early Silicon Valley start-up. After seeing the early success of this model, Wang continued to expand even more until 1989 when his company, now renamed Computer Associates (CA), became the first software company to earn more than a billion in annual revenues. Based in Long Island, it emerged as one of the most powerful corporations in the region, with some well-known Long Islanders serving on the company's board, eventually paving the way for Wang to later purchase the local hockey team, the New York Islanders.[19]

Through it all, CA was heavily criticized for its unsatisfactory customer service, as they would sell products but offer no way of updating, refining or evolving them, leaving their customers with products that would soon become obsolete and without any helpful service. *Fortune* magazine would later describe CA as a "4 billion dollar corporation run like a twenty person start-up," where the only thing that mattered was the sales department and how many sales it could push forward, with all other departments being essentially ignored. But who had time to care for the customers when Computer Associates was making so much money? It was this brash attitude that prompted Wang to attempt some hostile takeovers of other tech companies and in 1988, he was even sued for claims of bribery in a hostile bid to take over a computer consulting company. As the acquisition binge continued, Computer Associates made one acquisition that heavily changed the course of their existence. CA acquired UCCEL, originally a college start-up in Texas, for a sum of $800 million but even more important was their pickup of Sri Lankan immigrant Sanjay Kumar.

Kumar, who had fled Sri Lanka for South Carolina when he was just a teen, had advanced rapidly through the UCCEL system, despite having no college degree. At Computer Associates, he advanced even further and by 1993, Charles Wang's older brother Tony Wang was forced to retire just to

---

[19] The New York Islanders has some bad luck with fraudster owners, as it was first owned by Stephen Walsh and Paul Greenwood of WG Trading, and then by Kumar and Wang.

make room for Kumar on the board. Kumar then made his way up to CFO in the '90s and, during that tenure, CA continued its success through buying more companies, including Platinum Technologies for $3.5 billion in what was then the software industry's largest acquisition.

But as the end of the '90s neared, Computer Associates faced a throng of negative publicity over ill-advised stock options. Wang, Kumar, and Artzt had taken stock options totaling $1.1 billion, an amount equal to the entire revenue of CA that year. Although some corporate greed is acceptable, this exorbitant amount was simply unprecedented. Now, CA didn't just have unhappy customers; even shareholders were displeased. In the ensuing melee, Wang was forced out as CEO and he rechanneled his bombastic efforts to focus on running the New York Islanders, where his signature moves included firing a general manager after six weeks and replacing him with the backup goalie, along with dishing out (possibly) the worst sports contract in history, giving goalie Rick DiPietro a fifteen-year contract that lasted well beyond his playing years.

It came to the relief of many that Kumar was given full reign as CEO of CA. After all, while Wang's pompous nature did a lot of good for the company, including its many acquisitions, his neglect of consumer and public relations left a black mark on the firm. With a wiry frame and sporting a thin moustache, Kumar projected an aura of serenity and promised to bring a calmer reign and "gold standard" to CA. He even managed to convince legendary former SEC accountant Walter P. Schuetze, an eventual member of the Accounting Hall of Fame, to join the board, which was previously comprised of insiders and members of the Wang family.

But if anybody thought Kumar was an improvement, they were markedly wrong. In a scheme that had preceded the stock option debacle, Kumar had already been cooking CA books for a few years. Conspiring with the head of sales, Stephen Richards, Kumar had been inflating CA revenues using the "35-day month." Kumar had left the books of the company open for five days extra after every month, adding five days' worth of revenue to each month's accounts, ballooning their overall annual revenues. Richards helped by having the sales department back-date all the contracts to match the cooked books.

The effects of these changes were enormous. For all of the quarters in 2000 alone, they were inflated above 20% in each quarter and in one of those quarters, revenues were over-inflated by more than 50%. For one quarter in 2001, revenues were overstated by more than 60%. What about the internal accounting department? Well, true to the CA model that only sales mattered, the *New York Times* would later report that CA's internal accounting division consisted of only five employees, including part-time staff. That was for a company that by then had $6 billion in annual sales and 20,000 employees.

But after shareholders filed a suit against CA, a federal investigation ensued. Kumar resigned as CEO in April 2004 and by that September, he was indicted by a Brooklyn grand jury. With his sentencing done a week after Enron executive Jeffrey Skilling was sentenced to twenty-four years in prison, Kumar was not expected to get off lightly. In the end, he received twleve years in prison and an $8 million fine for his role in the scam, for attempting to pay $3.7 million to a potential witness as well as lying to federal investigators. Stephen Richards was also sentenced to seven years of prison but there was no evidence that Wang was connected in any way, and he continued to run the New York Islanders.

As a company, Computer Associates almost shut down and had arranged to pay $225 million in restitution just to stay alive. Replacing Kumar as CEO was Canadian IBM veteran John Swainson to bring calm to the hectic company. Among the sweeping changes he implemented were developing codes of ethics for the salespeople and placing ethics-promoting signage across the company building. In 2007, the new board released a statement accusing Charles Wang of being behind the Kumar fraud, as well as claiming that he instilled a "culture of fear" that led his employees to disregard rules simply to please him. Wang denied the assertions and since the statute of limitations had already passed, the Feds didn't bother investigating it. Whether he was involved in the fraud, we may never know.

As for Russell Artzt, he was never charged and continued to work at CA until his retirement in 2015.

Key Takeaways

As we saw with Parmalat's Calisto Tanzi, corporate fraud does not happen in a vacuum. It is company culture that drives individuals to "hit their numbers" at any cost. It is culture that drives subordinates to enter deep into the grey zone of dishonesty and even deliberately deceiving when necessary. When that culture is coupled with fear, employees are tempted to "do whatever it takes" to please their single-minded superiors.

Blatant disregard for customers and even shareholders is almost always a red flag, suggesting that management may do whatever is necessary to advance their own interests at the expense of others.

Furthermore, how a company reports and how much it invests in advancing transparency is a telltale sign of its respect for its partners and shareholders. Much like with Madoff's one-man auditor, for a company like CA with 20,000 employees and $6 billion in annual sales to have only five employees in accounting, is simply inconceivable and an actively waved red flag on a very high flagpole.

* * *

It is a capital mistake to theorize before one has data. Insensibly one begins to twist facts to suit theories instead of theories to suit facts

—Sherlock Holmes

TURNING THE TABLES ON THE LEGEND OF SIR FRANCIS DRAKE

The bogus fortune scam is one of the most popular scams in history. Savvy salespeople approach a naïve investor claiming that they could be the beneficiaries of a massive fortune, if only they could contribute to the legal fees necessary to battle for it. In the early twentieth century, these scams were almost as commonplace as sliced bread, but none did it better than Oscar Hartzell's abuse of the "Drake fortune."

The story begins back in 1596 with the passing of Sir Francis Drake, a legendary admiral in the English navy. Drake was born to a simple farming family. However, with untamed ambition, he led a group of English and French sailors in a brazen attack on a Spanish fleet at a time when Spain's King Philip II's kingdom seemed virtually untouchable. The coup netted £40,000, as well as subsequent funding from various English nobles to sail the sea. He claimed northern California for England and captured a treasure ship off the coast of Peru, all the while paving the way for England to become a colonial power. The Spanish called him a pirate and demanded for him to be executed. Queen Elizabeth responded by knighting him. His expeditions gave Queen Elizabeth a reported £100,000 (the equivalent of many billions today), but he kept more than his fair share for himself. Playing a large role in England's 1588 battle against the Spanish Armada, Sir Francis' legend only grew, and when he died leaving no heir, rumors grew aplenty about where his fortunes would go.

The rumors continued for centuries and led many Drakes to begin asking about the fortune. It was only in 1900 that this really took off as a fraud and for that, Richard Rayner (whose book on the topic is the source of much of this information) credits the arrival of the telephone. Con men began gathering the people named Drake in the phonebook and called them about how they were setting up pools to fund the legal battles to reclaim Sir Francis' fortune. Of course, no such fortune, nor any legal battles actually existed, but it worked like a charm.

One of these tricksters, Susie Whittaker, recruited lawyer Milo Lewis to work with her on selling the rights to the Drake fortune. Traveling through the farming town of Monmouth, Illinois, they arrived at the door of the Hartzell home. Whittaker claimed that she was the cousin of a "George Drake" and needed the money to battle for the fortune, and Hartzell's mother dished out $6,500 to Whittaker and Lewis, who subsequently disappeared. When Mrs. Hartzell's son Oscar heard about this, he began asking around the neighborhood and found that many fell prey to Whittaker and Lewis but still believed that they would get their money back and that the team had merely gone to fight the required legal battles.

Hartzell soon realized that there was a market for this fraud and he was intrigued by its possibilities. After spending time as a local deputy sheriff, he had been in a number of failed businesses and was looking for a new opportunity. He traveled to the Sioux City library to look into the Drake legacy and then used his sheriff connections to locate Whittaker and Lewis. Instead of arresting them, he jokingly forgave them and told them that as a team, they could turn this into a major league enterprise.

Forming the Sir Francis Drake Association, they began selling the rights to the Drake fortune, first only to those with the surname Drake. As success came, they began targeting anybody at all, with the continued claim that Whittaker's cousin was "George Drake" and investors would rake in the proceeds they donated plus interest. When Illinois authorities began frowning upon the association and disbarred Lewis, Hartzell conveniently booted out Whittaker and Lewis and claimed his own relation to the Drake family.

Unfortunately for many, the Illinois authorities never determined that Hartzell was selling a fraud and this allowed him to drive his enterprise to a whole new level. With the Roaring '20s paving the way for ridiculous investor optimism, Hartzell used his charming smile and personality to win over farmers who wanted a piece of the Drake fortune and built a network of agents to sell with him. Even as the crash of 1929 happened and the subsequent mistrust of Wall Street, Hartzell's farming background endeared him to his targets, despite dressing with the panache of a Wall Street banker. He eventually amassed an investor base of 80,000 individuals and moved to London with his ill-gotten proceeds. Far from the gazes of his investors and, more importantly, the reaches of the law, Hartzell began living lavishly. He continued sending to his faithful investors updates on how the battle was proceeding and reassuring them that they would soon see the fruits of their investments.

Authorities all over the world knew something was up but Hartzell cleverly avoided them. With his time as deputy sheriff giving him sufficient legal knowledge, he made sure to commit no crime while in London and didn't send out anything that would constitute mail fraud, while still receiving the monies pouring in. While the US State Department, FBI, Scotland Yard, and US Post Office Department were all building cases against him, they had little concrete information, virtually nothing they could try him on and no one that would bear witness against him. But as is oftentimes the case, there was one determined man to finally bring him down, a fellow Westerner named John Sparks.

A towering figure at 6'2" and 235 pounds, Sparks was a straight-shooting Lutheran who worked for the Post Office Inspection Service, whose main purpose was to sniff out frauds. The Post Office knew something was up by 1928 and sent Sparks to Iowa to do some research. Initially, he found nothing but dead ends, as Hartzell's investors believed so firmly in him that they would not testify. But as the crash of 1929 occurred, exposing or indirectly ending numerous other frauds, Sparks decided to make this case his baby, moving his entire family to Sioux City to snuff it out.

Sparks recruited people to send letters to Hartzell, hoping to nab him for mail fraud when he replied, but even in London, Hartzell was afraid that someone was after him and sent terse replies to "see his local agents." After trying to gather information from Hartzell's family and failing, he decided to go after his agents and struck gold there. He collected enough evidence from them to try Hartzell on mail fraud and had him deported from London and put on trial in 1933. What Hartzell hadn't factored in was that not only was it illegal to send fraudulent mail, but it was also illegal to recruit others to do it for you.

Throughout the trial, Hartzell's investors stood by his side. Prosecutor Harry Reed was turned into a local villain, and even when Hartzell was imprisoned in Kansas, his agents continued selling rights for the Drake fortune. Proclaiming his own innocence, Hartzell himself went insane and was transferred to a medical center in Springfield, Missouri in 1936. He died there in 1943. In total, Hartzell's investors lost an estimated $2,000,000, or the equivalent of over $300,000,000 today.

Key Takeaways

The first takeaway here is the wariness of an "upfront fee." There are certainly areas of commerce where an upfront fee is warranted, often in domains where the vendor could be abused by the customer and/or where there is meaningful work to be done upfront or any industry that employs retainers. In most instances, however, a fee is not warranted until value has been transferred or created, as there's nothing stopping many from taking the upfront fee and disappearing or simply not bothering to do their job. One should be especially wary when the fee is directed to something vague, like the fight for a mythical estate, as opposed to very specific and concrete expenses (e.g. a specific license, the billable hours of specific professionals, etc.) with defined outcomes and time horizons.

In addition, there needs to be an ongoing audit or analysis, ensuring that someone is not living pretty off the fees that are being generated. This speaks to the issue of aligning incentives. If someone is making a comfortable livelihood off the case (even assuming that it is real) with incentive to drag it out for as long as possible, this puts the sponsor of the suit at odds with the investors therein.

Today, litigation finance is a growing and, at times, highly profitable strategy. There are numerous legitimate and capable

institutions who are financing cases and resolving a market ineffi-
ciency, by matching those who have capital and those who need it
to pursue their legitimate claims. The key takeaway for the investors that finance these suits is to ensure their alignment of interest
with all the parties involved. Just imagine a lawyer is told that
any case he takes on will be financed by some hedge fund. How
discerning will they be in selecting their cases since they're getting
paid to bill, not win? And, more importantly, what's the probability that the investors of that fund will be satisfied with the results?
Alignment across the entire value creation chain is paramount.

The second takeaway revolves around basic due diligence.
At the same time Hartzell was conducting his scam, William
Cameron Morrow Smith was performing a similar swindle in
Pennsylvania, selling the rights to the "Baker" estate that supposedly included the Liberty Bell, the tomb of Benjamin Franklin
and much of downtown Philadelphia. Unlike Hartzell, Smith
required his investors to be named Baker, Becker or Barker, but
he still conned over 3,000 investors using a fake will until he
was accosted in 1936. These were just two of the many fraudsters to jump on this bandwagon, and the number of victims
from this scam is almost immeasurable. Yet, all could have been
avoided with basic due diligence. It's easy to claim ownership of
tons of real estate and historic landmarks and it's equally easy to
verify if those claims are actually true. The Baker estate professed
to cover historic landmarks such as Benjamin Franklin's grave,
Independence Hall, and others. Swept up by the gold-fever men-
tality, nobody caught up in this scam actually bothered to check.

* * *

Fool me once, shame on you; fool me twice, shame on me

—George Horne

HOW TO MANIPULATE $360 TRILLION: THE CURIOUS CASE OF LIBOR AND THOMAS HAYES

Have you ever taken out a mortgage on a house, a loan on a car or a business? If so, you were probably affected by the LIBOR (London Interbank Offered Rate), a rate used worldwide by banks to determine interest rates that affect over $360 trillion worth of loans. And, in one of the most brazen financial scandals in recent memory, this incredibly important LIBOR rate was manipulated by a British trader named Tom Hayes.

Despite having a generic name and a bland face that may be overlooked in even the smallest of crowds, there was something highly unusual about Tom Hayes. He slept in a bed with superhero linen well into his twenties. He drank hot chocolate when others drank alcohol, and according to one friend, he had "terrible taste in clothing." He was unusually direct and awkward in his communications. The first questions he would ask people at parties was how much they earned and would comment on their weight. He didn't seem to connect with fellow coworkers, so much so that he was nick-named "Rain Man" after the autistic Dustin Hoffman character in the 1988 movie of the same name. Sure enough, he would eventually be diagnosed with Asperger Syndrome, a form of autism, but for the time being, he was simply regarded as odd. Odd, but brilliant.

Still in his twenties, Hayes was a highly successful trader who had earned a math degree and then worked for the Royal

Bank of Scotland and the Royal Bank of Canada before moving to Tokyo to focus on derivatives while trading for UBS. Even when the market began its downturn in 2007, derivatives still traded well and so did Hayes, making $70 million in positive trades over the first eight months of 2008. Nonetheless, he had made the unfortunate miscalculation that interest rates, including LIBOR, would remain stable. He had bet an enormous amount of money based on that assumption, only to be shocked with the news that Lehmann Brothers collapsed. Fearing that the increased market risk would cause LIBOR to rise, Hayes knew that he had only one way to keep his profits up: by manipulating LIBOR.

Monitored by the British Banking Association, LIBOR was set daily by a committee of banks gathering information to help calculate how much it would cost for one bank to borrow money from another and then submitting their estimates. Hayes had met many of those submitters during his time as a trader and what struck him was that these submitters would make their estimates by asking trading brokers. If you knew the right brokers, you'd be able to control what information goes to set LIBOR.

Hayes set out to work immediately after the Lehmann Brothers crash. He sent out emails to brokers asking them to report the lowest rates possible, even promising one of them a cash reward of $50,000-$100,000 to do so. Hayes also sent a message to an acquaintance at ICAP, the world's largest inter-dealer broker who would publish a daily estimated prediction of LIBOR, to have that prediction lean toward the lowest possible estimate. Sure enough, despite the crash of Lehmann Brothers and the fact that banks were surely not going to lend other banks without demanding heightened returns, still, LIBOR stayed low.

While likely the mastermind, Hayes was not the only one who knew about his little scheme. The *Wall Street Journal* reported that when Citigroup's Asia department tried to lure away Hayes from UBS with a $3.4 million signing bonus, his boss at UBS emailed an executive that "Hayes' strong connections with LIBOR setters in London are invaluable." It was this knowledge that made Hayes so highly sought after, but when push came to shove UBS was not willing to match Citigroup's bonus offer and less than a year after his LIBOR scam, Hayes moved to Citigroup's Tokyo branch.

His new boss at Citi's Tokyo branch, a transported American named Chris Cecere, knew all about Hayes' LIBOR connections and tried to get Citibank to then join the ranks of those setting TIBOR, the Tokyo version of LIBOR, as well as getting Citibank's London operations "in" on LIBOR trading. After contacting the right people in Citi's London branch, Cecere was all but assured that Citi would make sure to lower the London LIBOR rates. The problem? The guy in charge in London was Andrew Thursfield, a no-nonsense fellow who didn't feel like altering anything just to get a little ahead on a few investments. Additionally, Thursfield was told that it was coming from LIBOR expert Tom Hayes and Thursfield had been turned off by Hayes in their only previous encounter in which Hayes essentially boasted about how good he was. The result? Thursfield did not lower the rates and he even launched an internal investigation as to why he was asked to lower them in the first place.

In the meantime, the low LIBOR rates began to attract the interest of many in the financial world. Many business journalists thought banks were intentionally setting LIBOR at low rates to hide the fact that they were short on cash and the American Commodities Futures Trading Commission began a full-scale investigation. All along, Hayes tried getting Thursfield to change, but the looming investigation scared the London team even more, to the point where Citi eventually let Hayes go in 2010. With the investigation brewing, Hayes offered to keep his mouth shut for a hefty sum. Citigroup ignored his offer and let him and his hefty bonus go.

No longer the hotshot trader, Hayes returned to London a lesser man. One good thing did come out of his Tokyo trip, however. He met a young British lawyer named Sarah Tighe at a Tokyo swimming pool. He married her shortly after coming back to London and after having a son, they bought a seven-bedroom house in southern England.

In the meantime, the news of LIBOR rigging began to go public. In June 2012, British bank Barclays agreed to pay a $100 million settlement to forty-three US states and the District of Colombia, which put serious pressure on London's Serious Fraud Office (SFO) to look into LIBOR. They did, and six months later, they came knocking at Hayes' door. After hearing that UBS was forced to reach a $1.5 billion settlement and that the US attorney general would go after Hayes personally, Hayes knew where the tide was turning and spilled everything to the SFO. He named twenty-five other people involved.

Hayes would be sentenced to fourteen years in prison, with Judge Jeremy Cooke saying he wanted to send a message to financial traders. Chris Cecere got off completely and went on to work for hedge funds in New York, and while two other LIBOR-manipulating bankers were charged by the American Department of Justice, they received only one-to-two years' prison time. Six London traders who were charged by the SFO were eventually acquitted in 2016. However, the big banks got their fair share of fines. Germany's Deutsche Bank, the Royal Bank of Scotland, and the French Bank Societe Generale were fined over $2 billion by US and UK authorities, while Deutsche Bank ended up paying another $2.5 billion in 2015 to European and US authorities.

UK authorities founded the Financial Conduct Authority (FCA) to regulate financial areas, including LIBOR. However, fewer people began to rely on LIBOR and by July 2017, the FCA announced that it would phase out LIBOR by 2021 and is currently searching for LIBOR's replacement.

Key Takeaways

Initially, the moral of the LIBOR story is hard to see, as it happened on such a macro behind-the-scenes setting. Average investors generally do not question why interest rates are fixed at their current rate; that's for the governments and big banks to deal with. What the story does, however, is remind investors that they need to employ the healthy discipline of looking at illogical market conditions and asking why.

Almost every time that capital markets are under stress and liquidity gets tight due to looming crisis or uncertainty, the spread between low-risk bonds like US Treasuries and riskier debt like the bonds of most corporations blows out. In other words, during periods of instability, people or institutions need much more incentive to lend money, and that translates into considerably higher interest rates. After the virtually unprecedented collapse of Lehmann Brothers, then one of the largest financial institutions on the planet, it was unfathomable that interest rates would not spike through the roof, and yet it didn't (immediately) happen. This should have prompted investors to ask "Why?" And even though they wouldn't have discovered the answer until the LIBOR scandal unfolded over time, the very discipline of asking "why" will lead them to making better decisions.

As well, the LIBOR story is yet another example of misaligned incentives. Putting aside Hayes involvement, and even if no trader attempted to manipulate LIBOR, there was a real possibility that the banks themselves would have skewed LIBOR lower, because by raising their submissions to higher interest rates, they would be effectively acknowledging that they are short on cash. And with the collapse of Lehman Brothers, no bank wanted to get in line behind them or to have their stock prices pummeled by signaling their own problems to the market. And since they submit these rates with virtually no oversight, their incentive was to keep LIBOR artificially low, albeit divorced from the fundamentals of the market.

* * *

If you don't know where you are going, you'll end up someplace else

—Yogi Berra

It is not the strongest of the species that survive, not the most intelligent, but the one most responsive to change

—Charles Darwin

THE FUTURE
OF FRAUD

As the famous Wayne Gretzky quote goes, "Skate to where the puck is going, not where it has been." Much of this book has focused on the frauds of the past. Of even greater importance, however, is anticipating the frauds of the future.

With the turn of the century, we have witnessed unprecedented technological advances that have transformed every market. From shopping for groceries to filing taxes, technology has renovated every facet our lives; investing is no exception. New investment opportunities, platforms, and methods of analysis have arisen via the internet. Artificial intelligence, algorithmic models, blockchain, and big data have been introduced to transactions. This affects how people invest as well as how the investment community is regulated and accredited. In fact, as of 2019, one will need to pass an artificial intelligence section to become a Chartered Financial Analyst.

In short, the finance of the future will be profoundly different from the finance of the past. And, as for the six factors of fraud detection, they will change considerably as well.

Third-Party Verification

The first element of fraud that we discussed is the need for third-party verification. Whether it be through auditors, administrators or verification of agency or other confirmatory bodies, we saw firsthand the folly of taking scam artists at their word. With modern-day technology, third-party verification takes on a completely new meaning.

Today, F. Bam Morrison could not go to Wetumka and convince its residents that he represented Bohn's circus, as a Google search of Bohn's circus yields no results. Similarly, if a modern-day George Parker attempts to sell you the deed to the Brooklyn Bridge, a quick search will tell you that the New York City Department of Transportation maintains it. From looking up SEC filings to searching a company's office location on Google Earth, there are now many freely available data points and verifiers online to help us distinguish fact from fiction, weeding out many potential charlatans in the process.

Furthermore, verification systems are improving. Auditors, for example, have historically been forced to rely on imperfect information, as there are usually mountains of data to sift through and they are in no position to guarantee that everything in the financial statements is 100% correct. In fact, one of the caveats of the auditing profession is that an auditor's objective is to give "reasonable assurance" that the financial statements are "free of material misstatements," as combing through every piece of a company's inventory is virtually impossible. Accounting giant Ernst and Young has already deployed "EY Helix," a technology platform to help them manage data in an audit and other big accounting firms have followed suit.

Similarly, administrators have begun to embrace technology as well. In one example, a Bermuda-based administrator, Opus, which now serves over 425 funds with a combined $14 billion under management, limits its exposure to human verifiers. To enhance objectivity and remove human biases, such as being convinced by a persuasive client to overvalue investments based on subjective factors, its use of algorithms to value investments will lead to more objectivity and less potential for manipulation.

For those that believe accountants and administrators cannot be manipulated, you haven't been paying careful attention. In one notable case not covered in this book, Eddie Antar, the owner of "Crazy Eddie." double-counted his inventory to prop up his books while taking his company public. As part of the process of taking his company public, Antar made sure to get big-named auditors. And while they were slaving away on his file, Eddie made it his business to treat them to the finest dinners and subtly greased them in any way that he could. In the process, he made sure that the glaringly obvious red flags in his operation were graciously overlooked. In fact, when Antar felt that his assigned auditor was immune to "grease," he would file a complaint with the firm to try to get a new auditor assigned.

While the objectivity of fact-based and data-rich technology is promising, *The Globe and Mail* reported that a study by the Association of Certified Fraud Examiners (Silcoff 2017) found that just four percent of external auditors caught fraud perpetrated by their client and, surprisingly, software tools caught even less. It will take a while for software to develop to the point where it can truly sniff out fraud, so our own continued vigilance is essential.

Checks and Balances

Checks and balances aren't only important in government. As the Allen Stanford case reminds us, it's imperative for a financial institution, bank or custodian to have an active, independent board of directors, to limit the power of any single individual with access to the capital of others.

Technology has limited human folly here as well. In 2014, a Japanese venture capitalist firm, Deep Knowledge, officially placed a robot named VITAL (Validating Investment Tool for Advancing Life Sciences) to its board of directors. VITAL's purpose was to analyze trends in life science companies to find good investments, and it has successfully introduced two companies, Pathway Pharmaceuticals and Insilico Medicine, to Deep Knowledge's portfolio. Though the primary purpose of VITAL is not the prevention of fraud, rather the identification of better investment opportunities, the presence of a VITAL on a board would add a layer of independence to a decision-making process to act a firm "check" on others. A future Allen Stanford could not convince VITAL to pour money into his dubious investments, no matter how many times he was knighted and by whom.

While the online world provides a measure of protection, it also increases potential abuses. Fraudsters can no longer be geographically contained. They could do plenty of damage from the cloud. This has been particularly true with cryptocurrencies.

Cryptocurrency, perhaps best known by its most prominent variety, Bitcoin, is virtual currency that is created and traded online. While most cryptocurrencies are not backed by any intrinsic value or any specific sovereignty, its legitimacy as a currency is based on the fact that all trades are recorded on a public ledger (known as a blockchain). It has a limited supply and decentralized nature, with many miners that keep the blockchain intact. Bitcoin is far and away the most popular, with a well-publicized blockchain that is confirmed and real; Bitcoin is only issued as a reward for people who "mine" the Bitcoin blockchain and keep it intact. Over 100,000 merchants now accept Bitcoin and Bitcoin ATMs have popped up all over the world. That said, while the emergence of cryptocurrencies was premised on the checks and balances of the masses, the emergence of new cryptocurrencies has converted this nascent asset class into a haven for swindlers, through it's utilization of Initial Coin Offerings (ICOs).

An ICO is a way for a cryptocurrency issuer to raise capital, issuing cryptocurrency in exchange for cash. ICOs have become a perfect tool for fraudsters who claim to issue a new cryptocurrency of their own and receive cash or another already functioning cryptocurrency in exchange for their own newly issued cryptocurrency. With no regulations and a product that the average investor doesn't fully understand, issuing a fake cryptocurrency for real value is relatively easy. One notable example was the Swiss company Ecoin, which began issuing its own cryptocurrency and pitched it to investors who didn't realize that, unlike Bitcoin, Ecoin wasn't distributed on any network or blockchain. It was simply stored on Ecoin's own servers. Essentially, Ecoin concocted its own worthless currency and began selling it for cash. It amassed over four million Swiss francs before Swiss authorities shut it down and revealed that they were looking into eleven other cryptocurrencies that they believed to be fake.

In *The Atlantic*, David Z. Morris notes how in the realm of cryptocurrencies, frauds can often do better than real cryptocurrency, citing how developer Gnosis and Mumbai-based start-up

OneCoin began issuing their cryptocurrency on the same day. While Gnosis was a well-respected operation using top-flight engineers and receiving generous coverage from the *Wall Street Journal*. It managed to raise $12 million in its first twelve minutes and did well but not exceedingly well. On the other hand, its competitor OneCoin proceeded to do much better, raising over $350 million in its ICO. The unfortunate reality: Gnosis did develop a currency on blockchain's distributed network, whereas OneCoin did not. It was a simple Microsoft Excel spreadsheet with numbers that, for all practical purposes, had no ability to function as a medium of exchange. Before Indian authorities could react to the fraud, the funds had been transferred abroad and investors were left holding the empty bag.

With the absence of checks and balances in the Wild-West world of ICOs, we have the potential to be victimized by a crime that's premised on avoiding the very pain it causes.

Compliance and Regulation

Rudy Kurniawan's wine fraud demonstrated how a lack of regulation tends to invite foxes into the henhouse. With no rules for them to obey and no guidelines for investors to demand, charlatans tend to thrive in such environments. The advancement of technology had both improved compliance and opened new arenas where fraudsters can operate more freely than ever before.

Consider domains such as insider trading which have heretofore been regarded as almost unregulatable. The line between public and insider information has been murky and keeping track of billions of daily trades makes catching culprits like finding a needle in a gargantuan haystack. While the SEC eventually caught up with individuals like Ivan Boesky, Martha Stewart and Raj Rajaratnam due to their immense reputations, finding random people who obtain tips from an insider would be virtually impossible for regulators to catch.

In 2010, however, the SEC founded the Analysis and Detection Center as part of their Market Abuse unit, which uses big data to comb through fifteen years of trades, looking for individuals who consistently pulled off well-timed trades ahead of big corporate revelations. Between 2014 and 2016, the Analysis and Detection Center was responsible for bringing nine insider trading cases to justice. In many cases, it identified insider trading where no one would've looked, such as a forty-seven-year-old plumber named Gary Pusey who was trading based on inside information he received from a friend that worked at Barclays. Pusey completed ten well-timed trades between 2014 and 2015; and he paid a heavy price for it. That's merely one example of an industry that technology helped regulate.

Conversely, there are now several domains that are actively evading the eye of regulatory bodies. One simple example of this is the growing peer-to-peer (P2P) lending industry.

Starting in the United Kingdom, by 2006 P2P made its way to the US with the founding of San Francisco-based Prosper, a marketplace and has since skyrocketed worldwide. The motivation behind P2P lending is fundamentally a reaction to banks overcharging or setting the bar for borrowers too high. The solution? Let people dis-intermediate the banks and borrow from one another directly. The theory goes that, among today's nearly eight billion global citizens, there should be enough direct lenders who could be matched to direct borrowers based on their unique constraints, be it the borrower's credit score, the rate of return, the size and duration of loan, et al. And numerous platforms, like Zopa or Prosper, match people up based on their unique requirements, almost like a dating website.

The idea took off on the heels of the 2008 financial crisis, when banks became even more reluctant to lend and catapulted peer-to-peer lending into a sizable cottage industry. With over two billion pounds being dished out in the market by Zopa alone, and small-business owners beginning to jump into the fray, the peer-to-business lending took off. While the SEC immediately began regulating P2P by regarding them as securities, not all of these platforms have developed safeguards to prevent executives from raiding the cookie jar. And among the ugly cast of characters, Ezubao, an infamously prominent example, stood out.

Ezubao, once considered a Chinese darling with numerous government affiliations, was China's largest peer-to-peer platform. Set up in July 2014, it quickly gathered over $9 billion from 900,000 investors with promises of returns as high as fourteen percent. Thankfully, the euphoria didn't last long and within one year, the doors of the operation came off. The entire enterprise was revealed as a scam, with 95% of the investment opportunities having been falsely contrived. Instead, the money was consumed by Ezubao's executives, and earlier investors were repaid by subsequent investors. Unlike other investment frauds, which only happened after a fund experienced financial troubles, this was started as a scam from the get-go, demonstrating the ease with which executives can raid and exploit a duplicitous online investment opportunity.

Similar risks were seen in the rise of the crowdfunding industry, which collected over $34 billion in 2015 according to a Cambridge study. One notorious example was Ascenergy, an energy company, which was aggressive on social media and put out a short YouTube clip in 2014, pushing their "high reward, low risk" investment opportunity, describing itself as "highly diversified, fiscally conservative and generous in its gross revenue sharing." The clip also included supposed testimonials from experts raving about their oil and gas reserves.

Oddly enough, at the same time, Ascenergy claimed that it would gladly exchange its reserves for some real estate (red flag!). Setting up platforms on a few crowdfunding sites, Ascenergy and its CEO Joey Galbadon raised $5 million from euphoric investors all over the world. The SEC would later reveal that Ascenergy was neither an energy nor a gas company and it did not have any reserves. So where did the money go? Galbadon had immediately diverted $1.2 million into other businesses he controlled and toward his day-to-day expenses such as buying music on iTunes. Needless to say, that wasn't what his investors signed up for.

Cryptocurrencies have had similar regulatory gaps, which is why India has responded by banning cryptocurrencies altogether, while Japan and Taiwan have taken a subtler approach by simply demanding regulation. Thailand now requires cryptocurrency sellers to register with the Thai SEC within ninety days, with fines and possible jail time for those who continue to sell without registering. Additionally, Thai authorities began treating cryptocurrency like any other currency when it comes to money laundering and similar crimes. As of May 2018, the *New York Post* reported that US feds were looking into the possibility of regulating Bitcoin.

The scary reality is that ICOs have been booming, tens of millions being raised for them each month. If they continue to go unregulated, it only might be a matter of time before the lessons of Ecoin and OneCoin are forgotten, setting the stage for a Madoff-scale fraud to emerge.

While regulation is beginning to make its way into the crowdfunding and cryptocurrency industry, with costs of implementation being beyond the SEC's current budget, there is currently little to prevent a swindler from making any imaginable claim on a crowdfunding platform. This will inevitably lead to abuse, which will diminish trust and limit its growth. That is, unless it falls under the current regulatory regime and compliance is adhered.

Quality of People

As we mentioned, it's important to know the quality of people you are dealing with. Avoiding those with checkered pasts and not giving people undue credibility has always been important for investors who want to avoid fraud, but it will become increasingly so in the digital age.

The internet is currently rife with impostors claiming undue credibility. Built on the simple premise that average people believe what they read online, swindlers use the internet to create entire identities, companies and networks that don't exist. While social media or business networking platforms like LinkedIn are helpful for securing references or testimonials, they could easily be fabricated as well. British Columbia's Better Business Bureau named "social media influencers" as one of the top scams of 2017. Anthony De Angelis, The Salad Oil King, at least went through the trouble of setting up a major manufacturing plant, with large oil tankers, and numerous employees, to construct his sham business. Now, all scammers need to do is create a website and some social media pages for a nonexistent company.

Another thought to keep in mind is that fraudsters will try to leverage existing branding and credibility. A perfect example was the aforementioned cryptocurrency market, where fraudulent cryptocurrencies like Ecoin and OneCoin took millions from investors' pockets. It's important to note that similar to Whitaker Wright's "consol" trick, both of these frauds chose names very similar to Bitcoin, the most legitimate cryptocurrency in the market, to gain undue credibility. Other real cryptocurrencies, like Gnosis, did not feel the need to resort to these tactics.

Yet another innovation in this new world order is communications, and the diminishing reliance on human-to-human interactions. Between email, messaging apps, chat rooms and innovations in social media, oftentimes we don't know who we are actually dealing with. This has allowed impostors to reach those that would normally have stayed away from them. One of the most famous online scams has been the fake Nigerian prince scam, where random people are emailed about the potential of lending a Nigerian prince substantial amounts of money to help him regain his inheritance and in exchange reap the rewards when the inheritance is recovered. While it was known for a while that the Nigerian prince emails were nothing more than complete scams, in 2018 a sixty-seven-year-old Louisiana Caucasian man named Michael Neu was arrested as one of its architects. Needless to say, in person, he'd have a hard time convincing anybody that he was a Nigerian prince. Cross-globe communication can allow people to hide and conceal their real selves, making it hard to ascertain the quality of people.

The bottom line is, while it has always been important to know the quality of people you are dealing with and ensure you have meaningful human-to-human interactions with them, it is especially vital when operating in our newly impersonal world.

Validity of Opportunity

As the digital age progresses, the need to clarify the validity of any investment opportunity has become simultaneously more critical and murkier.

While everyone is excited by the idea of "hitting it big," spotting the next "unicorn" or industry disruptor, the overwhelming majority are also clueless as to the inputs of complicated algorithms, artificial intelligence, and other black-box methodologies that are being touted today to produce returns.

Lawrence Salander was able to take advantage of investors who didn't know much about art with claims that he could produce outrageous returns. Similarly, new tech-savvy fraudsters will claim to find or develop new technology solutions or investment vehicles and prey on ignorant investors who will follow them blindly.

Many Ponzi schemes have sprung up claiming that their fantastic new technology allows them to generate exceptional returns, when in fact they're simply siphoning money to themselves and distributing new capital to earlier investors. This has been done using fancy algorithms, as demonstrated by Gabriel Bitran, a professor and associate dean at MIT's Sloan School of Business. This distinguished academic claimed to have an algorithm that could generate returns between sixteen and twenty-three percent. Along with his son Marco, he founded a hedge fund and they raised $500 million on that premise. In reality, father and son were really paying themselves generous commissions while paying earlier investors using subsequent investor money. The SEC discovered this when they began looking into Bernie Madoff's Ponzi scheme. By then, $140 million in investor money had been lost.

Algorithms, however, aren't the only new arena that few understand. The previously discussed cryptocurrency market is equally murky, where an increasing number of people want to be "in" on the new, hot investment without understanding how cryptocurrencies or blockchain truly works. Playing on this ignorance, shady characters and intermediaries emerge, promising to replicate the exorbitant returns they've "achieved" in this "asset class" to others. Of course, in reality no one has any magical method of generating predictable or extraordinary returns through cryptocurrencies, which are highly volatile and subject to the whims of the masses. And those that claim to are likely engaging in something nefarious. Allegedly, that's what Brooklyn trader Nicholas Gelfman did, soliciting $600,000 from eighty clients in a Bitcoin Ponzi scheme, claiming he had a special method of algorithmic trading. In September 2017, he was sued by the US Commodities Futures Trading Commission, and the case is ongoing.

The lesson for investors is that no matter what fantastic new software someone seems to have developed, verifying the validity of the opportunity is critical. And the claim of unusually high, predictable returns should be the same red flag for you in the 2020s as it should have been for Charles Ponzi's investors in the 1920s.

Consistency and Alignment

The need to make sure that your fund manager or investment operator's interests align with your own is paramount. The same way scammers of the past used schemes like the Drake estate to garner upfront payments that would never go for their intended purpose, modern-day fraudsters have done the same.

We already referenced the vast online crowdfunding industry. A Wharton study conducted by Professor Ethan Mollick in 2015 surveyed about 500,000 projects that were found on Kickstarter, an online crowdfunding platform specializing in arts-related projects and creativity. He found that about 9% of crowdfunding options do not deliver as promised and that only 13% of the time would the investor receive a refund. While oftentimes that is due to projects failing, with the high number of creative projects and start-ups using Kickstarter being inherently riskier, it is also a situation ripe for small charlatans, like Erik Chevalier, who will gladly take upfront payments in exchange for exotic promises.

Chevailer started a campaign trying to fund the creation of a board game called The Doom of Atlantic City, supposedly designed by two reputable board game artists. Over 1,000 people contributed and Chevalier raised $122,000. Of course, he did not spend the money on developing the board game, rather spending it on rent, a move to Oregon and other projects that he was working on. The Federal Trade Commission cracked down on him and this became the first action taken against a crowdfunding scam. The FTC ordered at least $111,000 of the investments to be refunded.

That didn't stop others like Alex Fundora, who raised $114,000 for his dinosaur survival game, The Stomping Land, and proceeded to vanish without a trace, until one of his investors found an online reference that he was now living in Colombia. Frauds have arisen, and will likely continue to rise, in the realm of equity crowdfunding, as hordes of investors are trying to find the next big hit. We already referenced the case of Joey Galbadon, whose company Ascenergy gathered $5 million of capital that was simply used for Galbadon's personal expenses.

This is a recurring challenge with crowdfunding platforms, where alignment of interest or how much skin in the game one has cannot be easily verified or established, and where investors have limited tools to assess the consistency of the claims relative to the plans and actions of the individual.

It's imperative for investors to remember that when alignment of interest cannot be verified and consistency between words and actions cannot be ascertained, the risk being undertaken is likely much greater than the potential reward.

Key Takeaways

History has shown that frauds flourish during times of rapid change and heightened uncertainty. Whether it's geopolitical disruptions, economic shifts, or technological revolutions, all societal shakeups are ripe environments for fraudsters to display their craft. So, in this rapidly changing world of artificial intelligence, cryptocurrencies, robotics, crowdfunding, big data, etc., how can investors "skate to where the puck is going?"

We now know that in 2007, online frauds constituted roughly one-fifth of all cases of fraud. By 2011, that number rose to forty percent. And today you are many times more likely to be robbed through your computer or phone than to be held up in the street. The unfortunate reality is that most of us are paralyzed by the overwhelming complexity of it all. The knowledge of all the digital platforms for fraud, along with their respective intricacies, will be feasible for the very few. That said, by becoming more familiar with the six factors of detecting fraud and employing the principles in this book, one can stay clear of most financial shenanigans.

By merely applying some of the simple heuristics—such as recognizing when something sounds too good to be true, dealing only with people you know intimately well, being able to verify the integrity of the cash flows (i.e. productive capital rather than other investors' money)—even the most technologically luddite investors can avoid being a case study for the frauds of the future.

* * *

IS ARTIFICIAL INTELLIGENCE CAPABLE OF DETECTING FRAUD?

As it happens, the combination of statistics, machine learning and algorithms are driving a great deal of insight in the domain of fraud detection. One such example is the utilization of Benford's Law. Benford's Law states that most naturally occurring data sets follow somewhat of a pattern, which is predictive of how often any given integer will begin a data set. For example, in roughly 30 percent of randomly selected data sets the first digit will be a 1. In approximately 18 percent of randomly selected data sets it will begin with a 2. Conversely, in only 5 percent of random data sets will it start with a 9. This insight has uncovered red flags by detecting financial data sets that have likely been contrived, doctored or manufactured, by virtue of them having no resemblance to the frequency distribution of Benford's Law.

CLOSING THOUGHTS

We need trust

After reading about dozens of callous individuals and complex cases of fraud, one could hardly be blamed for developing a serious issue with trust. While we have now emerged from blissful ignorance, our challenge now is being willing and able to believe.

Heightened awareness and sensitivity to fraud should not lead us down the wrongful path of eroding trust in our day-to-day lives. Just as healthy babies need to trust that the tall human holding them will take care of them, we need to trust that the people in our world are generally good and are not out to screw us.

Numerous studies on the subject have demonstrated that countries, people and institutions that lacked trust were far less productive and fulfilled than countries, people and institutions with higher trust quotients. The research suggests that higher generalized trust is accompanied by better mental health and physical wellbeing, stronger relationships, increased happiness, greater ability to take risks and outsource, build stable organizations, and express generosity. These people were not ignorant. To the contrary, higher generalized trust was correlated with higher intelligence. These more-trusting individuals merely saw their world not for what it was, but for what it ought to be and their lives were richer because of it.

Fraud won't disappear

Perhaps the least exciting caveat I can offer is that fraud will never be fully eliminated or extinguished. It is part of human nature, and perhaps even necessary for our evolution.

Researchers such as behavioral economist Dan Ariely and psychologist Robert Feldman, who have spent their careers studying deception, claim that deception is somewhat engrained in our DNA[20], with the average person lying more than three times in a typical ten-minute conversation.

By internalizing the best practices of this book, one can likely deflect the majority of frauds that one will confront, but there will always be that probability that someone will concoct a fraud so elaborate and brilliant that you will not be able to shield yourself from it. The purpose of this book is not to make investors impenetrable, but to make them more aware of the most sophisticated financial frauds committed and ensure that they are prepared when they confront the next iteration thereof.

Stop on red

The stories and cases throughout this book have offered us dozens of takeaways. In an effort to make these more useful, I have attempted to summarize these lessons through a listing of Red Flags you will find in the appendix ahead.

While we've outlined the importance of trust, we are not advocating for blind or naïve belief in the face of these red flags—"He's such a nice guy; he'd never do that to me." I've

---

[20] Deception and fraud are also visible in the animal world. For example, Frencesca Barbero, a researcher at the University of Turin, discovered that caterpillars and butterflies that invade ant colonies have learned how to mimic the sounds of queen ants. As a result, instead of removing their intruders, the ants provide these duplicitous insects with more care, food and protection than they would for their fellow ants. Even in times of shortage, these pretend ant queens are still treated like royalty.

included these to help you cycle through them when neccessary and remain vigilant when confronted by them. Please note that the existence of any of these red flags in isolation does not neccessarily suggest fraud, but any pattern of them should inspire investors to apply a critical eye.

The combination of red flags is important because, as we have seen throughout the book, fraud is often an amalgamation of circumstantial or financial pressures, coupled with the opportunity to deceive and the weak moral fortitude of the actors involved. With the presence of this trifecta—pressure is high, opportunity is high, and integrity is low—the probability of fraud is significant. When the opposite is true, fraud is unlikely.

By simply being concious of the red flags that point to these three variables you can sleep easier and sidestep even the most sophisticated snakeoil salesman.

* * *

APPENDIX I:
RED FLAGS BASED ON KEY TAKEAWAYS

Third Party Verification

- No external auditors for any or all affiliates.
- Size of enterprise disproportionally larger than size of auditor or third-party verifiers.
- No independent verification of ownership, asset existence, agency or previous transaction history.
- No verifiable track record of results (only promises of a bright future).
- Unconfirmed associations to established brands or known entitites.
- Absence of third-party adminstrators for valuation of funds.
- Ambiguity on the strength of the counterparty on any claims.
- Contrived social media and press releases, without independant verification of facts by third-party agencies.
- Unexplained resignation or high volume in turnover of third-party verifiers (i.e. auditors & administrators).
- No ability to get external references or survey prior employees, partners and investors.

Checks and Balances

- No independent board or functioning governance structure.
- Direct and unmitigated access to client funds.
- Absence of independent custodian.
- Principals too focused on hobbies, not watching the shop.
- Additional intermediary when intermediary is not needed.
- Absence of pre-desired processes and systems (allowing for quick, emotion-driven investments under stress).
- Irrationally generous terms offered to clients or vendors.
- Unusually profitable transactions near ends of accounting periods.
- Unexplained changes in financial statements or balances and lack of transparency.
- Growing difficulty in collecting receivables.
- Principals who are involved in multiple, conflicting businesses.

Compliance and Regulation

- Company based in unregulated industries, markets or far less regulated locales.
- Lack of proper licensing or registations, especially vis-a-vis securities.
- Revoked licenses or registrations.
- Principals do not respect lines of authority or pride themselves on "beating the system".
- Overly aggressive tax-saving schemes.
- Ongoing or recurring problems with regulators and/or tax authorities, history of bankruptcy.

Quality of People

- Unreasonably optimistic rate of return expectations.
- Individuals with any confirmed history (or even allegations) of deception, or overpromising (aggressive sales culture) and underdelivering.
- Principals' backgrounds cannot be checked or verified.
- Individuals that excessively leverage the credibility of others.
- Promoters who don't intimately know the principals they are promoting.
- Individuals project entitlement and/or moral superiority.
- Excessive gambling habits or involvement in speculative activities.
- Individuals cannot manage their personal commitments or obligations or experienced severe financial loss.
- Substance abuse or addictive behavior.
- Significant litigation.

Validity of Opportunity

- Returns that are simply too good to be true.
- Winning abnormally high percentage of market anticipatory bets.
- Inconsistent profitablity or return profiles with comparables in the same market, industry or business model.
- Over-reliance on jargon and high-falutin terminology without ability to explain how money is actually made.
- Religious messaging mixed with financial messaging to pull at investors' emotional or religious strings.
- Unclear or overstated liquidity of an investment.

- Opportunity divorced from simple supply and demand dynamics.
- Opportunities that are light on details and verifiable track record, but heavy on promises.
- Excessive borrowing or leverage inherent in the success of the strategy.
- Combining many bad investments to create a good one.

Consistency and Alignment

- Recurring changes within management teams.
- Asset-liability mismatch (e.g. ability to get liquidity in assets that are illiquid).
- Market-investment mismatch (e.g. stable returns in volatile markets or inconstancy between market results and reported results of specific investment vehicle).
- Compensation that is heavily front-end loaded versus back-end loaded (e.g. significant upfront payments versus profit sharing).
- Lack of skin in the game, with no personal money at stake.
- Gross undercharging.
- Too much dependence on one counterparty.
- Living ostentatiously and beyond one's means.
- Strategy drift and/or diversions from the core business.
- Inability to convey bad news as efficiently as one conveys good news.
- Lacking critical infrastructure or resources commensurate with scale of enterprise.

APPENDIX II:
REFERENCES BY CASE

Part 1: Third Party Verification

How Ivar Kreuger's Matches Set the SEC on Fire

Partnoy, Frank. *The Match King: Ivar Kreuger, the Financial Genius Behind a Century of Wall Street Scandals*, New York: Public Affairs. 2010.

Shaplen, Robert. *Kreuger, Genius and Swindler*. New York: Garland, 1986.

"The Match King." *The Economist*. December 19, 2007. Accessed November 8, 2018. https://www.economist.com/christmas-specials/2007/12/19/the-match-king.

Stanley Goldblum: If They're In On the Scam, Keep them on Payroll

"Equity Funding." David R. Hancox. Accessed November 8, 2018. http://davehancox.com/equity-funding/.

Messing, Brett, and Steven Sugarman. *The Forewarned Investor: Don't Get Fooled Again by Corporate Fraud*. Franklin Lakes, NJ: Career Press, 2006.

Stelnick, Rick, and Al. "Equity Funding Wall Street Scam: How It Happened." Decoded Science. July 17, 2013. Accessed November 8, 2018. http://www.decodedscience.org/mainframe-madoff-size-money-monstrous-misapplication-loop/4927.

Woolf, Emile. "The Equity Funding Story." Originally published in *Accountancy*. Downloaded from http://www.emilewoolfwrites.co.uk/wp-content/uploads/2012/11/The-Equity-Funding-Story.pdf

The Count Who Sold the Eiffel Tower

"Eiffel Tower Key Stats: The Tower in Numbers." La Tour Eiffel. Accessed November 8, 2018. https://www.toureiffel.paris/en/the-monument/key-figures.

Eofys, James. "Legendary Landmark Scams." Neatorama. Accessed November 8, 2018. http://www.neatorama.com/2007/07/02/legendary-landmark-scams.

James, Geoffrey. "Top 14 Financial Frauds of All Time." CBS News. March 03, 2011. Accessed November 8, 2018. http://www.cbsnews.com/8334-505183_162-57195447-10391735/top-14-financial-frauds-of-all-time/?pageNum=2.

"The Man Who Sold the Eiffel Tower." Today I Found Out. May 06, 2018. Accessed November 8, 2018. http://www.todayifoundout.com/index.php/2015/01/man-sold-eiffel-tower-twice/.

"The Man Who Sold the Eiffel Tower. Twice." Smithsonian.com. March 09, 2016. Accessed November 8, 2018. http://www.smithsonianmag.com/history/man-who-sold-eiffel-tower-twice-180958370/?no-ist.

"Victor Lustig." Wikipedia. October 11, 2018. Accessed November 8, 2018. https://en.wikipedia.org/wiki/Victor_Lustig.

Bre-X Minerals and the Canadian Gold Rush

Bergslien, Elisa. *Introduction to Forensic Geoscience.* 2012.

"Bre-X Geologist Mike De Guzman Rumoured to Be Alive." The Canadian Encyclopedia. Accessed November 8, 2018. http://www.thecanadianencyclopedia.ca/en/article/bre-x-geologist-mike-de-guzman-rumoured-to-be-alive/.

Coulson, Michael. *An Insiders Guide to the Mining Sector: How to Make Money from Gold and Mining Shares.* Petersfield: Harriman House, 2008.

Gerber, Jurg, and Eric L. Jensen. *Encyclopedia of White-collar Crime.* Westport. Conn.: Greenwood Press, 2007.

Salinger, Lawrence M. *Encyclopedia of White-collar and Corporate Crime.* Thousand Oaks, CA: Sage Reference, 2013.

Wyatt, Edward. "Small Investors and Big Money Taken by Tale of Jungle Gold." The New York Times. May 06, 1997. Accessed November 8, 2018. http://www.nytimes.com/1997/05/06/business/small-investors-and-big-money-taken-by-tale-of-jungle-gold.html.

Marc Dreier: The Man Most Likely to Succeed (in Jail)

Burrough, Bryan, and Nigel Parry. "Bryan Burrough on Marc Dreier." The Hive. January 31, 2015. Accessed November 8, 2018. http://www.vanityfair.com/news/2009/11/marc-dreier200911.

Parten, Constance. "Diary of a Scam: The Fall of Power Attorney Marc Dreier." CNBC. April 13, 2011. Accessed November 8, 2018. http://www.cnbc.com/id/42572204.

"The Impersonator." Daily Intelligencer. Accessed November 8, 2018. http://nymag.com/news/features/55863/index2.html.

Weiser, Benjamin. "Lawyer Gets 20 Years in $700 Million Fraud." The New York Times. July 14, 2009. Accessed November 8, 2018. http://www.nytimes.com/2009/07/14/nyregion/14dreier.html?_r=0.

Sucker Day: In Commemoration of F. Bam Morrison

"AMERICANA: The Mysterious Americans." Time. August 14, 1950. Accessed November 8, 2018. http://content.time.com/time/magazine/article/0,9171,858888,00.html.

Eaton, Kristi. *The Main Streets of Oklahoma: Okie Stories from Every County.* Charleston, SC: History Press, 2014.

Goldsmith, Earl. "Earl Goldsmith." Thehenryettan.com, Your News Place. Accessed November 8, 2018. http://www.thehenryettan.com/index.php?option=com_cont ent&view=article&id=843:wetumka-and-sucker-day&catid=13&Itemid=128.

Nash, Jay Robert. *Hustlers and Con Men: An Anecdotal History of the Confidence Man and His Games.* New York: M. Evans, 1976.

Choosing De Niro Over Dinero and the Valuation Practices of Edward Strafaci

Scharfman, Jason A. *Hedge Fund Governance: Evaluating Oversight, Independence, and Conflicts.* San Diego: Elsevier, 2015.

Vickers, Marcia. "The Fallen Financier." Bloomberg.com. December 8, 2002. Accessed November 8, 2018. https://www.bloomberg.com/news/articles/2002-12-08/the-fallen-financier.

Whitehouse, Kaja. "Ex-Koch Deputy Mayor Ken Lipper Close to Getting Reputation Back." New York Post. June 10, 2011. Accessed November 8, 2018. http://nypost.com/2011/06/10/ex-koch-deputy-mayor-ken-lipper-close-to-getting-reputation-back/.

Horses, Libraries and Hockey: The Story of WG Trading

Hurtado, Patricia. "Deloitte & Touche Wins Dismissal of Suit Over Ponzi Scheme." Bloomberg.com. January 23, 2013. Accessed November 8, 2018. http://www.bloomberg.com/news/articles/2013-01-23/deloitte-touche-wins-dismissal-of-iowa-pension-fund-suit-1-.

"Investment Manager Principal of WG Trading Company LP and WG Trading Investors Pleads Guilty in Manhattan Federal Court to Role in Several-Hundred-Million-Dollar Fraud Scheme." FBI. April 25, 2014. Accessed November 8, 2018. https://www.fbi.gov/contact-us/field-offices/newyork/news/press-releases/investment-manager-principal-of-wg-trading-company-lp-and-wg-trading-investors-pleads-guilty-in-manhattan-federal-court-to-role-in-several-hundred-million-dollar-fraud-scheme.

Jaitly, Rajiv. *Practical Operational Due Diligence on Hedge Funds Processes, Procedures and Case Studies.* Chichester: Wiley, 2016.

Kouwe, Zachery. "2 Money Managers Held in New Wall St. Fraud Case." The New York Times. February 25, 2009. Accessed November 18, 2018. https://www.nytimes.com/2009/02/26/business/26scam.html?_r=0.

Willis, Nico R. *Death of the American Investor: The Emergence of a New Global Eshareholder.* Phoenix: NetWorth Publications, 2011.

Part 2: Checks & Balances

Antigua's CD Player: The Story of Sir Allen Stanford

Gough, Leo. *The Con Men: A History of Financial Fraud and the Lessons You Can Learn.* Harlow: FT Publishing, 2013.

Meyer, Bill. "SEC Missed Numerous Red Flags Surrounding Texas Investment-fraud Suspect Allen Stanford." Cleveland.com. February 22, 2009. Accessed November 8, 2018. https://www.cleveland.com/nation/index.ssf/2009/02/sec_missed_numerous_red_flags.html.

Roan, Dan, and Patrick Nathanson. "Defiant US Fraudster Allen Stanford Vows to Clear Name." BBC News. January 11, 2016. Accessed November 8, 2018. http://www.bbc.com/news/world-35283297.

The Talented Xanthoudakis Who Could Make Money Disappear

Jaitly, Rajiv. *Practical Operational Due Diligence on Hedge Funds Processes, Procedures and Case Studies.* Chichester: Wiley, 2016.

Livesey, Bruce. *Thieves of Bay Street: How Banks, Brokerages, and the Wealthy Steal Billions from Canadians.* Toronto: Vintage Canada, 2013.

Marotte, Bertrand. "Cinar Founder Weinberg given Nearly Nine Years in Fraud Case." The Globe and Mail. May 16, 2018. Accessed November 8, 2018. http://www.theglobeandmail.com/report-on-business/industry-news/the-law-page/cinar-founder-ronald-weinberg-two-others-sentenced/article30557421/.

"Norshield Victims." Norshield Victims. January 01, 1970. Accessed November 8, 2018. http://norshieldvictims.blogspot.ca/.

Calisto Tanzi's Spoiled Milk: The Rise and Fall of Europe's Enron

Clikeman, Paul M. *Called to Account: Financial Frauds That Shaped the Accounting Profession.* London: Routledge, 2013.

Landler, Mark and Daniel J. Wakin. "The Rise and Fall of Parma's First Family." The New York Times. January 11, 2004. Accessed November 8, 2018. https://www.nytimes.com/2004/01/11/business/the-rise-and-fall-of-parma-s-first-family.html?mcubz=1.

Popham, Peter. "Calisto Tanzi: The Family Man Who Milked His Own Dairy Empire." The Independent. September 12, 2013. Accessed November 8, 2018. https://www.independent.co.uk/news/people/profiles/calisto-tanzi-the-family-man-who-milked-his-own-dairy-empire-73632.html.

Smith, Tony. "The Latin America Factor in the Scandal at Parmalat." The New York Times. January 13, 2004. Accessed November 8, 2018. https://www.nytimes.com/2004/01/13/business/the-latin-america-factor-in-the-scandal-at-parmalat.html?mcubz=1.

Wearing, Robert. *Cases in Corporate Governance.* London: Sage, 2009.

America's Most Notorious Moral Warrior: Charles Keating and Savings & Loan Scandal

Binstein, Michael, and Charles Bowden. *Trust Me: Charles Keating and the Missing Billions.* New York: Random House, 1993.

Day, Kathleen. *S & L Hell: The People and the Politics Behind the $1 Trillion Savings and Loan Scandal.* W. W. Norton &, 1993.

Nichols, Lawrence T., and Nolan J. James, II. "The Lesson of Lincoln: Regulation as Narrative in the Savings and Loan Crisis." In *The Savings and Loan Crisis: Lessons from a Regulatory Failure*, 143-71. Kluwer Academic Publishers, 2004.

Seidman, Lewis William. *Full Faith and Credit: The Great S & L Debacle and Other Washington Sagas.* Washington, DC: Beard Books, 2000.

"The Lincoln Savings and Loan Investigation: Who Is Involved." The New York Times. November 22, 1989. Accessed November 8, 2018. https://www.nytimes.com/1989/11/22/business/the-lincoln-savings-and-loan-investigation-who-is-involved.html

Want to Make it Big? Start a Charity!

"Four Cancer Charities Accused of Pocketing $187M in Donations." ABC News. May 19, 2015. Accessed November 9, 2018. https://abcnews.go.com/US/cancer-charities-accused-pocketing-187m-donations/story?id=31160723.

Graham, David A. "How Four Alleged Scam Charities Stole $187 Million Meant for Cancer Patients." The Atlantic. May 21, 2015. Accessed November 9, 2018. https://www.theatlantic.com/business/archive/2015/05/are-you-donating-to-charity-or-lining-someones-pockets/393725/.

Ruiz, Rebecca R. "4 Cancer Charities Are Accused of Fraud." The New York Times. December 21, 2017. Accessed November 9, 2018.

"Give, and I Shall Taketh From You": The Lies of Gerald "Double Your Money" Payne

Fager, Chuck. "Fraud: Greater Ministries Leaders Get Lengthy Prison Terms." Christian History | Learn the History of Christianity & the Church. June 28, 2017. Accessed November 9, 2018. https://www.christianitytoday.com/ct/2001/october1/15.21.html.

"THE INDUCTEES: Gerald Payne." Con Artist Hall of Infamy: Gerald Payne. Accessed November 9, 2018. http://archive.pixelettestudios.com/hallofinfamy/inductees.php?action=detail&artist=gerald_payne.

"The Lyin' King: Gerald Payne and the Greater Ministries International $500 Million Fraud." Fraud News America. April 17, 2014. Accessed November 9, 2018. http://www.fraudnewsamerica.com/fraud-news-america-articles/the-lyin-king-gerald-payne-and-greater-ministries-international-500-million-fraud/.

Part 3: Compliance and Regulation

Rudy Kurniawan vs. Bill Koch: Guess Who is Still Standing?

Corie Brown | Times Staff Writer. "$75,000 a Case? He's Buying." Los Angeles Times. December 01, 2006. Accessed November 9, 2018. http://articles.latimes.com/2006/dec/01/entertainment/et-rudy1/3.

Massett, Philippe, and Caroline Henderson. *Wine as an Alternative Asset Class.* PDF. August 2009.

Sour Grapes. Met Film Production, 2016. https://www.netflix.com/Title/80029708.

Steinberger, Michael. "Rudy Kurniawan and the Largest Known "Wine" Fraud in History." The Hive. January 30, 2015. Accessed November 9, 2018. https://www.vanityfair.com/culture/2012/07/wine-fraud-rudy-kurniawan-vintage-burgundies.

Hellman, Peter. *In Vino Duplicitas: The Rise and Fall of a Wine Forger Extraordinaire.* The Experiment, 2017.

Sovereign Promises: Sir Gregor MacGregor & the Dominion of Melchizedek

Barrett, William P. "Boy, Do We Know Tzemach Ben David Netzer Korem." Forbes. August 11, 2011. Accessed November 9, 2018. https://www.forbes.com/sites/williampbarrett/2010/10/08/boy-do-we-know-tzemach-ben-david-netzer-korem/#7bfd7e04ef39.

"Cyberfraud: The Fictitious Dominion of Melchizidek." Asia Pacific Media Services. Accessed November 19, 2018. http://www.asiapacificms.com/articles/cyberfraud_melchizedek/. First published in The Nation (Bangkok) May 30, 1999.

Knecht, G. Bruce. "A 'Nation' in Cyberspace Draws Fire From Authorities." The Wall Street Journal. February 09, 1999. Accessed November 9, 2018. https://www.wsj.com/articles/SB918510801235641000.

Pasztor, David. "Scam Without a Country." Dallas Observer. May 2, 1996. Accessed November 9, 2018. https://web.archive.org/web/20080307050942/http://www.dallasobserver.com/1996-05-02/news/scam-without-a-country/full.

"The King of Con-men." The Economist. December 22, 2012. Accessed November 9, 2018. https://www.economist.com/christmas-specials/2012/12/22/the-king-of-con-men.

Tillman, Robert. *Global Pirates: Fraud in the Offshore Insurance Industry.* Boston, MA: Northeastern University Press, 2002.

Martin Frankel: The Anxious Nerd who Forced a Global Manhunt

Gerst, Eric D. *Vulture Culture: Dirty Deals, Unpaid Claims, and the Coming Collapse of the Insurance Industry.* New York: AMACOM, 2008.

Lohse, Deborah, and Leslie ScismStaff Reporters of The Wall Street Journal. "How Martin Frankel Built Insurance Empire So Fast." The Wall Street Journal. July 02, 1999. Accessed December 03, 2018. https://www.wsj.com/articles/SB930866246297872088.

Pollock, Ellen Joan, and Deborah LohseStaff Reporters of The Wall Street Journal. "A Portrait: Martin Frankel Was Ambitious, Cocky and Insecure." The Wall Street Journal. June 25, 1999. Accessed November 9, 2018. https://www.wsj.com/articles/SB930267024742820296.

Salinger, Lawrence M. *Encyclopedia of White-collar and Corporate Crime*. Vol. 1. Los Angeles: Sage Publications, 2013.

Segal, David. "Faked Out at Aching Gump?" The Washington Post. July 01, 1999. Accessed November 9, 2018. https://www.washingtonpost.com/archive/business/1999/07/01/faked-out-at-aching-gump/362c29dd-6997-4a8a-a9b8-9a6461086235/?utm_term=.3144acb21fad.

Lookout for the Repeat Antics of Roc Hatfield

Huddleston, Pat. *The Vigilant Investor: A Former SEC Enforcer Reveals How to Fraud-proof Your Investments*. New York: American Management Association, 2012.

Meinhardt, Jane. "Hatfield's Dealings Draw Government Attention Once Again." Bizjournals.com. April 29, 2002. Accessed November 9, 2018. https://www.bizjournals.com/tampabay/stories/2002/04/29/story6.html

"Product Liability." Findlaw. Accessed November 9, 2018. https://injury.findlaw.com/product-liability.html.

"SEC Seeks Contempt Order Against Repeat Offender For Alleged Violations Of Previous Injunction - Federal Judge Freezes Respondents' Assets, Schedules Contempt Hearing." Mondo Visione. Accessed November 9, 2018. http://www.mondovisione.com/news/sec-seeks-contempt-order-against-repeat-offender-for-alleged-violations-of-previ/.

The Rise and Fall of Panama's Escape Artist: Marc Harris

Associated Press. "Expelled Financier Denied Bond in Money Laundering Case." Boca Raton News. June 14, 2003. Accessed November 10, 2018. https://news.google.com/newspapers?id=n88PAAAAIBAJ&sjid=Ro4DAAAAIBAJ&pg=3278,5584807.

"David Marchant (journalist)." Wikipedia. September 06, 2017. Accessed November 9, 2018. https://en.wikipedia.org/wiki/David_Marchant_(journalist).

"Marc Harris." Wayback Machine. Accessed November 9, 2018. http://web.archive.org/web/20060423163946/http:/www.quatloos.com/groups/m-harris.htm.

"Marc Harris." Wikipedia. February 21, 2018. Accessed November 9, 2018. https://en.wikipedia.org/wiki/Marc_Harris.

Shapiro, Glen. "Marc Harris Faces 17 Year Jail Sentence." Tax-News.com - Global Tax News. June 2, 2004. Accessed November 10, 2018. https://www.tax-news.com/news/Marc_Harris_Faces_17_Year_Jail_Sentence____16197.html.

Spiro, Leah Nathans, and Geri Smith. "Marc Harris: Tax Haven Whiz Or Rogue Banker?" Bloomberg.com. May 13, 1998. Accessed November 9, 2018. https://www.bloomberg.com/news/articles/1998-05-31/marc-harris-tax-haven-whiz-or-rogue-banker.

YBM Magnex: The Story of the Brainy Don who Loved Canada

Huddleston, Pat. *The Vigilant Investor: A Former SEC Enforcer Reveals How to Fraud-proof Your Investments.* New York: American Management Association, 2012.

Livesey, Bruce. *Thieves of Bay Street: How Banks, Brokerages, and the Wealthy Steal Billions from Canadians.* Toronto: Vintage Canada, 2013.

Part 4: Quality of People

Richard Whitney: The Dark Knight of Wall Street

Beschloss, Michael. "From White Knight to Thief." The New York Times. September 13, 2014. Accessed November 11, 2018. https://www.nytimes.com/2014/09/14/upshot/from-white-knight-to-thief.html?_r=0.

Krebs, Albin. "Richard Whitney, 86, Dies; Headed Stock Exchange." The New York Times. December 06, 1974. Accessed November 11, 2018. https://www.nytimes.com/1974/12/06/archives/richard-whitney-86-dies-headed-stock-exchange-leader-in-stopping-29.html?_r=0.

Mackay, Malcolm. "Meet Richard Whitney, Wall Street's 1930s Version of Bernie Madoff." History News Network. Accessed November 11, 2018. https://historynews network.org/article/151925#sthash.EJ8ORnxu.dpuf.

"United States History." Douglas MacArthur. Accessed November 11, 2018. https://www.u-s-history.com/pages/h1808.html.

Martha's Rush to the Door: A Case Study in Insider Selling

"ImClone Stock Trading Case." Wikipedia. September 26, 2018. Accessed November 21, 2018. https://en.wikipedia.org/wiki/ImClone_stock_trading_case.

Stewart, James B. *Tangled Webs: How False Statements Are Undermining America: From Martha Stewart to Bernie Madoff.* New York: Penguin Books, 2012.

Toobin, Jeffrey. "A Bad Thing." The New Yorker. July 06, 2017. Accessed November 11, 2018. https://www.newyorker.com/magazine/2004/03/22/a-bad-thing.

John Mabray and Ben Marks's Two-Faced House in Two Counties

Hatfield, Elaine, and Richard L. Rapson. *Flimflam Artists: True Tales of Cults, Crackpots, Cranks, Cretins, Crooks, Creeps, Con Artists, and Charlatans.* Bloomington, Ind.: Xlibris, 2011.

Reading, Amy. *The Mark Inside: A Perfect Swindle, a Cunning Revenge, and a Small History of the Big Con.* New York: Vintage Books, a Division of Random House, 2013.

The Man Who Couldn't Face the Music

Bendici, Ray. "The CT Files: The Double Life-and Dealings-of Philip Musica." Connecticut Magazine. March 06, 2017. Accessed November 11, 2018.

http://www.connecticutmag.com/history/the-ct-files-the-double-life-and-dealings-of-philip/article_1ca9e27c-b7f8-599c-a88b-a2733b662ee1.html.

Block, Lawrence. *Gangsters, Swindlers, Killers, and Thieves: The Lives and Crimes of Fifty American Villains.* Oxford: Oxford University Press, 2004.

Clikeman, Paul M. *Called to Account: Financial Frauds That Shaped the Accounting Profession.* London: Routledge, 2013

"The Inductees: Philip Musica (aka F. Donald Coster)." Con Artist Hall of Infamy. Accessed November 11, 2018. http://archive.pixelettestudios.com/hallofinfamy/inductees.php?action=detail&artist=philip_musica.

Ferdinand Ward: How to Fool a President and Become the Best Hated Man in America

Gordon, John Steele. "Pyramid Schemes Are as American as Apple Pie." The Wall Street Journal. December 17, 2008. Accessed November 11, 2018. https://www.wsj.com/articles/SB122948144507313073.

Huddleston, Pat. *The Vigilant Investor: A Former SEC Enforcer Reveals How to Fraud-proof Your Investments.* New York: American Management Association, 2012.

Stiles, T. J. "'A Disposition to Be Rich,' by Geoffrey C. Ward." The New York Times. June 29, 2012. Accessed November 11, 2018. https://www.nytimes.com/2012/07/01/books/review/a-disposition-to-be-rich-by-geoffrey-c-ward.html?_r=0&mtrref=undefined&gwh=0A4379EE749A248BF57568AB981BFF19&gwt=pay. (*NY Times* book review about book about Ward)

Whitaker Wright: A Ballroom Under a Lake is of Little Consol-ation

Mount, Harry. "Witley Park in Surrey: The Story behind Whitaker Wright and Britain's Most Bizarre Folly." Daily Mail Online. November 08, 2011. Accessed November 11, 2018. https://www.dailymail.co.uk/news/article-2058772/Witley-Park-Surrey-The-story-Whitaker-Wright-Britains-bizarre-folly.html.

Plazak, Dan. *A Hole in the Ground with a Liar at the Top: Fraud and Deceit in the Golden Age of American Mining.* Salt Lake City: University of Utah Press, 2006.

"The Conservatory Under a Lake." Sometimes Interesting. September 06, 2016. Accessed November 21, 2018. https://sometimes-interesting.com/2015/04/22/the-conservatory-under-a-lake/.

Rape, Plunder and Loot: The Story of the Fugitive Financier

Clikeman, Paul M. *Called to Account: Financial Frauds That Shaped the Accounting Profession.* London: Routledge, 2013

Davison, Phil. "A VERY BIG FISH INDEED." The Independent. October 23, 2011. Accessed November 11, 2018. https://www.independent.co.uk/arts-entertainment/a-very-big-fish-indeed-1591664.html.

(EDT), Fortune Magazine. *Scandal!: The Amazing Tales of Cheats, Crooks and Criminals, and How They Helped Create the Modern Economy.* Little Brown &, 2008.

Herzog, Arthur. *Vesco: From Wall Street to Castros Cuba: The Rise, Fall, and Exile of the King of White Collar Crime.* New York: Authors Choice, 2003.

Kandell, Johnathan and Marc Lacey. "A Last Vanishing Act for Robert Vesco, Fugitive." The New York Times. May 03, 2008. Accessed November 11, 2018. https://www.nytimes.com/2008/05/03/world/americas/03vesco.html?mcubz=1&m-trref=undefined&gwh=504554EE9BC5B3825B34D95AFDC86E3F&gwt=pay.

"Robert Vesco." The Economist. May 29, 2008. Accessed November 11, 2018. https://www.economist.com/obituary/2008/05/29/robert-vesco.
"The Inductees: Bernard Cornfeld." Con Artist Hall of Infamy. Accessed November 11, 2018. http://archive.pixelettestudios.com/hallofinfamy/inductees.php?action=detail&artist=bernard_cornfeld.

Part 5: Validity of Opportunity

Charles Ponzi: The Man who Promoted Peter and Paul

"Charles Ponzi, The Financial Idiot Who Drove Boston Money Mad in 1920." New England Historical Society. July 24, 2017. Accessed November 11, 2018. http://www.newenglandhistoricalsociety.com/charles-ponzi-the-financial-idiot-who-drove-boston-money-mad-in-1920/.

Darby, Mary. "In Ponzi We Trust." Smithsonian.com. December 01, 1998. Accessed November 11, 2018. https://www.smithsonianmag.com/history/in-ponzi-we-trust-64016168/#jlME9ospplHq6t4Q.99.

Grossman, Samantha. "Top 10 Swindlers." Time. March 07, 2012. Accessed November 11, 2018. http://content.time.com/time/specials/packages/article/0,28804,2104982_2104983_2104997,00.html.

Trex, Ethan. "Who Was Ponzi & What Was His Scheme?" Mental Floss. December 16, 2008. Accessed November 11, 2018. http://mentalfloss.com/article/20377/who-was-ponzi-what-was-his-scheme.

Veronese, Keith. "The Ladies' Deposit: Created by Women for Ripping Off Women." Io9. December 16, 2015. Accessed November 21, 2018. https://io9.gizmodo.com/5915425/the-ladies-deposit-created-by-women-for-ripping-off-women.

Zuckoff, Mitchell. *Ponzis Scheme: The True Story of a Financial Legend.* New York: Random House Trade, 2006.

Oprah's Carpet Cleaning Mogul Stealing Grandma's Jewelry: The Crazy Life of Barry Minkow

"Barry Minkow." Wikipedia. November 02, 2018. Accessed November 11, 2018. https://en.wikipedia.org/wiki/Barry_Minkow#Conviction_and_prison.

Gzfraud. "Mark Morze: Catching the Crooks who Cook the Books, Part 1." YouTube. September 05, 2011. Accessed November 11, 2018. https://www.youtube.com/watch?v=PsjmsONPU-E.

Gzfraud. "Mark Morze: Catching the Crooks who Cook the Books, Part 2." YouTube. September 05, 2011. Accessed November 11, 2018. https://www.youtube.com/watch?v=uWRNbaOSjjA.

Miller, Alan C. "Barry Minkow--His Dream Born in a Garage Turns Sour." Los Angeles Times. January 19, 1988. Accessed November 11, 2018. http://articles.latimes.com/1988-01-19/local/me-37107_1_barry-minkow.

Murphy, Kim. "'Like the 3 Stooges' : ZZZZ Best: How the Big Bubble Burst." Los Angeles Times. March 30, 1989. Accessed November 11, 2018. http://articles.latimes.com/1989-03-30/news/mn-622_1_barry-minkow/2.

Skylinegtr94, and Roulette. "Hall of Fame Con Men: Mark Morze–Part 2 of 2." Wall Street Oasis. June 16, 2013. Accessed November 11, 2018. https://www.wallstreetoasis.com/blog/hall-of-fame-con-men-mark-morze-part-2-of-2.

"THE INDUCTEES: Barry Minkow." Con Artist Hall of Infamy. Accessed November 11, 2018. http://archive.pixelettestudios.com/hallofinfamy/inductees.php?action=detail&artist=barry_minkow.

Gzfraud. "Mark Morze: Catching the Crooks who Cook the Books, Part 1." YouTube. September 05, 2011. Accessed November 11, 2018. https://www.youtube.com/watch?v=PsjmsONPU-E.

Gzfraud. "Mark Morze: Catching the Crooks who Cook the Books, Part 2." YouTube. September 05, 2011. Accessed November 11, 2018. https://www.youtube.com/watch?v=uWRNbaOSjjA.

Even the Jargon Couldn't Save Him: How Kirk Wright Got Sacked

Huddleston, Pat. *The Vigilant Investor: A Former SEC Enforcer Reveals How to Fraud-proof Your Investments.* New York: American Management Association, 2012.

McDonald, Ian, and Valerie Bauerlein. "Troubles at Atlanta Hedge Fund Snare Doctors, Football Players." The Wall Street Journal. March 09, 2006. Accessed November 11, 2018. https://www.wsj.com/articles/SB114187533315493405.

Tierney, Mike. "Kirk Wright's Death Does Not Stop Lawsuit by Ex-N.F.L. Players." The New York Times. June 02, 2008. Accessed November 11, 2018. https://www.nytimes.com/2008/06/02/sports/football/02wright.html?_r=0&mtrref=undefined&gwh=E8875AC1A74875B87BDC77AC2243DB76&gwt=pay.

The Crocodile Tears of Lawrence Salander

Amore, Anthony M. *The Art of the Con: The Most Notorious Fakes, Frauds, and Forgeries in the Art World.* New York: St. Martins Press, 2016.

Boroff, Philip. "What Art Collectors Can Learn From Art Thief Larry Salander." Barron's. May 16, 2015. Accessed November 11, 2018. https://www.barrons.com/articles/what-art-collectors-can-learn-from-art-thief-larry-salander-1431741126.

Eligon, John. "Lawrence Salander Sentenced for Art Fraud Scheme." The New York Times. August 03, 2010. Accessed November 11, 2018. https://www.nytimes.com/2010/08/04/nyregion/04salander.html?_r=0&mtrref=undefined&gwh=154FC11BD10A5BA715C9AA911B897255&gwt=pay.

Ewell, Bernard. *Artful Dodgers: Fraud & Foolishness in the Art Market*. Abbott Press, 2014.

The Salad Oil King Who Toppled AMEX and Elevated Buffet

Geisst, Charles R. *Wheels of Fortune: The History of Speculation from Scandal to Respectabilit*. John Wiley & Sons, 2004.

Markham, Jerry W. *A Financial History of the United States*. Armonk, NY: M.E. Sharpe, 2011.

Middleton, Kathleen M. *Bayonne Passages*. Charleston, SC: Arcadia, 2000.

Taylor, Bryan. "How The Salad Oil Swindle Of 1963 Nearly Crippled The NYSE." Business Insider. November 23, 2013. Accessed November 11, 2018. https://www.businessinsider.com/the-great-salad-oil-scandal-of-1963-2013-11.

Boiler Rooms and Superloaders: How Walter Tellier Ruled the '50s

Elfenbein, Eddy. "Archives." Crossing Wall Street RSS. January 14, 2018. Accessed November 17, 2018. http://www.crossingwallstreet.com/archives/2018/01/the-lost-bull-market-1949-1955.html.

Fisher, Ken. *100 Minds That Made the Market*. Hoboken: John Wiley & Sons, 2010.

Lenzner, Robert. "Bull Markets Last Five Times Longer Than Bear Markets." Forbes. January 02, 2015. Accessed November 17, 2018. https://www.forbes.com/sites/robertlenzner/2015/01/02/bull-markets-last-five-times-longer-than-bear-markets/#68da85002dd5.

"The Inductees: Walter Tellier." Con Artist Hall of Infamy. Accessed November 26, 2018. http://archive.pixelettestudios.com/hallofinfamy/inductees.php?action=detail&artist=walter_tellier.

Nami's Yen: Came Down from Heaven and Went Up in Smoke

AFP. "The Most Notorious Financial Frauds in History." The Telegraph. June 06, 2016. Accessed November 28, 2018. https://www.telegraph.co.uk/money/consumer-affairs/the-most-notorious-financial-frauds-in-history/kazutsugi-nami/.

Hayashi, Yuka. "Mr. Nami's 'Yen From Heaven'." The Wall Street Journal. February 09, 2009. Accessed November 28, 2018. https://www.wsj.com/articles/SB123412358924861075.

Kelly, Tim. "Japan's Bernie Madoff." Forbes. June 19, 2013. Accessed November 28, 2018. https://www.forbes.com/2009/02/22/dispatch-japan-fraud-markets_0223_tokyo_dispatch.html#6be514ef4714.

"L&G Execs Arrested over Investor Fraud." The Japan Times. February 6, 2009. Accessed November 28, 2018. https://www.japantimes.co.jp/news/2009/02/06/national/lg-execs-arrested-over-investor-fraud/#.W_yKuPZFzZb.

McCurry, Justin. "Kazutsugi Nami of L&G Arrested on Suspicion of Fraud." The Guardian. February 05, 2009. Accessed November 28, 2018. https://www.theguardian.com/business/2009/feb/05/japan-kazutsugi-nami-ladies-gentlemen.

An Eccentric Vigilante's War on the World's Biggest Pigeon Fraud

Mooallem, Jon. "Birdman." The New York Times. March 06, 2015. Accessed November 28, 2018. https://www.nytimes.com/2015/03/05/magazine/the-pigeon-king-and-the-ponzi-scheme-that-shook-canada.html?_r=0&mtrref=undefined&gwh=910A02C251A3FBFB7D3176A3F716E29C&gwt=pay.

William Miller: The 520% Man

Nash, Jay Robert. *Hustlers and Con Men: An Anecdotal History of the Confidence Man and His Games*. New York: M. Evans, 1976.

Skarda, Erin. "Top 10 Swindlers." Time. March 07, 2012. Accessed November 28, 2018. http://content.time.com/time/specials/packages/article/0,28804,2104982_2104983_2104992,00.html.

Train, Arthur Cheney. *True Stories of Crime from the District Attorney's Office*. C. Scribner's Sons. 1908.

From Cowsheds to Laundromats: The Rastogi's Imaginary Empire

"Asians = Corruption - Stormfront." Stormfront RSS. Accessed November 28, 2018. https://www.stormfront.org/forum/t22253/.

Reporter, Daily Mail. "Businessmen Jailed for Running a £340m Scam from Cow Shed in India." Daily Mail Online. June 05, 2008. Accessed November 28, 2018. https://www.dailymail.co.uk/news/article-1024505/Businessmen-jailed-running-340m-scam-using-fake-addresses--including-cow-shed-India.html#ixzz47R2DV300.

"The Inductees: Rastogi Brothers." Con Artist Hall of Infamy. Accessed November 28, 2018. http://archive.pixelettestudios.com/hallofinfamy/inductees.php?action=detail&artist=rastogi_brothers.

Rudy Giuliani's Big, Greedy Fish: The Story of Ivan Boesky

Chermak, Steven, and Frankie Y. Bailey. *Crimes of the Centuries. Notorious Crimes, Criminals, and Criminal Trials in American History. 3 Vols*. Santa Barbara: ABC-CLIO, 2015.

Cramer, James J. "Bad Boys, Bad Boys." Daily Intelligencer. Accessed November 29, 2018. http://nymag.com/nymetro/news/bizfinance/columns/bottomline/n_9352/.

Gerber, Jurg, and Eric L. Jensen. *Encyclopedia of White-collar Crime.* Westport. Conn.: Greenwood Press, 2007. Wayne, Leslie. "Wall St. Saw a Tough 'Arab'." The New York Times. November 22, 1986. Accessed November 28, 2018. http://www.nytimes.com/1986/11/22/business/the-worlds-of-ivan-f-boesky-wall-st-saw-a-tough-arab.html?pagewanted=all.

Sterngold, James. "BOESKY SENTENCED TO 3 YEARS IN JAIL IN INSIDER SCANDAL." The New York Times. December 19, 1987. Accessed November 29, 2018. http://www.nytimes.com/1987/12/19/business/boesky-sentenced-to-3-years-in-jail-in-insider-scandal.html?pagewanted=all.

Stewart, James B. *Den of Thieves.* New York: Simon & Schuster, 2010.

The Taped Insider: A Glimpse into the Rise and Fall of Raj Rajaratnam

Ahmed, Peter Lattman and Azam. "Hedge Fund Billionaire Is Guilty of Insider Trading." The New York Times. May 11, 2011. Accessed November 29, 2018. https://dealbook.nytimes.com/2011/05/11/rajaratnam-found-guilty/?mtrref=undefined&gwh=99414A20214A23FFBD5BC4A93A2885D7&gwt=pay.

Kouwe, Zachery. "A Look at the Hedge Fund Chief Accused of Fraud." The New York Times. October 16, 2009. Accessed November 29, 2018. https://dealbook.nytimes.com/2009/10/16/a-look-at-the-accused-hedge-fund-manager/?mtrref=dealbook.nytimes.com&gwh=2F4E0314D8852197C0C103684EE89082&gwt=pay.

Pulliam, Susan, and Chad Bray. "Trader Draws Record Sentence." The Wall Street Journal. October 14, 2011. Accessed November 29, 2018. https://www.wsj.com/articles/SB10001424052970203914304576627191081876286.

Saloon, Divorce. "NEW YORK: Raj and Asha Rajaratnam's 3 Kids Could Lose Their Inheritance." Divorce Saloon Blog. September 18, 2010. Accessed November 29, 2018. http://www.divorcesaloon.com/2009/10/18/raj-and-asha-rajaratnams-3-kids-could-lose-their-inheritance/.

Rothfeld, Michael, Susan Pulliam, and Chad Bray. "Fund Titan Found Guilty." The Wall Street Journal. May 12, 2011. Accessed November 29, 2018. https://www.wsj.com/articles/SB10001424052748703864204576317060246641834.

Part 6: Consistency & Alignment

The Defrauded Fraudster: The Unbelievable Bayou Story

Lawson, Guy. *Masters of Delusion Sam Israel, the Octopus, and the Inside Story of the Wildest, Craziest Fraud in the History of Wall Street.* Crown Pub, 2012.

Wood River's Sunset in Sun Valley

Hedge Fund Shain, Randy. *Hedge Fund Due Diligence: Professional Tools to Investigate Hedge Fund Managers*. Hoboken, NJ: Wiley, 2008.

Hibbard, Justin. "Wood River's Founder: A Rich Novice?" Bloomberg.com. October 19, 2005. Accessed November 29, 2018. https://www.bloomberg.com/news/articles/2005-10-19/wood-rivers-founder-a-rich-novice.

Jaitly, Rajiv. *Practical Operational Due Diligence on Hedge Funds Processes, Procedures and Case Studies*. Chichester: Wiley, 2016.

"Wall of Shame - Fund Fraudsters." CheckFundManager. Accessed November 29, 2018. http://www.checkfundmanager.com/wall_of_shame.html. Zuckerman, Gregory, and Ian McDonald. "Lack of Response To Wood River Draws Questions." The Wall Street Journal. October 12, 2005. Accessed November 29, 2018. https://www.wsj.com/articles/SB112908334782866304.

Subprime-Rich and Cash-Poor: The Story of Ralph Cioffi and the Downfall of Bear Stearns

Abelson, Max. "Ralph Cioffi, After the Fall." Observer. August 18, 2010. Accessed November 29, 2018. http://observer.com/2010/08/ralph-cioffi-after-the-fall/.

Goldstein, Matthew, and David Henry. "Bear Stearns' Bad Bet." Bloomberg.com. October 11, 2007. Accessed November 29, 2018. http://www.bloomberg.com/news/articles/2007-10-11/bear-stearns-bad-betbusinessweek-business-news-stock-market-and-financial-advice.

McCool, Grant. "Jury Acquits Ex-Bear Stearns Hedge Fund Managers." Reuters. November 11, 2009. Accessed November 29, 2018. http://www.reuters.com/article/bear-stearns-idUSLNE5AA00120091111.

Weidlich, Thom. "Cioffi, Tannin to Pay $1.05 Million to Settle SEC Lawsuit." Bloomberg.com. February 13, 2012. Accessed November 29, 2018. http://www.bloomberg.com/news/articles/2012-02-13/ex-bear-stearns-managers-cioffi-tannin-to-pay-1-05-million-in-sec-suit.

The Unsafe Harbor of Portus Asset Management

Gordon, Sheldon. "Canadian Financier's Rapid Climb Ends." The Forward. June 03, 2005. Accessed November 29, 2018. https://forward.com/news/3596/canadian-financier-e2-80-99s-rapid-climb-ends/.

Jaitly, Rajiv. *Practical Operational Due Diligence on Hedge Funds Processes, Procedures and Case Studies*. Chichester: Wiley, 2016.

McFarland, Janet. "OSC Settles for $8.8-million–but Portus Co-founder Can't Pay." The Globe and Mail. April 30, 2018. Accessed November 29, 2018. https://www.theglobeandmail.com/globe-investor/osc-settles-for-88-million-but-portus-co-founder-cant-pay/article4502716/.

Yew, Madhavi Acharya-Tom. "Failed Hedge Fund Co-founder Gets Four Years in Jail." Thestar.com. May 26, 2011. Accessed November 29, 2018. https://www.thestar.com/ business/economy/2011/05/26/failed_hedge_fund_cofounder_gets_four_years_in_ jail.html.

The Only Hitter with a .966 Batting Average: Bernard L. Madoff

"Madoff Investment Scandal." Wikipedia. November 22, 2018. Accessed November 30, 2018. https://en.wikipedia.org/wiki/Madoff_investment_scandal.

Markopolos, Harry, and David Fisher. *No One Would Listen: A True Financial Thriller.* Hoboken, N.J: Wiley, 2011.

Staff, Investopedia. "Option." Investopedia. August 04, 2018. Accessed November 30, 2018. https://www.investopedia.com/terms/o/option.asp.

Being Too Early Doesn't Count: Michael Berger's Doomsday Bet

Anderson, Jenny. "The Bankruptcy Development That Has Wall St. Worried." The New York Times. February 23, 2007. Accessed November 30, 2018. https://www.nytimes.com/2007/02/23/business/23insider.html?mtrref=undefined& gwh=F83FDA25A2531D2EF48DD1B390961D95&gwt=pay.

"Fugitive Banker Caught in Austria." The Wall Street Journal. July 10, 2007. Accessed November 30, 2018. https://www.wsj.com/articles/SB118401289257261240.

Grontzki, Philipp, and David Glovin. "U.S. Hedge Fund Fugitive Berger Caught in Austria." The New York Sun. July 10, 2007. Accessed November 30, 2018. https://www.nysun.com/national/us-hedge-fund-fugitive-berger-caught-in-austria/ 58135/. Originally published in *The Bloomberg News.*

Kurdas, Chidem. "Does Regulation Prevent Fraud? the Case of Manhattan Hedge Fund." *Independent Review*, January 1, 2009, 325-43.

Computer Associates: Creating the 35-Day Month

Berenson, Alex. "CA Says Its Founder Aided Fraud." The New York Times. April 14, 2007. Accessed December 02, 2018. https://www.nytimes.com/2007/04/14/technology/ 14compute.html?_r=0.

De La Merced, Michael J. "Ex-Leader of Computer Associates Gets 12-Year Sentence and Fine." The New York Times. November 03, 2006. Accessed December 02, 2018. https://www.nytimes.com/2006/11/03/technology/03computer.html?mcubz=1.

"Sanjay Kumar (business Executive)." Wikipedia. October 25, 2018. Accessed November 30, 2018. https://en.wikipedia.org/wiki/Sanjay_Kumar_(business_executive).

Varchaver, Nicholas. "CA: America's Most Dysfunctional Company." Skullcandy: The World's Coolest Headphones - Dec. 30, 2008. November 16, 2006. Accessed November 30, 2018. http://archive.fortune.com/magazines/fortune/fortune_archive/ 2006/11/27/8394334/index.htm.

Turning the Tables on the Legend of Sir Francis Drake

Farquhar, Michael. *A Treasury of Deception: Liars, Misleaders, Hoodwinkers, and the Extraordinary True Stories of Historys Greatest Hoaxes, Fakes, and Frauds.* New York: Penguin, 2005.

Matulich, Serge, and David M. Currie, eds. *HANDBOOK OF FRAUDS, SCAMS, AND SWINDLES: Failures of Ethics in Leadership.* S.l.: CRC PRESS, 2017.

Nash, Jay Robert. *Hustlers and Con Men an Anecdotal History of the Confidence Man and His Games.* New York: Evans, 1976. Regarding the Baker Estate.

Rayner, Richard. *Drakes Fortune the Fabulous True Story of the Worlds Greatest Confidence Artist.* New York: Anchor Books, 2003.

How to Manipulate $360 Trillion: The Curious Case of LIBOR and Thomas Hayes

Doyle, Larry. "Sense on Cents." Sense on Cents Bernie Madoff Upbringing Tag. February 8, 2013. Accessed December 02, 2018. http://www.senseoncents. com/2013/02/libor-scam-tom-hayesgoes-much-higher-than-me/#more-32750.

Enrich, David. "Libor's Mastermind: The Unraveling of Tom Hayes, Convicted in a Global Financial Scandal - Part Five." The Wall Street Journal. September 17, 2015. Accessed December 02, 2018. http://graphics.wsj.com/libor-unraveling-tom-hayes/5.

Goodley, Simon. "Tom Hayes, the Libor-rigging Scandal's 'ringmaster'." The Guardian. August 03, 2015. Accessed December 02, 2018. https://www.theguardian.com/business/ 2015/aug/03/libor-rigging-tom-hayes-sfo.

McBride, James. "Understanding the Libor Scandal." Council on Foreign Relations. October 12, 2016. Accessed December 02, 2018. https://www.cfr.org/backgrounder/ understanding-libor-scandal.

Ridley, Kirstin. "Insight - How Libor Whiz Rain Man Became 'the Guy Everyone Was...'" Reuters. August 03, 2015. Accessed December 02, 2018. https://uk.reuters. com/article/uk-libor-hayes-insight/insight-how-libor-whiz-rain-man-became- the-guy-everyone-was-going-to-blame-idUKKCN0Q81OE20150803.

Treanor, Jill. "Libor Interest Rate to Be Phased out after String of Scandals." The Guardian. July 28, 2017. Accessed December 02, 2018. https://www. theguardian.com/business/2017/jul/27/libor-interest-rate-phased-out-scandals.

Vaughan, Liam, and Gavin Finch. "Libor Scandal: The Bankers Who Fixed the World's Most Important Number | Liam Vaughan and Gavin Finch." The Guardian. January 18, 2017. Accessed December 02, 2018. https://www.theguardian.com/business/2017/ jan/18/libor-scandal-the-bankers-who-fixed-the-worlds-most-important-number.

Vaughan, Liam, and Gavin Finch. *The Fix: How Bankers Lied, Cheated and Colluded to Rig the Worlds Most Important Number.* Hoboken, NJ: Wiley/Bloomberg Press, 2017.

The Future of Fraud

AFP. "Insider Trading in the Digital Age: Use Post-it Notes." Yahoo! News. September 19, 2014. Accessed December 02, 2018. https://www.yahoo. com/news/insider-trading-digital-age-post-notes-195824560.html.

Alois, JD. "The First Investment Crowdfunding Fraud. What Does This Mean for the Industry?" National Crowdfunding & Fintech Association of Canada. December 02, 2015. Accessed December 02, 2018. https://ncfacanada.org/ the-first-investment-crowdfunding-fraud-what-does-this-mean-for-the-industry/.

Andersen, Travis. "Ex-MIT Official, Son Sentenced to Federal Prison for Hedge Fund Scheme - The Boston Globe." BostonGlobe.com. December 16, 2015. Accessed December 03, 2018. https://www.bostonglobe.com/metro/2015/12/16/mit-official-son-sentenced-federal-prison-for-hedge-fund-scheme/KY5APWCLKOteqkyYT4huhK/story.html.

"Artificial Intelligence in AML and KYC: Enhancing Accuracy and Reducing Costs Hot Topic Q&A." FICO® | Decisions. Accessed December 02, 2018. https://www.fico.com/en/latest-thinking/executive-brief/artificial-intelligence-in-aml-and-kyc-enhancing-accuracy-and-reducing-costs.

Cheng, Evelyn, and Kayla Tausche. "Jamie Dimon Says If You're 'stupid' Enough to Buy Bitcoin, You'll Pay the Price One Day." CNBC. October 16, 2017. Accessed December 03, 2018. https://www.cnbc.com/2017/10/13/ jamie-dimon-says-people-who-buy-bitcoin-are-stupid.html.

Cox Business Editor @JosieCox_London, Josie. "How Thousands of Britons Are at Risk from 'world's Biggest Online Scam'." The Independent. July 29, 2017. Accessed December 02, 2018. https://www.independent.co.uk/news/business/news/online-scam-thousands-pounds-life-savings-trading-binary-options-fraud-pensioners-fca-a7865856.html.

Franklin, Joshua. "Swiss Shut down 'fake' E-Coin in Latest Cryptocurrency Crackdown." Reuters. September 19, 2017. Accessed December 03, 2018. https://www.reuters.com/ article/us-swiss-cryptocurrency/swiss-shut-down-fake-e-coin-in-latest-cryptocurrency-crackdown-idUSKCN1BU0ZT.

Fredman, Catherine. "Fund Me or Fraud Me? Crowdfunding Scams Are on the Rise." Product Reviews and Ratings - Consumer Reports. October 5, 2015. Accessed December 03, 2018. https://www.consumerreports.org/cro/money/crowdfunding-scam.

Gough, Neil. "Online Lender Ezubao Took $7.6 Billion in Ponzi Scheme, China Says." The New York Times. February 01, 2016. Accessed December 03, 2018.

Harris, Sheryl. "Crazy Eddie CFO Shares How Companies Trick Auditors and Fleece Investors: Plain Dealing." Cleveland.com. December 19, 2014. Accessed December 03, 2018. https://www.cleveland.com/consumeraffairs/index.ssf/2014/12/crazy_eddie_cfo_gives_an_insid.html.

"Kickstarter Fulfillment Report." Kickstarter. Accessed December 03, 2018. https://www.kickstarter.com/fulfillment.

Kim, Tae. "Billionaire Bitcoin Skeptic Howard Marks Admits It Could Be Legit Currency, but Is Still a 'Speculative Bubble'." CNBC. September 08, 2017. Accessed December 03, 2018. https://www.cnbc.com/2017/09/08/billionaire-marks-still-says-bitcoin-is-a-speculative-bubble.html.

Mac, Dominic. "The KYC and AML Landscape in 2017." Refinitiv. November 16, 2018. Accessed December 02, 2018. https://www.refinitiv.com/perspectives/financial-crime/kyc-aml-landscape-2017/.

"Machine-learning Promises to Shake up Large Swathes of Finance." The Economist. May 25, 2017. Accessed December 02, 2018. https://www.economist.com/finance-and-economics/2017/05/25/machine-learning-promises-to-shake-up-large-swathes-of-finance.

Morris, David Z. "The Rise of Cryptocurrency Ponzi Schemes." The Atlantic. May 31, 2017. Accessed December 03, 2018. https://www.theatlantic.com/technology/archive/2017/05/cryptocurrency-ponzi-schemes/528624/.

Reuters. "Here's How the SEC Is Using Big Data to Catch Insider Trading." Fortune. November 1, 2016. Accessed December 02, 2018. http://fortune.com/2016/11/01/sec-big-data-insider-trading/.

Roose, Kevin. "As Elites Switch to Texting, Watchdogs Fear Loss of Transparency." The New York Times. July 06, 2017. Accessed December 02, 2018. https://www.nytimes.com/2017/07/06/business/as-elites-switch-to-texting-watchdogs-fear-loss-of-transparency.html.

Scannell, Kara. "Insider Trading Schemes Using Encrypted Apps Alarm FBI." Financial Times. August 20, 2017. Accessed December 02, 2018. https://www.ft.com/content/7fad3fca-8438-11e7-94e2-c5b903247afd?mhq5j=e5.

Silcoff, Shaun. "Could a Robot Catch the next Madoff? Ottawa Startup Bets AI Can Root out Fraud." The Globe and Mail. June 16, 2017. Accessed December 03, 2018. https://beta.theglobeandmail.com/report-on-business/international-business/ottawa-ai-firm-training-machines-to-blow-whistle-on-fraudsters-poised-for-breakout/article35325475/?ref=http://www.theglobeandmail.com&._

"The European Alternative Finance Industry Is Lagging Far behind the US and UK." Business Insider. September 07, 2016. Accessed December 03, 2018. https://www.businessinsider.com/the-european-alternative-finance-industry-is-lagging-far-behind-the-us-and-uk-2016-9. -and-uk-2016-9

Vardi, Nathan. "Feds Call Full Tilt Poker A Massive Ponzi Scheme." Forbes. September 20, 2011. Accessed December 03, 2018. https://www.forbes.com/forbes/welcome/?toURL=https://www.forbes.com/sites/nathanvardi/2011/09/20/feds-call-full-tilt-poker-a-massive-ponzi-scheme/&refURL=https://www.google.ca/&referrer=https://www.google.ca/.

Walsh, Eric. "CFTC Files Civil Charges over Alleged Bitcoin Ponzi Scheme." Reuters. September 21, 2017. Accessed December 03, 2018. https://www.reuters.com/article/legal-cftc-bitcoin/cftc-files-civil-charges-over-alleged-bitcoin-ponzi-scheme-idUSKCN1BW2DF.

Weichel, Andrew. "Top Scams of 2016 Include Fake Endorsements from Online 'influencers'." British Columbia. March 02, 2017. Accessed December 02, 2018. https://bc.ctvnews.ca/top-scams-of-2016-include-fake-endorsements-from-online-influencers-1.3307091.

YouTube. Ascenergy, LLC. May 23, 2014. Accessed December 02, 2018. https://www.youtube.com/watch?v=DfQ2amtKrv8.

Anecdote Sources

"2016 ACFE Report to the Nations." Ponzi Schemes | Association of Certified Fraud Examiners. Accessed December 03, 2018. https://www.acfe.com/rttn2016/about/executive-summary.aspx.

Albrecht, W. Steve., Keith R. Howe, and Marshall B. Romney. *Deterring Fraud: The Internal Auditors Perspective*. Altamonte Springs, FL: Institute of Internal Auditors Research Foundation, 1984.

Evans, Martin. "Cyber Crime: One in 10 People Now Victim of Fraud or Online Offences, Figures Show." The Telegraph. July 21, 2016. Accessed December 03, 2018. https://www.telegraph.co.uk/news/2016/07/21/one-in-people-now-victims-of-cyber-crime/.

Feldman, Robert S. *The Liar in Your Life: The Way to Truthful Relationships*. New York: Twelve, 2010.

"FINRA Foundation Research Reveals Fraud Victims Vulnerable to Severe Stress, Anxiety and Depression." Types of Investments | FINRA.org. March 09, 2015. Accessed December 03, 2018. http://www.finra.org/newsroom/2015/finra-foundation-research-reveals-fraud-victims-vulnerable-severe-stress-anxiety-and.

Gray, Jeff, and Janet McFarland. "Crime without Punishment: Canada's Investment Fraud Problem." The Globe and Mail. May 11, 2018. Accessed December 03, 2018. https://www.theglobeandmail.com/report-on-business/crime-and-no-punishment-canadas-investment-fraud-problem/article13938792/?page=all.

Haywood Hunt & Associates. "Top 10 Fraud Statistics That Can't Be Ignored." Haywood Hunt & Associates Inc | Private Investigators Toronto & Mississauga. March 21, 2017. Accessed December 03, 2018. https://www.haywoodhunt.ca/top-10-fraud-statistics-that-cant-be-ignored/.

Huddleston, Pat. *The Vigilant Investor: A Former SEC Enforcer Reveals How to Fraud-proof Your Investments*. New York: American Management Association, 2012.

Konnikova, Maria. *The Confidence Game: Why We Fall for It Every Time*. New York: Viking, 2016.

KPMG. *Https://www.richmondfed.org/~/media/richmondfedorg/banking/education_for_bankers/fraud_awareness/pdf/who_is_the_typical_fraudster.pdf*. PDF. 2011.

Rebovich & Layne, 2000; Kerley & Copes, 2002; AARP 2003a

Maglich, Jordan. "A Ponzi Pandemic: 500 Ponzi Schemes Totaling $50 Billion in 'Madoff Era'." Forbes. February 12, 2014. Accessed December 03, 2018. https://www.forbes.com/sites/jordanmaglich/2014/02/12/a-ponzi-pandemic-500-ponzi-schemes-totaling-50-billion-in-madoff-era/#187c98356925.

Raaij, W. Fred Van. *Understanding Consumer Financial Behavior Money Management in an Age of Financial Illiteracy.* New York: Palgrave Macmillan US, 2016. (Pratkanis & Shadel, 2005) - Researchers have found that victims are psychologically reluctant to come forward.

Shadel, Doug, and Karla Pak. "Investment Fraud Survey." AARP. February 01, 2017. Accessed December 03, 2018. https://www.aarp.org/research/topics/economics/info-2017/investment-fraud-survey.html.

Shadel, Doug, and Karla Pak. "The Psychology of Consumer Fraud." Longevity.stanford.edu. Accessed December 03, 2018. http://longevity.stanford.edu/2012/02/26/the-psychology-of-consumer-fraud/.

Small, Bridget. "Fraud Affects 25 Million People: Recognize Anyone You Know?" Consumer Information. March 13, 2018. Accessed December 10, 2018. https://www.consumer.ftc.gov/blog/2013/04/fraud-affects-25-million-people-recognize-anyone-you-know.

Stephenson, Debbie, and K. Hartford. "10 Famous Investment Scams." The DealRoom. June 23, 2015. Accessed December 03, 2018. https://www.firmex.com/thedealroom/10-famous-investment-scams/.

The Shame Campaign–Revealing the Secrets of the Ill-Dark-And-Naughty. April 12, 2014. Accessed December 03, 2018. http://theshamecampaign.com/2014/04/12/snake-oil-salesman-william-rockefeller-taught-his-son-well/.

Titus, Richard M., F. Heinzelmann, and J. Boyle, 1995. Victimization of persons by fraud. Crime & Delinquency Vol. 41, No. 1, 54-72.

Kerley, K. and H. Copes (2002). 'Personal Fraud Victims and Their Official Responses to Victimization,' Journal of Police and Criminal Psychology, 17(1): 19–35

UT Dallas. "Study Examines Social Connections and Impacts of Financial Fraud." Phys.org - News and Articles on Science and Technology. August 7, 2017. Accessed December 10, 2018. https://phys.org/news/2017-08-social-impacts-financial-fraud.html#jCp.

* * *

APPENDIX III:
SUGGESTED READINGS THAT INSPIRED THIS BOOK

Abagnale, Frank W. *The Art of the Steal: How to Protect Yourself and Your Business from Fraud.*

Albrecht, W. Steve. *Fraud: Bringing Light to the Dark Side of Business.*

Ariely, Dan. *The Honest Truth about Dishonesty.*

Babiak, Paul, Robert D. Hare. *Snakes in Suits: When Psychopaths Go to Work.*

Chancellor, Ed. *Devil Take the Hindmost.*

Fisher, Kenneth L. and Hoffmans, Lara W. *How to Smell a Rat: The Five Signs of Financial Fraud.*

Huddleston, Pat. *The Vigilant Investor: A Former SEC Enforcer Reveals How to Fraud-Proof Your Investments.*

Jennings, Marianne M. *The Seven Signs of Ethical Collapse.*

Konnikova, Maria. *The Confidence Game.*

McLean, Bethany and Nocero, Joseph. *All the Devils Are Here.*

Markopolos, Harry. *No One Would Listen: A True Financial Thriller.*

Moffitt, Donald. *Swindled! Classic Business Frauds of the Seventies.*

Partnoy, Frank. *The Match King: Ivar Kreuger. The Financial Genius behind a Century of Wall Street Scandals.*

Perino, Michael. *The Hellhound of Wall Street.*

Rosen, Al and Rosen, Mark. *Swindlers: Cons & Cheats and How to Protect Your Investments from Them.*

Sarna, David E. Y. *History of Greed: Financial Fraud from Tulip Mania to Bernie Madoff*

Schilit, Howard M. and Jeremy Perler. *Financial Shenanigans: How to Detect Accounting Gimmicks & Fraud in Financial Reports,*

Zuckoff, Mitchell. *Ponzi's Scheme: The True Story of a Financial Legend.*

CPSIA information can be obtained
at www.ICGtesting.com
Printed in the USA
LVHW092154011119
636126LV00001B/2/P